Michael Ondaatje

Twayne's World Authors Series

Canadian Literature

Robert Lecker, Editor

McGill University

TWAS 835

MICHAEL ONDAATJE
Photograph by Jerry Bauer. © Jerry Bauer

Michael Ondaatje

Douglas Barbour

University of Alberta

Twayne Publishers • New York
Maxwell Macmillan Canada • Toronto
Maxwell Macmillan International • New York   Oxford   Singapore   Sydney

Michael Ondaatje
Douglas Barbour

Twayne Publishers
Macmillan Publishing Company
866 Third Avenue
New York, New York 10022

Maxwell Macmillan Canada, Inc.
1200 Eglinton Avenue East
Suite 200
Don Mills, Ontario M3C 3N1

Library of Congress Cataloging-in-Publication Data

Barbour, Douglas, 1940–
    Michael Ondaatje / Douglas Barbour.
        p.   cm. — (Twayne's world authors series ; TWAS 835. Canadian literature)
    Includes bibliographical references (p.   ) and index.
    ISBN 0-8057-8290-7 (alk. paper)
    1. Ondaatje, Michael, 1943–   —Criticism and interpretation.
    I. Title.   II. Series: Twayne's world authors series ; TWAS 835.
    III. Series: Twayne's world authors series. Canadian literature.
    PR9199.3.O5Z58   1993
    818'.5409—dc20   92-27095
                                                             CIP

The paper used in this publication meets the minimum requirements
of American National Standard for Information Sciences—Permanence
of Paper for Printed Library Materials. ANSI Z3948-1984. ∞™

10 9 8 7 6 5 4 3 2 1 (hc)

Printed in the United States of America

"has developed and bred new strain of spaniel, 'The Sydenham Spaniel,'
Candn. Kennel Club 1970, with Livingstone Animal Foundation Kennels"
> Michael Ondaatje,
> in *Canadian Who's Who,* vol. 25, ed. Kieran Simpson
> (Toronto: University of Toronto Press, 1990), 718

"I'm a great believer in the mongrel."
> Michael Ondaatje to Catherine Bush

Contents

Preface

As a poet whose richly metaphoric prose texts have won him an international reputation, Michael Ondaatje has tended, when he has not refused by means of evasion to even deal with such questions, to discuss his own writing in terms of analogy and ambiguity. Unlike such fellow writers and admirers as Robert Kroetsch and George Bowering, he does not enjoy theorizing about his own poetics. Nevertheless, his career demonstrates a consistent intent to enlarge the possibilities of his craft, and he has always sought new ways to approach his materials.

As he approaches fifty, he has achieved a rare international success for a Canadian writer, and it seems clear that he does not intend to rest upon his laurels. During the past couple of years, as I was working on this study, he entered the Canadian Centre for Advanced Film Studies, where he wrote the script for *Love Clinic*, a film produced by his fellow students, and completed work on a new novel, *The English Patient*, published in the autumn of 1992 and winner of the Booker prize. He continues to write poetry, as "Breeze," his moving elegy for bpNichol, a close friend and fellow poet, demonstrates. Given the fact that he is still very much a writer "in process," a study such as this can in no way even pretend to be definitive. In the pages that follow, I trace the growth and complication of a complex poetic, paying especial attention to Ondaatje's longer works, the long poems and fictions upon which his international reputation is built. Using the concept of indeterminacy as a way of showing how his work has moved from later modernism to postmodernism, I have tried to enter into the spirit of each of his books up to the 1987 novel, *In the Skin of a Lion*. I attempt no conclusions beyond those implicit in the individual readings precisely because his career is so obviously far from finished; clearly there are many other approaches to his work which would yield insights.

Acknowledgments

No book is the product of a single hand, and I owe much to other readers of Michael Ondaatje's work, even when I disagree with their conclusions. I am grateful for conversations over the years with various friends, who have patiently listened to my thinking: George Bowering, Frank Davey, Paul Hjartarson, Smaro Kamboureli, Robert Kroetsch, Stephen Scobie, Stephen Slemon, and Lola Tostevin. Sharon Barbour has always been there; once again her editorial insights have pointed the way. Two Graduate Research Assistants, Kathryn Harvey and Adam Muller, sought out many elusive references. A grant from the Social Sciences and Humanities Research Council of Canada freed me from teaching in 1990–91 and gave me time to write this study. Finally, I want to express my gratitude to Michael Ondaatje for having written the poetry and prose that over the years has pleased me as I read and taught it, and that proved itself more than capable of sustaining the lengthy rereadings out of which a study such as this proceeds.

I am also grateful to Michael Ondaatje for permission to quote from:

The Dainty Monsters. Toronto: Coach House Press, 1967.
the man with seven toes. Toronto: Coach House Press, 1969.
The Collected Works of Billy the Kid: Left Handed Poems. New York: Norton; Toronto: House of Anansi, 1970
Rat Jelly. Toronto: Coach House Press, 1973.
Coming Through Slaughter. New York: Norton; Toronto: House of Anansi, 1976; London: Marion Boyars, 1979.
There's a Trick with a Knife I'm Learning to Do: Poems 1963–1968. New York: Norton; Toronto: McClelland and Stewart, 1979.
Running in the Family. New York: Norton; Toronto: McClelland and Stewart, 1982.
Secular Love. Toronto: Coach House Press, 1984.
In the Skin of a Lion. New York: Alfred A. Knopf; Toronto: McClelland and Stewart, 1987.
The Cinnamon Peeler: Selected Poems. London: Pan Books, 1989; New York: Alfred A. Knopf, 1991.

Chronology

1943   Philip Michael Ondaatje born 12 September in Colombo, Ceylon (Sri Lanka).

1949–1952   Attends St. Thomas College, Colombo.

1952–1962   Attends Dulwich College, London, England.

1962   Immigrates to Canada.

1962–1964   Attends Bishop's University, Lennoxville, Quebec.

1964–1965   Attends University College, University of Toronto, B.A. 1965.

1965–1967   Attends Queen's University, Kingston, Ontario, M.A. 1967.

1965   Ralph Gustafson Poetry Award.

1966   Selection of his poems included in *New Wave Canada*, edited by Raymond Souster.

1967–1971   Begins teaching at the University of Western Ontario, London, Ontario. President's Medal, University of Western Ontario (for "Paris").

1967   *The Dainty Monsters.*

1968   Dramatic performance of *the man with seven toes*, Vancouver, British Columbia.

1969   *the man with seven toes.*

1970   *The Collected Works of Billy the Kid* (receives Governor General's Award in 1971). *Leonard Cohen.* Film: *Sons of Captain Poetry.* Editor at Coach House Press.

1971   Joins Department of English, Glendon College, York University.

1971   Edits *The Broken Ark: A Book of Beasts.* Dramatic reading of *The Collected Works of Billy the Kid*, Toronto.

1972   Film: *The Clinton Special.*

1973   *Rat Jelly.* Play of *The Collected Works of Billy the Kid,* Stratford, Ontario. Chalmer's Award finalist for *Billy the Kid.*

1976   *Coming Through Slaughter.* Receives *Books in Canada* First
        Novel Award.

1977   Edits *Personal Fictions: Stories by Munro, Wiebe, Thomas and
        Blaise.*

1979   *There's a Trick with a Knife I'm Learning to Do* (receives
        Governor General's Award for Poetry in 1980). *Elimina-
        tion Dance.* Edits *The Long Poem Anthology.*

1980   Play of *Coming Through Slaughter*, Toronto. Receives
        Canada-Australia Literary Prize.

1981   Visiting professor, University of Hawaii.

1982   *Running in the Family. Tin Roof.* Professor, Department of
        English, Glendon College.

1984   *Secular Love.*

1985   Contributing editor of *Brick: A Journal of Reviews.*

1987   *In the Skin of a Lion.* Receives (1988) City of Toronto Book
        Award, Trillium Book Award; finalist, Ritz Paris Hem-
        ingway Award (no award given).

1988   Receives Order of Canada.

1989   *The Cinnamon Peeler: Selected Poems* (Great Britain).

1990   Edits *From Ink Lake: Canadian Stories.* Visiting professor,
        Brown University.

1991   *The Cinnamon Peeler: Selected Poems* (United States). Coed-
        its, with Linda Spaulding, *The Brick Reader.*

1992   *The English Patient.* Receives Booker Prize (1992) and
        Governor Generd's Award for fiction (1992).

Chapter One
Crossing Borders in Life and Writing

The 1960s was a generative decade for Canadian literature. Many significant writers published their first books then: Margaret Atwood, George
Bowering, Timothy Findley, Robert Kroetsch, Gwendolyn MacEwan,
Daphne Marlatt, Alice Munro, and bpNichol among them. But, as
Margaret Atwood points out in her introduction to *The New Oxford Book
of Canadian Verse in English,* when something of a "Canadian cultural
'renaissance' . . . took place in the sixties,"[1] due to an unprecedented
increase in the audience for poetry and a newly determined cultural
nationalism, "poetry became, for a decade and partly by default, the
predominant literary form in Canada" (Atwood, xxxvii). Michael Ondaatje
came to Canada at the beginning of that heady decade, and discovered an
atmosphere in which "meeting poets and having enthusiastic teachers
brought things into focus for me and I began to write."[2] He pursued his new
craft with diligence and energy. Although he was, like many of us, an
immigrant, he was a very recent one, and the richly evocative imagery of his
first volume of poems, *The Dainty Monsters* (1967), won critical praise upon
its appearance in 1967. In 1982 Margaret Atwood concisely summed up his
impact: "Michael Ondaatje evades categorization, but his exotic imagery
and violent mini-plots have gained him a reputation as one of the most vital
and inventive of the younger poets" (Atwood, xxxviii).

Although *The Dainty Monsters* established Ondaatje as a poet, he is
best known today for his innovative prose, which combines various forms
of experimentation with a visceral emotional energy that attracts a wide
range of readers in many countries. In achieving an international reputation, he has joined a still select group of Canadian writers who publish
in the United States and the United Kingdom as well as Canada, and
whose new books are regularly reviewed in such major periodicals as the
New York Times Book Review and the *Times Literary Supplement.* His 1990
anthology of Canadian short stories, *From Ink Lake,* published simultaneously in Britain, the United States, and Canada, received enthusiastic
reviews for both content and organization.

How he has achieved such prominence is an interesting story, for Ondaatje has neither followed trends nor played to any crowd. Although he is a jealous guardian of his private life, he has proven an intelligent promoter of his own work, managing both to write what he wanted and to find the best publishers for each work. Beginning with a poetry collection from the small experimental Coach House Press, with which he has maintained ties, he moved to the slightly larger House of Anansi Press for his first major work, *The Collected Works of Billy the Kid,* and later published selected poems and his two most recent prose works with McClelland and Stewart, also known as "The Canadian Publishers" (the four longer works plus the selected poems also having their own publishers in the United States and Britain).[3]

Michael Ondaatje was born to Philip Mervyn Ondaatje and Enid Gratiaen Ondaatje in Colombo, Ceylon (now Sri Lanka), on 12 September 1943. His paternal grandfather was a wealthy planter in Kegalle, and Ondaatje's memories are of " 'a great childhood' filled with aunts, uncles, many houses, and . . . gossip and eccentricity."[4] The "gossip and eccentricity" would eventually become the controlling formal tropes of his "fictional memoir," *Running in the Family* (1982). Ondaatje attended St. Thomas College in Colombo. After his parents' separation in 1948, he stayed in Colombo until 1952, when he followed his mother, brother, and sister to London and attended Dulwich College. Finding the English school system unsatisfying, he eventually followed his older brother, Christopher, to Montreal in 1962. At Bishop's University, Lennoxville, in the Eastern Townships of Quebec, he majored in English and history. As Ondaatje tells it: "Around 1962, after I came to Canada [I started to write poetry]. I was 19 then and had never read much poetry to that point, although I used to read a great many novels and biographies, and still do. Then meeting poets and having enthusiastic teachers brought things into focus for me and I began to write. My first teacher at Bishop's was Arthur Motyer and I owe him a great deal for he introduced me to poetry in the best possible way" (*Manna,* 19). While enthusiastically reading the poetry of everyone from Browning to Eliot and Yeats at Bishop's, he also met a number of practicing poets there, especially D. G. Jones, who had already published two books of poetry. The absence of an overwhelming history or "great tradition" in Canada and the fertile contemporary atmosphere gave Ondaatje the freedom to write.

Early in his career, in 1964, Ondaatje married artist Kim Jones, with whom he had two children, Quintin and Griffin, during the next two years. Completing his B.A. studies at the University of Toronto in 1965, he won the Epstein Award for poetry and came in contact with Raymond Souster, who included Ondaatje's poetry in his landmark anthology, *New Wave Canada* (1966). He also met Wayne Clifford, a poet and editor at Coach House Press, who invited him to submit a manuscript for publication. While Ondaatje chose not to do so in 1965, he offered Coach House a manuscript he was sure of two years later. In late 1965, he entered the M.A. program in English at Queen's University, Kingston, Ontario. He completed both his thesis on the poetry of Edwin Muir and the manuscript for *The Dainty Monsters* in 1967. While at Queen's, he also became one of the editors of *Quarry,* a university literary magazine that had just gone national and quarterly.

In the fall of 1967 Ondaatje became an instructor in English at the University of Western Ontario in London, and published his first book of poetry to critical accolades. Over the next few years he completed his second book, *the man with seven toes,* wrote a short critical study, *Leonard Cohen,* and began work on *The Collected Works of Billy the Kid. The man with seven toes* was performed as a dramatic reading for three readers in Vancouver in 1968 and at Stratford in 1969, the second performance directed by Paul Thompson, who became a close friend and collaborator. They collaborated on the 1972 film *The Clinton Special,* based on Theatre Passe Muraille's *The Farm Show,* directed by Thompson, and the 1980 stage adaptation of *Coming Through Slaughter* (Martin Kinch directed the 1971 stage adaptation of *Billy the Kid*).

When, in 1971, the University of Western Ontario insisted that he complete a Ph.D. to be granted tenure, Ondaatje left Western to take a position as assistant professor at Glendon College, York University, where he has taught ever since. That year he won Canada's most prestigious literary award, the Governor General's Award, for *The Collected Works of Billy the Kid.* While at Glendon, Ondaatje has taken time to write and to travel: in recent years that has included teaching stints in Hawaii (1979), Rome and Turin (1986), and Rhode Island, at Brown University (1990).

While working on another manuscript in the early 1970s, Ondaatje was sidetracked by a "cryptic newspaper reference: 'Buddy Bolden, who became a legend when he went berserk in a parade.'"[5] Five years later he published *Coming Through Slaughter.* As he put it, "I wanted everything about this person. I read that reference in the newspaper. I became obsessed with him while I was working on another book. I realized that I was going to have to face this character. He took over and I started writing about him instead and left the other thing" (Witten, 9–10).

Ondaatje's obsession led him into new territory fictionally, and the result of his endeavors was widely praised, winning the *Books in Canada* award for the best first novel by a Canadian in 1976. At the end of that year, Ondaatje visited India for a Commonwealth Literature conference; this was the closest to his birthplace he had been in 24 years. On sabbatical leave in 1978, he traveled to Sri Lanka and spent five months with his sister and relatives. *There's a Trick with a Knife I'm Learning to Do,* his Governor General's Award–winning collection of 1979, contains a number of new poems based on that trip.

He returned to Sri Lanka in 1980, and the two journeys provided the impetus for his next major book, *Running in the Family* (1982), a memoir more of his parents' generation than of his own life and possibly more fictional than factual, certainly on a formal level. Ondaatje poses the problem of genre best in his acknowledgments: "I must confess that the book is not a history but a portrait or 'gesture.' And if those listed above disapprove of the fictional air I apologize and can only say that in Sri Lanka a well-told lie is worth a thousand facts."[6] In 1980, while he continued his work on this book, he separated from his wife and has since lived with Linda Spalding. His most recent collection of poetry, *Secular Love* (1984), in many ways his most personal statement, treats both the destructive pain of marriage breakup and the creative joys of newfound love.

Michael Ondaatje has always been fascinated by movies, and, when he has found the opportunity, he has tried his hand at them. In 1969, with *The Collected Works of Billy the Kid* in press, he directed *Sons of Captain Poetry,* a 35-minute documentary on the Canadian sound and concrete poet bpNichol (whose own small book on Billy the Kid, *The True Eventual Story of Billy the Kid,* along with three other works, also won a Governor General's Award the year *The Collected Works of Billy the Kid* did). In 1972, he made *Carry on Crime and Punishment,* a five-minute jeu d'esprit in which family and friends appear as dognappers of the family basset hound, Wallace. *The Clinton Special* (1972) is a longer documentary on the creation and performance of *The Farm Show,* a play in which the actors and director lived with the people they eventually portrayed on stage; as it clearheadedly examines the complex relationships between performers and farmers, both working at their craft, it reveals a fascination with the contradictory parallels between living and performing, which Ondaatje later explored in his own family history in Ceylon. In 1990, Ondaatje was named one of 16 students at Norman Jewison's

Canadian Centre for Advanced Film Studies near Toronto; there he has participated as writer in the making of a short film, *Love Clinic*.

For the most part, however, Ondaatje spent the 1980s finishing the book he calls "his first formal novel."[7] *In the Skin of a Lion* won the 1987 City of Toronto Book Award, the first annual Trillium Book Award, and was one of three nominees for the Ritz Paris Hemingway literary prize. In this book, Ondaatje turns his eye upon the city of Toronto, where he has lived for the past 20 years, finding in its unwritten history a reality as magical as any Gabriel García Márquez conjured in Colombia or he himself discovered earlier in New Orleans or Ceylon. Much more socially conscious than his previous books, it stakes a claim for itself as truly postcolonial in both subject matter and approach.

For the moment, then, Ondaatje has already created an oeuvre of some significance in both poetry and prose, not to mention his accomplishments in theater and film. He is a full professor at Glendon College, where he teaches Canadian and American literature, contemporary literature in translation, and creative writing. He often gets release time to work on his own writing or to teach elsewhere. He seems finally settled and at home in Canada, yet he is one of the best known and most highly praised Canadian writers in the United States, Britain, and the Commonwealth. In the fall of 1992, his newest and longest novel, *The English Patient* was published. It seems clear that he will continue to surprise and delight his large readership for many years to come.

Modernism, Postmodernism, and Postcolonialism

For much of his career, Michael Ondaatje has been associated with the Coach House Press, a press with strong postmodernist connections in Canada and abroad. Indeed, even when his books were published by other presses, most were still designed and printed at Coach House Press.[8] Among the major advantages of working with a small press are the personal contact and the resultant concern for craft in design. Coach House has long had a reputation for some of the best design in Canada, but its major reputation is as a publisher of innovative and experimental texts by many of the leading Canadian postmodernist writers, including George Bowering, Wayne Clifford, Victor Coleman, Frank Davey, Daphne Marlatt, Steve McCaffery, bpNichol, and Fred Wah. That Ondaatje was an integral part of Coach House's publishing program says much about its openness to writing that does not fit a narrow avant-garde or postmodern definition. What Wayne Clifford saw in Ondaatje's early

poems was their sharply etched imagery and the already powerful emotional suggestiveness of his lyric voice.

It was a voice more tied to Yeats, Eliot, and Stevens than to Pound and
Williams, to name the representatives of the two main traditions of
twentieth-century English-language poetry. Marjorie Perloff has exam-
ined the roots of those two traditions, exploring and analyzing the
writings of the one she first calls "indeterminacy."[9] In both *The Poetics of
Indeterminacy* and *The Dance of the Intellect*, Perloff makes a strong case for
reading the "moment" of modernism itself as already bifurcated, already
fully separated into the two streams of "symbolism" and "indeterminacy" (Perloff 1981, 4) or the two "traditions" of Pound and Stevens (to
choose two of the most representative figures of the modernist era).[10]
While most Coach House poets have always belonged to the Pound
tradition, as passed down through Williams to Olson, Creeley, Duncan,
Levertov and others in the United States, and so into Canada through
their teaching and reading in Vancouver, the young Ondaatje aligned
himself with Stevens, who makes a significant appearance in two of his
lyrics, and the symbolist poets in his tradition like Robert Lowell and
John Berryman.[11] Perloff maintains that "Stevens's rage for order, his
need to make analogies . . . is at odds with Pound's deployment of
metonymic linkages, his creation of Cubist surfaces or aerial maps where
images jostle one another," adding that the critics who complain of
Pound's "incoherence" are really attacking him for violating "the norms
of the lyric, specifically the Romantic lyric" (Perloff 1985, 17). In
"Postmodernism and the Impasse of the Lyric," she further explores the
problem of lyric subjectivity as ego-based retreat from formal exploration and linguistic/textual awareness, and finds even modernist "lyricism" trapped in what might be called *The Golden Treasury* syndrome
(Perloff 1985, 176–78): "In Pound's eyes, *The Golden Treasury* was
nothing less than a Chinese wall against modern poetry" (Perloff 1985,
178). In the context of Ondaatje's poetic career, I would argue that he
begins as a writer in the Stevens tradition, as a modernist lyricist, and
generally remains true to that tradition in his shorter poems before
Secular Love.

In his longer works, Ondaatje not only joins the Pound tradition, but
also becomes a specifically postmodern writer. Although the terms
postmodern and *postmodernism* may seem too vague, they are constantly
used and too ubiquitous to be displaced.[12] Brian McHale argues that
postmodernism is a poetics in which the *post* emphasizes "the element of
logical and historical *consequence* rather than sheer temporal *posteriority*.

Postmodernism follows *from* modernism, in some sense, more than it follows *after* modernism" (McHale, 5). Connecting this suggestion to Perloff's concept of the two traditions that emerged during the period of high modernism, I see her "poetics of indeterminacy" as his postmodernist poetics.[13]

The formal qualities of postmodernist poetics include extension and the mixing of genres. In a work such as *The Collected Works of Billy the Kid,* which has been called a paradigmatic "contemporary Canadian long poem,"[14] there is a mixture of prose and poetry "*{w}ithout privileging either medium,* lyric poem or 'prose instruction' . . . [; and the] corollary, equally important for postmodernism, is that the lyric voice gives way to multiple voices or voice fragments" (Perloff 1985, 183). And Ondaatje, although his original poetic impulse was toward the postromantic lyric in the Stevens mode, shifted toward the larger collage constructions of the Pound tradition partly under the influence of a particularly Canadian tradition, "the documentary poem."[15] In both *the man with seven toes* and *The Collected Works of Billy the Kid,* the use of documentation, however fragmented and parodied, makes possible a break from lyric subjectivity, as does the use of various voices out of legend. Moreover, the insistence on more than one voice in these longer works starts Ondaatje on the path toward what Mikhail Bakhtin would call the "novelization" of his poetry and eventually into forms of the novel itself.[16] In these two works he finds a way to attenuate lyric subjectivity while retaining lyric tone in the "speech" and "thoughts" of some of their "characters." In other words, once Ondaatje began writing in extended forms, he also began to write truly "heteroglossic" or "novelistic" texts.[17] The documentary impulse shares with the novelistic impulse the desire to listen to and re-present the voices of what Bakhtin calls "a diversity of social speech types (sometimes even diversity of languages) and a diversity of individual voices" (Bakhtin 1981, 262). It engages "the factual" and out of its compulsive collage or previous or invented "texts" it makes fictional worlds full of lively gaps. Ondaatje's desire to speak the inner worlds of figures silenced by either too much documentation (Billy the Kid) or far too little (Mrs. Fraser, Buddy Bolden) leads him to produce multivoiced texts full of epistemological gaps that yet create worlds that exist only in the writing that creates them.[18]

In his play with the possibilities of "documentation," Ondaatje makes the shift from modern to postmodern almost exactly as he makes the shift from lyric poem to long poem or poetic sequence. In his introduction to

The Long Poem Anthology, he refers to his chosen poems as "involved with process and perspective" (*LPA*, 11), and adds that "[t]he stories within the poems don't matter, the grand themes don't matter. The movement of the mind and language is what is important" (*LPA*, 12). He speaks from experience when he says, "[p]erhaps the documentary will always be a new form. . . . The need to chart what is around us, to say what is in the pot, creates at first strange bedfellows with the contemporary poetic voice" (*LPA,* 16). But, for him, the "physical world, its habit, what's 'given,' is the map or backdrop to these poems" (*LPA,* 16). The factual is only background and the term "documentary" has itself undergone transformation in these poems. Invention is at the core of the writing act out of which they emerge. Such invention will always seek new forms that refuse conventional narrative and ask readers to partici-pate in putting all the disparate pieces together anew each time they read. In making such a request, Ondaatje the anthologist and Ondaatje the writer join forces to create postmodern texts, full of gaps and paradoxes, leaps of imagination and vocal gymnastics, fragmented col-lages of fact and fiction: the thoroughly carnivalized writing of his longer works.[19] Robert Kroetsch points out that such works "treat of *real* legendary people. This basic tension, then, in the Canadian long poem: a) the temptation of the documentary, b) the scepticism about history. And as a consequence: a kind of madness in the recording" (Kroetsch, 119).

As various commentators have pointed out, there are modernisms and postmodernisms; neither term can serve as a monolithic sign.[20] The roman-tic sensibility of Ondaatje's early poetry remains active in the later, longer works, yet comes under questioning scrutiny from the postmodernist for-malism he adopts. This is not to deny that Billy the Kid, Buddy Bolden, and Ondaatje's own father all share attributes of the romantic figure of the self-destructive artist. While it is a figure with whom Ondaatje seems obsessed, it is one he refuses to become, no matter how attractive he finds it as tropic center for his texts. His interest in such American poets of self-destruction as John Berryman, Robert Lowell, and Sylvia Plath, which is not shared by those Canadian writers with whom he has usually been associated, has not led him to imitate their lives. Rather, the formal shift away from a poetics of symbolism to one of indeterminacy makes possible his textual escape from romantic self-immolation (which is an utterly "lyric" impulse, monologic in the extreme; the necessary dialogism of documen-tary, whether simple or parodic, will not allow it).

If Ondaatje becomes a postmodern writer in his longer works while still writing at the edge of modernism in his poetry, in *In the Skin of a Lion* and some recent poems, he takes a sideways step, perhaps, or one into a separate stream, towards postcolonialism.[21] Such a step involves a much more open articulation of the political sphere in the writing, for, as Hutcheon argues of feminism, postcolonialism has a distinct political agenda "and often a theory of agency that allow[s it] to go beyond the postmodern limits of deconstructing existing orthodoxies into the realms of social and political action" (Hutcheon 1989, 150). Ondaatje himself says early in his career that he is "not interested in politics on [a] public level" (*Manna,* 20), although he enjoys writing by others that "starts from the personal and moves out" and "which is about [the self] and yet also political."[22] Of the background for *In the Skin of a Lion,* however, he says, "this is Toronto history, but the people who actually built the goddamn bridge were unspoken of. They're unhistorical!" and "Canada has always been a very racist society, and it's getting more so" (Turner, 21). Clearly, he has changed perspective. When viewed from the outside, the change has a lot to do with the question of representation, and how it is affected by postmodern or postcolonial fictional directives.

By following his own desire to "start each new book with a new vocabulary, a new set of clothes,"[23] Ondaatje has consistently moved into new textual territory, traversing modes of late modernism, postmodernism, and postcolonialism in his continuing search for the new. How he does so, and what the various results are like, is the burden of the following chapters. Although the theoretical thinking I have been addressing here underpins the study that follows, it remains essentially a reading of a series of poetic writings in which the engagement with language in its microparticulars tends to be foregrounded in the texts, and in my readings of them.

Chapter Two

The Early Poetry

From today's perspective, *The Dainty Monsters* does not appear quite as spectacularly new as it did in 1967; for one thing, there is all of Ondaatje's later work to judge it by. Nevertheless, it is more complex and mature than is usual for a young poet, and has far fewer poems for the older author to be ashamed of than do most such collections, though it has a few pretensions the older writer will slough off. A good argument could be made that Ondaatje's epigraphs to his various books reveal his growing sophistication during the past two and a half decades, as they move from traditional literary sources in *The Dainty Monsters* to pop culture, nonfiction, ancient texts, and translations from more marginalized contemporary writers in the later texts. The epigraphs to *The Dainty Monsters*, useful introductions to each section, also hint at Ondaatje's essentially modern stance in these poems.

The title and the epigraph to the first section, "Over the Garden Wall," taken from W. H. Auden's "The Witnesses,"[1] is the title of one of the central poems, a fanciful fictional autobiography that continues the emphasis on animals in many poems of this section. "The Witnesses," one of Auden's casual symbolic fables from the early 1930s, is full of the paranoia of that time. Its ironies have to do with the fact that its speakers are the watchers, not the watched. The lines quoted create an uneasy tone that hovers over individual poems, even when they appear innocent of fear or terror in themselves. The "something" that will "fall like rain" and not "be flowers" (Auden, 187) could all too easily be bombs, especially in the high Cold War days of the late 1960s. Equally, the lines suggest an allegiance with the symbolic tradition to which Auden belongs, and most of the poems in the book support such a view.

A look at even a few of the critical statements that attempt to categorize Ondaatje as a poet demonstrates a multiplicity of viewpoints on this subject. J. E. Chamberlin tells us that he "is a poet of contradictions."[2] Stephen Scobie describes him as a poet of "equilibrium" and "balance,"[3] adding that "irony, and the absence of shock, are constants in Ondaatje's poetry" (Scobie 1985a, 48). Susan Glickman reads the trajectory of his poetry as a gradually emerging violent myth of the romantic artist, who "needs to hone his edge, to keep himself painfully separate and aware . . . [while] the *man* longs for affiliation and comfort and family."[4] Tom Marshall, on the other hand, argues that, throughout his work, "the dominant metaphor . . . is 'layering,' . . . Palimpsest perhaps" and adds that " 'layering' may be another way of saying metaphor, and it may be that, on some level, these poems are 'about' the mind's poetic process itself."[5] Lynette Hunter agrees that metaphor is the core of Ondaatje's vision: "there is a conscious statement that poetry is a metaphor for all experience. While the poet uses metaphor to express yet control the energy within his own work, he also uses the poetry itself as a direct metaphor for how a man experiences reality."[6] Sam Solecki also says that "Ondaatje is a poet of reality,"[7] but for him, a "tension between mind and chaos is at the centre of Ondaatje's poetry; and its implications can be seen in the dualistic nature of his imagery, in the deliberate thematic irresolution of his major lyrics. . . . Ondaatje has written poems describing the fundamentally chaotic nature of experience" (Solecki 1985a, 94). Ondaatje's poetry, then, has always provided a map large enough to encompass a wide range of explorations. It is perhaps a testament to Ondaatje's imagistic invention that critics feel compelled to find such metaphors to describe his work. Images and metaphors, as well as highly symbolic figures, comprise much of the text in *The Dainty Monsters*: that alone signals its place on the boundary between modernism and postmodernism, as one poem can remain determinedly modernist while the next slips quietly into a postmodern mode.

Ondaatje's early poems are obsessed with animals and birds, often seen in some violent relation to humanity, as George Bowering, among others, points out: "In his twenties he explored and exploited the violence implied in the confrontation between people and animals, [. . . and was] interested in the experiential philosophy developing from a paradox pronounced early in his verse: [that] 'nature breeds the unnatural' " (Bowering, 167). The dry voice of many of these poems— poised, alert, and keeping a careful distance from what it describes—does not so much present animals in violent opposition to humanity as it presents them as self-sufficient and separate, even suggesting that they may be signs of an other evolution, taking place beside us yet directed toward a future where we have little, if any, place. That voice shares Auden's or Stevens's sense of understatement, placing everything in a photographic frame or freezing it in amber. There is a sense of control in Ondaatje's "habit of intensifying the world, of fashioning artifice"

(Bowering, 164), where the intensification is itself somehow artificial insofar as it creates that most desired of New Critical artifacts, "The Poem as Icon."[8] While Ondaatje will jettison the sense of closure in these early poems, they remain bright and powerful, and introduce many of the major themes of his first few books.

" 'Description is a Bird,' " the first poem in *The Dainty Monsters*, begins a series of animalistic discriminations that connect the first eight poems to one another and to another nine poems scattered through the rest of the first section. Humans seldom enter these poems; when they do, they are present only as observing or as analogical subjects, while the animals themselves serve as symbolic presences and figures whose symbolic nature can be deviously and parodically altered to the poem's purposes. " 'Description is a Bird' "[9] illustrates many of the early Ondaatje effects. Aspects of surrealism[10] and of the ironic symbolist heritage influence this writing. The language reaches for effect, the local effect often overriding the total one, or at least setting up jarring contrasts, as in the first two lines. An afternoon sun "twists down": a powerful image, possibly expressing potential violence, or simply an attempt to register the effect of the quickly moving clouds ("of horses") of the third line? The birds we do not yet know to be swallows "come piggle piggle piggle all around the air," and this childlike, comic image sharply contrasts with the implications of the first line. At the same time, the use of "piggle piggle piggle" both suggests the "confusion" and "disorderly jumble" of "higgledy-piggledy"[11] and offers in its repetition of the neologism a countering suggestion of order in the midst of apparent confusion. The sandswallows' "turn" on the stage of the beach, their movements paradoxically "quick and gentle as wind," are the "virtuoso performances" of the second stanza, done for the presumably "magnificent audience" of the poem's speaker, who "appears" in the poem only through this implication, and through the judgments it makes on the birds' behavior. But this is a self-conscious comment: except for that couplet, the images and metaphors of the rest of the poem are themselves "virtuoso performances / that presume a magnificent audience" in us.

The similes throughout have a surreal air: clouds are horses, or vice versa; the swallows' movements are like the wind; the leader "turns thinner than whims" while the others follow "[l]ike God"; and they scatter, finally, "with the discipline of a watch." Comparing actions with abstractions, these three give a paradoxical aura to the whole poem. Readers will accommodate the poem only insofar as they feel that whims are thin or insubstantial, that anticipation is godlike, or that a sudden scattering is the result of a discipline as mechanical as a watch's. Stated thus, the similes become less exotic than they at first appear. There is a satisfying finality to the poem: perhaps it simply demonstrates swallowness; there is no more to say.

But what if there is more to say? That sense of closure suggests the poem's alignment with the symbolist tradition: if we push at the metaphors and symbols enough we will comprehend it. Yet it will not do us much good to refer to a dictionary of symbols, for the poem simultaneously appears symbolic and refuses a symbolic reading of its figures. If birds are symbols of thought, imagination, and spirituality,[12] with crows in particular associated with divination and solitude (Cirlot, 71) and swallows sacred to Isis and Venus and connected to the spring (Cirlot, 322), how does their conjunction work in this poem? Especially if horses signify intense desire (Cirlot,152) while clouds suggest a state of continual metamorphosis between the formal and the nonformal, phenomena and appearances (Cirlot, 50). A possible interpretation: love is a performance against solitude which demands discipline in the midst of apparent chaos such as these birds display beneath twisting sun and roiling clouds; love is what these birds describe.[13] Or is it? This poem may have a satisfying sense of closure, but Ondaatje is already reaching toward "undecidability," a textual situation in which "the symbolic evocations generated by words on the page are no longer grounded in a coherent discourse, so that it becomes impossible to decide which . . . associations are relevant and which are not" (Perloff 1981, 18). Here the vexed question of "how influences work" makes it almost impossible to place this poem, or many others, in either tradition. It is not because there is no degree of "undecidability" to the symbols and metaphors, that I agree with George Bowering that these early poems belong in the tradition of "closed" verse rather than that of "open form," but "because they [are], by the time . . . the reader [gets] to them, over with; there [is] no mystery left, no labour for the reader, just puzzle or rue" (Bowering, 164). Although I can untangle the symbolic meaning in the poem, I prefer to respond to the movement of certain lines, like the second with its repeat of "piggle," or to the sharp insight of "the betrayals of a feather," or to the specific concreteness of the first two lines of the final stanza, in which the images are natural and therefore adequate symbols, as Pound demanded.[14]

"'Description is a Bird'" represents the kind of poem Ondaatje dropped from his selected poems a little over a decade later. A fine little poem of its kind, able to stand up to a close reading better than many poems of the period, it is both closed in itself and represents a poetry of closure that Ondaatje's restless imagination soon found too confining. Other poems in *The Dainty Monsters* hint at the direction of his future writing.

"Birds for Janet—The Heron" (*DM,* 12–13; *TK,* 2–3) is the first poem in the 1979 selected poems. In some ways it appears more consistently and insistently symbolic, if only because it names its central figure in the title. But here, more than in the first poem, the bird is created out of its description, which ranges away from the scientific into the analogical in a manner that will become Ondaatje's own: even when the images are sense-oriented they veer quickly into the qualitative mode. This shift of focus can be both exhilarating and confusing, forcing the reader to move back and forth between the world of impression and the world of abstraction. It is especially effective in this poem, where the clipped syntax, short lines, and six separate sections insist that the reader continually adjust to changes in perspective.

The opening line describes both the heron's step into flight and our own imaginative leap to identify with it: "The reach" (*DM,* 12; *TK,* 2). "[F]ingers stretching / backbones" both draws us in and confuses our response to the representation: it might be an allusive description of the long legs and neck of the bird; or it might be a physiological analogy, asking us to feel what such thin length is like. All three nouns lack a clear referent: whose reach, fingers, or backbones are they? The next stanza seems clearly to be "about" the heron of the title, but "fur," which is also applied to the eagles, maintains the sense of arbitrary estrangement: visual rather than accurate, it brings the birds down to earth and aligns them with animals. Although this poem is about birds, it keeps them on the ground, refuses them the air and all the symbolic associations that would thereby accompany them. "Reflections make them an hourglass" has a comic accuracy which brings the reader back to the visual presence of the bird, as does the first stanza of the second part, with its "hairless ankle" crossed over a "starved knee." That evaluative adjective is typical Ondaatje: it hints at some suffering yet neatly implies the purely visual thinness of a heron's leg. The next few stanzas indulge in exotic invention to further defamiliarize the subject of the poem. But the verb phrase "fingers his food" now suggests that the earlier "fingers" imaged the bird. In this way the poem draws us into a continual, active reappraisal of what we are reading. Such echoes hold the disparate parts of the poem together. The "stone container," although it seems to imply something small and manufactured, could just be a metaphor for river or lake, just as "blue zebra milk" could suggest the color of the water reflecting the heron as it ducks its head in it. But, like "leaf of banana," its exotic nature cannot help but draw attention to itself, and I wonder if by doing so it does not interfere with the gradual accumulation of meaning in the poem.

To this point, the descriptions, however odd, appear to refer to the physical presence of the bird; now the poem shifts into a metaphysical mode, working its psychology, a kind of existential paranoia that leads inevitably to the concept of suicide. There is an implication that the soul of such a bird is external, but no reason is given. The potential for pain may explain the apparent non sequitur of the next section. Herons symbolize the morning and generation, and have a favorable significance, while eagles symbolize height, the spiritual principle, warlike endeavor, even divine majesty, and always patriarchal power (Cirlot, 148; 91–92). Ondaatje reinvents the heron as a symbol here—for Janet?—until it achieves a kind of inverted nobility, its majesty disconnected from the power associated with "muscular henchmen" (*DM*, 13; *TK*, 3),the criminal hierarchy invoked in that phrase. It turns inward, contemplates the soul, seeks an absence to enter, and thus becomes "the true king." In this it is similar to such later figures as Buddy Bolden, Bellocq, and Mervyn Ondaatje—is perhaps their earliest avatar. Only in the fifth section does the human observer enter the text, and in doing so, this "we" seems to displace the other subject of the poem; or, that apparent subject chooses to disappear at this point, perhaps to commit suicide. The text seems to grant the heron the power to make such a choice, to evade the very net of words attempting to capture it. Reading backward from the later books, I might conclude that the heron drowns itself, as the ibis does in *Coming Through Slaughter*, but all this poem does is float such possibilities in a syntax that refuses consistent referentiality. Is it the path of a heron or only of its suicide? Did the bird or did "we" walk to the center of the lake? If tracks are "left empty," is there really any path? This stanza deconstructs its own meaning in the very process of making it. Like the other parts of the poem, part five is not part of a logical argument but another jewel on a string. So perhaps the final couplet's retreat to near banality is not all that disappointing; it is, after all, just something else to say about herons.[15] Yet it feels like a conclusion. Ondaatje's text swings uneasily between closure and open-endedness, and in so doing approaches a degree of indeterminacy that might mark it as postmodern.

Most of the animal poems stick closer to the model of "'Description is a Bird'" than to "Birds for Janet—The Heron." Some present their subjects without any obvious interaction with the human. They shift from the cool observation of "Pigeons, Sussex Avenue" to the gregarious humor of "The Sows" and "Sows, one more time," to the almost visionary fantasy of "Gorillas," but in them all, the observing eye maintains a discreet distance. In all of these poems the symbolic qualities of their titular figures are essentially ignored or undercut. The "Gorillas," for example, may symbolize baser forces and the dark undercurrent of unconscious activity (Cirlot, 212), but this text insists on their evolutionary potential, albeit in a tone of ambiguous prophecy (*DM*, 19). A similar tone animates the final two lines of "Early Morning, Kingston to Gananoque," where the subject of the poem's enunciation remains invisible, although it has been present in the awareness that the land beyond the highway is "too harsh for picnics," a place where—in one of Ondaatje's key early phrases—"nature breeds the unnatural" (*DM*, 21; *TK*, 5). The harsh vision of animal life and death under the dangerous aegis of human interference—cars, farming, etc.—leads to another prophetic conclusion: "Somewhere in those fields / they are shaping new kinds of women" (*DM*, 21; *TK*, 5). Like some other apocalyptic statements in the early poems, this appears to open up speculation while actually closing down all possibilities but the one given. There's a sense in which this apocalyptic close to the poem is simply a function of youthful romanticism, a tonal quality the young poet may have picked up from Leonard Cohen, for example. It is matched by the way "In Another Fashion" echoes both Yeats and Cohen in its directive to "build new myths" by provoking "new christs / with our beautiful women" and finding pale birds "to drink from clear bowls / to mate with our children" (*DM*, 34; *TK*, 14). But this poem, which begins with a cat's performance, lacks the nobility Yeats seeks, and directs itself to the dark underside of such breeding, painfully poking fun at the old attitudes with a punk's insouciance. Despite their black romantic tone, Ondaatje kept both these poems for the selected poems, as he did "Application for a Driving Licence," a comic poem in which Scobie's claimed "absence of shock" (Scobie 1985a, 48) is itself a kind of hyperbole, and, like the "shocking" images of mating birds as "a burst cottonball" (*DM,* 35; *TK*, 15), should not be taken too seriously.

A similar comic irony and absence of shock play across the title poem of the first section, "Over the Garden Wall." The paranoid overtones of the original phrase, which make themselves felt in many of the poems in this section of the book, are arbitrarily dispensed with here, and with its quick shifts of focus, its slapstick images of animals in drag, the poem becomes a surreal comedy of mistaken evolution. In a different kind of surreal comedy, based on the Buster Keaton–like seriousness of Henri Rousseau's paintings, "Henri Rousseau and Friends" (*DM*, 26–27; *TK*, 10–11) upholds by undercutting the romantic-symbolic desire for permanence and stasis in art. Even the title is ambiguous. Are the friends the animals frozen in place in the paintings or the writer's, to whom the poem is then addressed? By describing some of the more famous animal scenes in Rousseau's paintings, the poem asserts its affinity with them.[16] In its final stanzas, however, it goes beyond this to argue a strange economy of exchange between art and life: not the life depicted but the life of those who purchase. Standing beneath the paintings is "just as intense a society" (*DM*, 26; *TK*, 11) in which can be found "vulgarly beautiful parrots, appalled lions, / the beautiful and the forceful locked in suns / and the slight, careful stepping birds." The comedy here has the same edge as the other surreal comedies of evolution: it bites in both directions, and we are no longer sure exactly who is the target. Perhaps it's us.

Over and over again, these early poems invoke a fantastical vision of the evolutionary theme of "survival of the fittest" (*DM*, 36). But the later poems shift away from the world of nature strained through apocalyptic eyes to a more complex domestic vision in which the stringencies of the everyday haul the writing back toward the mundane, even if it is a mundane perceived in heightened terms. These two tendencies meet in "Dragon" (*DM*, 18; *TK*, 4): Ondaatje deliberately chooses a figure that is all symbolism[17] and reduces it to the antiromantic confines of the ordinary world. If "Over the Garden Wall" creates a provisional site for comically undercutting mythic expectations, by its very title "Dragon" reaches back to the epic inheritance of ancient myth only to discover its loss. So diminished is the dragon, it retains mere remnants of its former glory. The similes are as important as the scene in fulfilling this reduction; they suggest an earlier and lost period of upper-class formality as extinct as the weltanschauung in which dragons had their psychological place. If the opening line is a conventional juxtaposition of familiarity and surprise, the rest of the stanza, with its beaver dam, cocktails, and dragon's "tail, keeping the beat of a waltz, / sen[ding] a morse of ripples to my canoe," wrenches us into the here and now. The mixture of tones, where the nobility of "muted like dawns" contrasts with the shabby diminution of "the vague sheen on a fly's wing," continues into the final stanza, where "strangely fierce" opposes "pathetic loud whispers" and the odd note of "the excited spaniel"—which in most contexts might signify lighthearted play but here implies a savage violence—creates an

aura of unease in the final line. In the context of the other poems of
strange evolution, the group surrounding the pitifully tiny dragon
signals the end of all it stands for. Yet, if the world is a spiritually smaller
place, there is room in it for a homegrown mythology, and it is this that
Ondaatje attempts to create in the other lyrics of this first section, before
turning to larger, more ancient, tales in the second.

If some of the poems in "Troy Town" attempt to domesticate mythology, as the choice of Paris as a protagonist suggests, Ondaatje's lyrics of
family life mythologize domesticity. There is the same casual manner to
"The Diverse Causes" as in the animal poems, but the focus is on the
details of family life in a spring cottage. The epigraph sets the scene with
its invocation to renew the time-honored rites of relationship and service;
the medieval spelling only heightens the mood of ancient propriety that
the poem both supports and undercuts in its acknowledgment of contemporary gains and losses. The first line could belong to any number of
traditional Chinese poems, but these "Three clouds and a tree / reflect
themselves on a toaster" (DM, 22; TK, 6) in a cottage kitchen where the
"window hangs scarred, / shattered by winter hunters." The usual
contrasts of peace and violence are immediately established, but the
poem cannot, or will not, offer a simple separation of the two: inside "a
cell of civilised magic" "Stravinski roars at" a breakfast with powdered
milk. Is "at" only a temporal sign or is it also a sign of anger? While the
former is likely, the poem's slide toward indeterminacy allows for the
other possibility. If the "inside" contains potential violence in the midst
of its peace, the "outside" contains peace in the midst of its implicit
violence: the "minute birds walk confident" in the "world not yet of
men." The next long stanza presents the daily life of reclaiming a cottage
after winter—cleaning buckets, removing cobwebs, fetching water—
then turns to domestic peace: while "the children sleep . . . I turn a
page / careful not to break the rhythms / of your sleeping head on my
hip." Both "love and the god outside" and "my daughter burn[ing] the
lake / by reflecting her shoes in it" (DM, 23; TK, 7) create a love and
peace that refuse sentimental evasion. Beyond the boundary of the body,
fire can rage in a lover's dreams, and even his daughter burns her way
through boundaries between earth and water, dream and life. This is the
first poem in The Dainty Monsters to represent an apparently autobiographical "I," and that representation introduces new complexities into
the lyric voice of the poem as well as into our reading of it. The story told
here, despite its allusions to a May god, feels "real" in a way the fanciful
animal poems do not, yet it presents a world no less duplicitous, no less

dangerous, no less teetering between chaos and order. And the chaos and the order are intertwined, both part of the internal and external worlds of the figures in the poem. Because it maintains such a delicate balance between the two throughout, "The Diverse Causes"—and "diverse" now seems inevitable here—remains a paradigmatic early poem.

The poems of domestic love appear more traditionally "lyric" than the animal poems: many of them seek to capture a moment of emotion by freezing it in time, as "Four Eyes" (*DM,* 46; *TK,* 17) will put it, evoking a distinguishing characteristic of traditional lyric.[18] Still, these poems simultaneously undercut conventional romantic lyric attitudes in their insistence on family relationships rather than those of obsessive love. And there is an anecdotal quality to some of them which precludes a conventionally lyric response in the reader. A few even reach toward the momentary process of an event and, rather than trying to capture and hold it, allow it its transience. At this point, however, they generally fall back into closure, as "'Lovely the Country of Peacocks'" shows. After presenting a witty catalog of his baby daughter's actions, the speaker offers two conclusions: first, the observation that watching her, "we wear sentimentality like a curse" (*DM,* 41; *TK,* 16); and second, a commentary on her both illustrating that sentimentality and attempting to undercut it with a final humorous jab that doesn't quite succeed:

> Her body bears, inside the changing flesh,
> rivers of collected suns,
> jungles of force, coloured birds
> and laziness.
>
> (*DM,* 41; *TK,* 16)

This stanza evokes traditional symbolic meanings: the sun as "heroic and courageous force, creative and guiding" (Cirlot, 317); rivers signifying both "fertility and the progressive irrigation of the soil" and "the irreversible passage of time [with its concomitant] sense of loss and oblivion" (Cirlot, 274); the jungles reiterating the power of the sun; and birds suggesting "thought," "imagination," and "the swiftness of spiritual processes" (Cirlot, 28). All these imply a budding artist, perhaps, with "laziness" the twentieth-century cynical afterthought meant to keep us from utterly accepting the sentimentality that, by naming, the poem has partly excused, partly erased.

Even in the twentieth century, the lyric poet still wishes to find a way to offer the traditional poetic gift of celebration to his beloved. But there are difficulties for a self-aware writer. "Four Eyes" (DM, 46; TK, 17) offers a vision of the attempt and the problems, and even as it seems to achieve the necessary lyric closure, it admits the failure implicit in the success of artifice. The poem begins in an anecdotal medias res, with the lovers on a bed listening to music—signaling an ongoing process—and the lyric poet entering into the consciousness of the other to "pick this moment up / with our common eyes / only choose what you can see." Changeless things—photograph, picture, dress—are what these common eyes see, and the lyric poet breaks away from the shared act to record the moment, as solitary singer. Returning, he is forced to record more than that—the separate self-sufficiency of the other, and the refusal of a living being to stay put: "The music continuing / you were still being unfurled / shaped by the scene." Still, the lyric poet seeks the stasis of art: "I would freeze this moment / . . . / and in immobilised time / attempt to reconstruct" (DM, 46; TK, 17) As Solecki suggests, the poet has to sever himself from the scene in order to "record" it, and therefore finds that only metaphor will make that possible (Solecki 1985a, 96–97), and, as Scobie says, Ondaatje, like the painter Henri Rousseau, perceives the artist's task as that of freezing moments into stasis (Scobie 1985a, 54–55). Pianos and horses act as metaphors for the music the beloved is still, and continuingly, listening to, but the key words in the stanza are "would" and "attempt." The poem struggles with the contradiction that while it "may aspire towards the timelessness of the sleeping gypsy, the Grecian urn," both poet and reader remain "caught in flux and change" (Scobie 1985a, 56). This poem, like all poems, even those which attempt much more fully to articulate flux, is simply a way to "shape / and lock the transient" (TK, 47), but it still wants to argue that such immobilized time not only can, but should, be reconstructed. Yet, by its very deferral of certitude, its inability to say that it has done so, it reveals the paradox at the center of such lyric yearning: what is captured is only a version of a moment, not the moment itself. The pianos and horses are poetry's lies. The poem is one of apparent absolute closure: rhythmically, it comes to a complete stop. But the statement is insecure, a quixotic desire for an unattainable stasis: "you" begins to disappear into the metaphors as soon as the poet breaks to record the moment, already passed, already of the past. This paradoxical effect, and the various possible ways of dealing with it, will return in more complex form in later poems, but "Four Eyes" reveals its presence at the very beginning of Ondaatje's career. Perhaps because lyric finally cannot satisfactorily engage the problem, Ondaatje soon turns to longer forms, where spatial extension in the

writing implicates temporal continuations in both the reading and the events read.

In "The Time Around Scars" (*DM*, 49; *TK*, 19), Ondaatje queries some of the problems of separate existences in time, discovering how all signs of events, including writing itself, are only traces of what has happened, incapable of expressing the events themselves. Indeed, the speaker's awareness of this occurs when a girl he has not seen "for several years / writes of an old scar." The writing, hers and then his, is necessarily supplementary, and, like memory, secondary to what happens.[19] Like writing, scars separate us from presence, as well as the present: "We remember the time around scars, / they freeze irrelevant emotions / and divide us from present friends." But the attempt to "freeze" emotions and situations is precisely what "Four Eyes" sought. In addressing the romantic problem of life versus art, both these poems recognize how art and memory distance themselves from life. The speaker can "bring little to th[e] scene" of his wife's "scars like spread raindrops / on knees and ankles," because he was not there. Like writing itself, these scars are signifiers which can be "read" only as signifieds: for them, too, "[t]here is nothing outside of the text" (Derrida, 158). All he can do is read them now as part of the text of her body in time, in his life. Yet even if we do "remember the time around scars," all he brings to the scene of the scar he "gave" the girl is a cool appraising image of the event: "this scar I then remember / is medallion of no emotion," and has no significance. In the final stanza, the writing, which divides him, and us, from any present happening, reaches toward an ideal romantic transcendence of time even as it admits the impossibility of doing so: "I would wish this scar / to have been given with / all the love / that never occurred between us" (*DM*, 49; *TK*, 19). Once again "would" marks the failure of art to change life. Yet the poem moves us, representing a desire to give even memories lacking emotional weight some validity in our lives. The poem admits the paradoxical denials upon which it is built into the metaphoric structure of its argument. By contrasting the scar given with no love to one woman to the scars beheld with love but no knowledge in another, it suggests how separate even lovers are. In "Four Eyes," the poet cannot but choose to break away from the beloved in her reverie; here he cannot participate in her past. This emotional truth charges both poems, whatever their other meanings, with a sense of passionate loss. Part of Ondaatje's success as a writer is due to his ability, from the beginning of his career, to evoke emotional participation in his readers.

Another poem that does just that, although in an entirely different

manner, is "For John, Falling" (*DM*, 48; *TK*, 20). This is in many ways a frightening poem, expressing the shock of violence suddenly erupting into the ordinary world of the everyday. Lynette Hunter thinks this poem is one of Ondaatje's best early examples of the process of generating "a form that finds its release in the use of metaphor" (Hunter, 49–50). In its presentation of the general response to a construction accident, it "creates an increasing tension out of the uselessness of action, and the coincident frustration of inactivity" (Hunter, 50). It partly does this through an "excruciatingly prosaic" verse (Hunter, 50), although the images and metaphors are anything but prosaic or ordinary; and although each line seems to present precise information, it is difficult to figure out exactly what has happened. This confusion, deliberately invoked by the poem's formal denial of journalistic ordered description, is the confusion of the event. Has John "fallen over the edge of a pit" (Hunter, 50) or from a machine, or under one? It is hard to tell. The first stanza does not even mention the man; only in the second does he appear, alone and dying, where "[n]o one ran to" him. The first stanza suggests the immense power of the machines, how they overwhelm the human element in this situation. But once the machines are turned off, the enormity of the man's wound becomes apparent. The displaced syntax, the brutal and surreal similes of fist-sized holes or "hands clutched to eyes like a blindness," make no literal sense but the latter clearly suggests the approach of death. In the next two stanzas, what Chamberlin calls Ondaatje's general strategy of using "shifting tones and unexpected voices" creates tonal "shifts between what Walter Bagehot once called the pure, the ornate and the grotesque" (Chamberlin, 36). These changes bring us ever more into the scene, as parallel participants, trying like everyone else there to see and make sense of this horrible death. There is a grim humor to "ridiculous requests for air" as well as to the picture of the construction workers' desperate search for something useful to do. The final stanza's images press the sense of everyone's irrelevance even further.

> And the press in bright shirts,
> a doctor, the foreman scuffing a mound,
> men removing helmets,
> the machine above him
> shielding out the sun
> while he drowned
> in the beautiful dark orgasm of his mouth.
> (*DM*, 48; *TK*, 20)

The understatement is necessary if the final two lines are to achieve their climax. And it is presented as a climax, in a deliberate violation of

literary decorum that still has the power to shock after all these years. Although the "final line . . . rhythmically expands, and releases, the energy of the poem, the word 'beautiful' exercising a delicate control over the violence of the image" (Hunter, 50), the word "orgasm" is a scandalous intrusion: usually an abstract noun of intense emotional and physical release, it now becomes a horrific, visual resolution of the continuing collection of blood in the man's jaws since the second stanza. Thus the poem mimics the temporal movement it seeks to describe, catching us off guard with its final metaphor of death as love and as fulfillment, if only because it takes him out of pain. This final line demands a complexity of response that takes us beyond the lyric into something much larger. In a way, "For John, Falling" can be read as an episode in some larger story, the other episodes of which are missing; in that sense, it looks toward the episodic structures of Ondaatje's poem sequences. But however we read it, it retains a dark power of its own simply because it renders violent death in a way that violates our sense of what's proper, just as the death itself did for those who were there to experience it.

Ever since the Renaissance turn to Hellenism, young authors have found inspiration in classical sources. And although there was a change of direction in what "can be called the Renaissance of 1910, which recognized the archaic,"[20] Hellenic myth is still the most important storehouse for story most beginning writers can find. And at least since 1922, when *Ulysses* first appeared and T. S. Eliot argued that "[i]n using the myth, in manipulating a continuous parallel between contemporaneity and antiquity, Mr. Joyce is pursuing a method which others must pursue after him,"[21] writers have sought to wear the masks of various famous figures out of Homer and others. Homer is especially interesting because the works under his name are "the most ancient pages in Western literature" (Davenport, 23), and so point backward far further than history. Davenport argues that the *Odyssey* is the central modernist source, rather than the *Iliad*, which had held priority in the past. In choosing to write of "Troy Town," then, Ondaatje signaled his desire to continue in his own small way the modernist effort while not merely repeating what had already been done. In fact, as the section proceeds, it reaches far beyond Greek mythology into Egypt, the Bible, history, and finally a kind of invention, for its narrative impulses. And it approaches all its subjects in the light of its epigraph, Dmitry Karamazov's contradictory boast, or is it apology: "Indeed I can't help feeling that in telling you all about these inner struggles of mine, I've exaggerated a little in order to show you what a fine fellow I am. But, all right, let it be like that and to hell with all those who pry into the human heart."[22] This sets up certain expectations that perhaps the poems cannot live up to, especially since they are short and lack the psychological expansion of the novel. But it also suggests that contradiction, passionate struggle, and glimpses of character will occur.

Of the nine poems and sequences in this section, five are clear personae poems, while the other four imply a specific if unidentified speaker. Of these nine, only three, one of which is "Peter," the final sequence of the earlier book, appear in the selected poems. Perhaps Ondaatje chose to reject the rest because they depend so fully upon well-known mythical-literary pretexts without either subverting or supplementing them. This seems plausible, although simply by choosing Paris as a protagonist for the other sequence, he has undercut the heroic mode of the original, thus offering a somewhat new vision of the tale.

Three poems, "The Goodnight," the seven-part "Paris," and "O Troy's Down: Helen's Song," take up the Trojan War story in differing ways, forming a single sequence that demonstrates Ondaatje's subtle handling of an imagery of violence and passion, often with echoes of the poems in the first part of the book. Paris figures prominently throughout, an unheroic man of memory and sensation, who can at best articulate intense impressions rather than profound emotion and thought. Even when he gets to tell his version, he cannot really explain anything; all he can do is illustrate it. Moreover, "he" slips in and out of focus throughout, an early version of the indeterminate protagonist of Ondaatje's subverted documentaries, even if the documents here are classical myths. As will be the case in his later book-length poems, he chooses to deal with a given and complete story rather than with the continuing act of invention, with its "ironies inherent in the act of composition, [its] acknowledgement that a writer who participates in motion cannot 'freeze' a scene for the universal literary museum" (Bowering, 169), but he also chooses to leave most of the (already known) story in the interstices between lyric texts.[23] Thus he concentrates on text and narration, inviting readers to participate in the act of production as it occurs. As well, because the story itself contains a wealth of by now complex characters, he is able to assume their fictional solidity even as he uses them as lyric images or voices.

From known myth, Ondaatje turns to a historical figure of near-mythical dimensions, Queen Elizabeth I. "Elizabeth" (*DM*, 68–69; *TK*,

24–25) slides from child-voice through adolescent-voice to adult-voice, catching the intonations of each, and intimating the ways in which a complex and debilitating maturity forced itself upon the young ruler who would have to sacrifice passion to power. Death is ever present as both threat and memento mori, even to the young girl who "hid the apple in my room / till it shrunk like a face / growing eyes and teeth ribs" (*DM*, 68; *TK*, 24). But the control of voice holds our attention, as the nuances of childish awareness shift to adolescent awakening from one stanza to the next. First, "Daddy took me to the zoo" and "put a snake around my neck," then "Philip and I broke the ice with spades" and "he kissed me / with raw saltless fish in his mouth." The casual pun on "broke the ice" is typical here, as is the way images of snakes against humans and humans against fish play off each other to develop a growing sense of danger. That danger finally turns this Elizabeth away from sexual desire toward something more inverted, sly, and controlling, but again, it is the tonal slippage that best evokes her change, as she slides from thoughts of "Tom, soft laughing" and "turning / with the rhythm of the sun on warped branches, / who'd hold my breast and watch it move like a snail / leaving his quick urgent love in my palm" (*DM*, 69; *TK*, 25), to his beheading, and then to her later "cool" flirtations "with white young Essex."

Here again, proleptic mood-enhancing modifiers like "warped" push the narration forward, the general outlines of the story, as with the Trojan poems, being assumed. The names appear in some historical disorder, but they fit into a generalized image of the political betrayals and punishments of time: Elizabeth's "sister 'Bloody' Mary, Mary's husband Philip of Spain, the unfortunate or perhaps very foolish Tom Seymour, who was thought to have had a sexual dalliance with the young princess and was later executed for political reasons, and her late favorite the Earl of Essex (also, of course, executed—an irony not made explicit in the poem itself)" (Marshall, 86). The beheading stanza is almost cinematic: the gentle suggestion of "blush," grotesquely implying that Tom is merely ashamed to have waltzed so poorly into death, has a harsh, almost black comic, effect; the sudden, almost physical, "this way" shocks attention back to the speaker rather than to what she has described, and leads into the psychological distance of the final couplet, its insistence on control in "nimble rhymes." The whole poem is a remarkable performance, and it remains one of Ondaatje's most appreciated and anthologized poems.

"Peter" is widely considered the most formidable single poem in *The*

Dainty Monsters, and it's not hard to see why. An allusive transposition of the beauty and the beast tale, a fragmented story of brutality and creativity, it also engages the problems of an art that seeks to capture the violence of life. Despite its structural similarities to the mythic Trojan sequence, even to its seven sections, it seems at first to be a wholly original invention. In fact, there is a slight allusive connection to the Wayland Smith myth, in which Wayland, captured and hamstrung by King Nidhad, eventually rapes his daughter Beadohild and escapes on wings he has contrived.[24] The three central characters serve similar narrative functions in "Peter," but the actual story this particular narration evokes removes most of the mythic overtones of the original. Peter, especially, lacking the legendary stature of Volund, is not captured because he is a famous smith but begins to make cunning silverwork only after he is captured and hamstrung. "Peter" differs from "Paris," too, in its consistent external focalization on a figure seen both from within and without (see Rimmon-Kenan, 74–77); unlike Paris, who recalls, argues, and speaks directly to other figures in the story, Peter neither can nor will speak for himself, except perhaps in what he makes, which the narrative voice can only describe. Nevertheless, that narrative voice, although generally maintaining an "objective" distance from events, slips in and out of the point of view of various figures in the text. The resultant "shifting tones and unexpected voices" (Chamberlin, 36), already re-marked in some of the shorter poems, propels the narrative through violence to its violent conclusion.

On one level, "Peter" is a desperately romantic poem, addressing head-on the question of how personal experience enters works of art. In his own way, Peter is a figure of the romantic artist as tormented outcast, even if, in this story, others do much of the tormenting to him. But he is not simply a victim who eventually explodes into vengeful violence. In the only essay on this poem, Gillian Harding-Russell argues that it "creates a myth around a vindictive artist figure . . . [that] deftly objectifies the artist's dilemma by representing him as 'court monster' in a fairy-tale setting . . . [T]he artist in 'Peter' is ambivalently presented as victim and victimizer. This precludes our complete sympathy, and he finally proves himself a figure more negative than positive."[25] The ambiguities are present from the first line of part 1. "Peter" begins in violence, and the first violence is Peter's: "That spring Peter was discov-ered, freezing / the maze of bones from a dead cow" (*DM*, 71; *TK*, 26). The opening deictic phrase seems to point to a specific time, but any sense of history is soon dissolved by what follows; in fact, the narrative voice both focuses our attention by seeming to point to one single event and then leaves historical time for a sense of folktale, of "once upon a time," which hovers over the rest of the sequence. In the first line, Peter is passive, and those who discover him are unknown. With no specific reference, "freezing" at first seems to be Peter's state, then becomes perhaps his action with the bones of the dead cow. Harding-Russell reads the first stanza simply as Peter's "gruesome act of reconstructing a cow from its skeleton through ice sculpture" (Harding-Russell, 206), but the text does not allow a single reading here. That is, the dead cow might already be freezing, as the tense of "glazed" suggests, and Peter's carving "hollows of muscle," and "threading veins on its flank" could be either his artful reconstruction or his desperate search for food, as the second stanza implies. Neither reading is sure. The breakdown of syntax in the second stanza suggests the loss of formal control in violence, but that loss is general and not just Peter's. It leaves deliberately unclear whether the villagers who find the cow and Peter are the same people who attempt to capture him. It is not even clear if those are two separate events. The story remains unclear despite the narration's sharp focus on fragments of action. But then, outside of Peter, no one has been named, certainly not the narrator. It is as if everything is happening in a kind of void, perhaps a moral void, but not necessarily an artistic one if even now Peter can carve as he will later shape. At this moment, however, Peter seems to be feeding off the cow, feeding off his own carving. The sharply etched action of part 1 will draw readers in, but the contradictions the syntax has created may also leave them confused. Whatever the story is, it is not a simple one.

Part 2 maintains the confusion, with the apparent clarity of deixis (the situation of person, place, and time) shattered by the lack of referents. Although "they" (*DM*, 72; *TK*, 27) could be the villagers from the previous section, "they" also might not be. The "yard," the weapons, the "new science" all seem beyond a mere village or its inhabitants. But if it is clear who "they" are not, it is not yet clear who "they" are, and uncertainty on this matter will continue for at least one more section. There is a sense of development here: First they snare him, then they hamstring him, which leaves "him singing in the evening air," a phrase shocking in its restraint after the visceral description of their violence. Then he faints, and hypotaxis shifts to parataxis, with "and a brown bitch / nosed his pain," followed by "and he froze into consciousness." In part 1, Peter's "freezing" might have been into unconsciousness, but here, the attempts to hobble him, to "freeze" his movement, translates through a new chilling awareness into action on his own behalf. By this point, the concept of freezing has become wholly ambiguous, for "to numb wounds" (*DM*, 72; *TK*, 27) is to make movement possible, not to stop action in the pose of a piece of sculpture. Part 3 continues the refusal to place the scene anywhere specific in time or place. As months pass, Peter's "words were growls, meaning-less; / disgust in his tone burned everyone" (*DM*, 73; *TK*, 28). The arbitrary meaninglessness of Peter's words, although "everyone" under-stands his tone, suggests a folktale sensibility at work in the poem, but other aspects of it, such as the nonreferential use of pronouns (here the sudden shift from "everyone" to "you" to "they" in the first stanza), evoke a sensibility more post- than pre-modern, more literary than oral. The narrator, interestingly, may identify with "everyone" and that generalized "you," but not the "they" who "cut out his tongue." The explanatory tone of "difficult / to unpin a fish's mouth / without the eventual jerk / to empty throat of pin and matter" registers the uncaring casualness with which they once again violate him. Peter's months of "learning to speak with the air of his body, / torturing breath into tones" displays both the control of the artist who will work with whatever materials he is given to achieve some kind of communication and the horrific nature of the attacks upon his humanity. At this point the narrator suddenly enters the text to make a judgment: "it was despicable, / they had made a dead animal of his throat." To this point, Peter has been systematically dehumanized by the discourse of power, however much the narrator attempts to maintain a discreet distance from it. Thus, the descrip-tions have pretty well aped "their" desire to keep Peter as a "snared" animal, something "little more than a marred stone, / a baited gargoyle" firmly trapped in the court. But that one interjection renders Peter as almost wholly the victim, for by making "a dead animal of his throat," they have tried to destroy what makes him most human, his power of speech. And in a sense, although "baited"—and the ambiguity implies both that he is a kind of bait, only an animal again, and that they bait him, that is play with him as a human enemy—he does escape insofar as the image of "his feet arcing like a compass" "makes implicit a writing metaphor . . . , which indicates the artist's striving" (Harding-Russell, 207).

In part 4, place and persons are finally named, but the place is generic, "the court," while "they" becomes Jason (and his courtiers?) and his daughter Tara. If the two names have any symbolic significance the text seems uninterested in it.[26] It seems likely that sound more than sense joins them to another name whose symbolism is also ignored in this text.

By making "a hive for him" (*DM*, 74; *TK*, 29), "they" reveal once more the dehumanizing nature of their power. In terms of Jason's assumed mastery, Peter is only a pet, safe even for his daughter to play with: "She, with bored innocence, / would pet him like a flower" and thrill to "scowls and obscenities." But she is also "delighted at sudden grins / that opened his face like a dawn," which suggests he still has some self-control and even a capacity for joy. But he can act only as a pet, it seems, eating "bouldered at their feet, / vast hands shaping rice" and trailing them like a dog, "his legs dragged like a suitcase behind him." That final anachronistic simile wrenches both text and reader away from legend for just a moment and points to later works in which such self-conscious play with textual setting displays the contemporary implied author at work. Within the ongoing sequence, "bouldered" repeats the image of "marred stone" (*DM*, 73; *TK*, 28), while "shaping" brings out the possibility of craft in the carving image in part 1. So that, when part 5 finally shows Peter as an artist rather than as a victim of courtly violence, it does not seem so strange.

Only part 5 actually describes Peter's work, and it does so in order to reveal the nature of his art as well as its dangers: "All this while Peter formed violent beauty" (*DM*, 75; *TK*, 30). Such "violent beauty" might well include the poem we are reading, an act of self-reflexivity which now insists on the poem's questioning of a particular kind of art. If the first stanza's shift from "death on chalices" to animalistic utensils represents "the evolution of art from its function as useful craft and its part in religious ritual to its modern autonomy," while the "second stanza describes a selection process implicit in producing artistic impression," of "expressionistic exaggeration" (Harding-Russell, 208), the fixation in all the objects on mortality and the fragmentation of body and action also reveal character in action. Peter's art is expressionist, and what it expresses is his own sense of entrapment (even "an arm swimming" can only "nose *barricades* of water") and separation from wholeness of body and spirit. What he can see and what he can create are only parts, fragments, of what he desires, and thus his art is incomplete. In this sense, he is necessarily limited as a romantic artist who can only create out of experience, because his experience is all negative. The final stanza neatly balances the art against the loss in the ambiguous image of his pouring "all his strength / into the bare reflection of eyes." Do these silver fragments just barely reflect the eyes of the court, which look at them, or do they rather focus his naked artistic power into the eyes that reflect them? Both possibilities are equally, and simultaneously, present.

If the first five parts have focused on Peter, part 6 focuses through him on Tara, subtly shifting the narration's mood toward impending personal violence. Part 5's overview of passing time suggests the whole period of Peter's captivity. Part 6's hypotactic opening phrase, "Then Tara grew" (*DM*, 76; *TK*, 31), looks back to Part 4, where Tara appears as an innocent child, and it builds a configuration of sexual maturation as seen and felt by Peter. Even in the first long stanza, the sexual overtones of hips riding, thighs gripping, and "she bending over him" undercut the innocent picture of a playful young girl. The image of her as "tall, / ungainly as trees" conflates her youthful awkwardness with the perspective of the man on his knees, to maintain awareness of his position as captive court pet. Yet he also makes "golden spiders for her / and silver frogs, with opal glares." Although the spiders could be "an image for the artist who spins his web of creation" and the silver frogs may also "suggest transformation in which attributes of the moon or nature are purified by the 'silver' of the civilized arts" (Harding-Russell, 208, referring to Cirlot, 114–15), the gold and silver also suggest day and night, reflecting his growing desire to develop her interest in him. But she changes, growing older and therefore apart from him, until "she smiled cool at Peter now, / a quiet hand received gifts from him."

By its use of polysyndeton, part 6 manages to suggest change while holding temporal movement in a kind of suspension: time passes yet somehow all this happens at once in the imagination. Brilliantly mixing Peter's perceptions with a larger narrative vision, the burning of her body's awkwardness suggests the maturing poise synecdochically imaged in the last stanza while also hinting at sexual awakening. Describing various parts of her body in terms of their animal and bird analogies furthers this development. The fragmentation and bestial allusions represent Peter's fear of the very sexuality he desires, and provide a rationale for the violence of his eventual approach to her. As an adult woman, she has a power represented both in the kingly heron readers of the earlier poems will associate with the "long bird at her shoulder" and in the "new sea beasts," which by their very newness are beyond ordinary control. She is beautiful, but she is also a strong and therefore frightening woman who deals with Peter at a new distance, poised and in control. However, she also belongs to those who have held political power over him since he was captured, and the implications of the double bind all this places him in are explosive.

Part 7 presents the explosion: "An arm held her, splayed / its fingers like a cross at her neck," until "he shaped her body like a mould" and "poured loathing of fifteen years on her, / a vat of lush oil, staining, / the large soft body like a whale" (*DM*, 77; *TK*, 32). Critical responses to this conclusion are intriguing. Harding-Russell argues that the introduction of Christian imagery dramatizes "the vindictiveness of the artist" who "baits Tara and ignominiously exposes her" (Harding-Russell, 209). Refering to Tara "as the female counterpart for the sacrificial bull," she concludes that "a tactile metaphor of the cat's tongue 'rasping' her neck and breasts together with the archetypal metaphor of the whale combine to fulfil the requirements of an experiential post-modern art that looks for and finds deep-seated psychological precedent in the human mind" (Harding-Russell, 209). Lynette Hunter at least recognizes what is happening, although she couches her criticism in rather too gentle terms: "Since [Peter's] artistic expression has apparently failed, he turns again to direct communication and attacks the girl. . . . She is his new material; he shapes and moulds her body to provide the form through which energy mounts and releases in sexual love" (Hunter, 51). But if "love" is one force behind Peter's action, "loathing of fifteen years" is another, and so the text insists on the brutality of this rape (there is surely no other term for it). If part of the text renders an attempt at shaping, it also reveals the chaos that has slipped the net of art and erupted into criminal violation of another person, however strong the desire for revenge.

Moreover, in violating her, Peter violates himself, as the lack of affect in the first two lines indicates. It is not his arm nor are they his fingers which do this violence. Only when fear thrashes like an animal "at her throat," recalling how "they had made a dead animal of his throat" (*DM*, 73; *TK*, 28), does "he" feel something, as her silence now matches his. The image of the cross does imply that she is a sacrifice, but it is not clear to or for what. The continuing description is disturbingly ambivalent. Shaping her body may be a form of loving artistry, but it is also an act of remorseless control, to bring her frightening sexuality under his power; and so he especially tries to mold her breasts, those "sea beasts" of the previous section. As he pours his loathing on her, the adjective "lush" and the verb "staining" both carry a heavy load of implied degeneracy. And so she becomes both "soft," and therefore safe, and a "whale," from which lush oil is taken. The modifying words and phrases slip among possible referents to maintain a double view that reflects back across the whole implied story of the rest of the poem. No one is guiltless here.

Although the poem may be "about the process of art, about learning how to make metaphors so that one can find an equilibrium in life to control yet release energy" (Hunter, 51), it creates a myth in which the process is doomed to failure. The equilibrium that follows the artist's breakdown, his loss of control in the violent release of the manic energy of revenge, is a negative one. Peter and Tara are joined in a tableau of loss and suffering: "he lay there breathing at her neck / his face wet from her tears / that glued him to her pain." The act of revenge proves to be no escape at all; instead of freeing him of her (and in this "Peter" most fully deviates from the Wayland Smith legend that may have been its imaginative seed), it glues him "to her pain" in a closed textual universe of imaginative failure.[27] As has been the case throughout the narration, Peter's experiential art here lacks the necessary dimension of wholeness. At this point the poem's fragmentation simply provides a further metaphor of the artistic failure of its protagonist. Hunter criticizes "Peter" because "the poem is weak in its connections. . . . The isolation of each [unit] is emphasized because Peter never expresses himself directly except through action, yet there are no echoes even of a shape he carves" (Hunter, 51). It is true that Peter does not tell us anything the way Paris does, but the echoes are there, even to the shapes he carves, the "fragments of people" (*DM*, 75; *TK*, 30) becoming sea beasts (*DM*, 76; *TK*, 31), and then the breasts he shapes with "stub of tongue" (*DM*, 77; *TK*, 32) in the violent closure of rape. But the isolation is also there, and it is in his failure to transcend it that "Peter" reveals the dangers of an extremist art in which "the rhetoric of suffering becomes the mark of sincerity in the work itself, and, in popular mythology, the madness or suicide of the artist authenticates the *oeuvre*."[28] Peter is the first example of such an artist in Ondaatje's oeuvre, but "Peter," like the later works with such an artist figure, is an example of a different kind of rhetoric, in which balanced control, careful invention, and imaginative fiction making become the mark of artistic sincerity in the work. It is not, perhaps, wholly successful,[29] if only because the necessary ambivalences of its structure are sometimes undercut by slips in tone that create a disturbing emotional ambiguity that feels somewhat out of control.

Both the Trojan sequence and "Peter" demonstrate Ondaatje's early desire to escape the confines of lyric space while retaining lyric intensity. Although he will soon go much further, as he discovers the greater fictional expansiveness of the book-length documentary poem, the shift that took place from one to another of these apprentice works indicates how quickly he learned simultaneously to remake and reject the given story. While "Peter" uses only one narrative voice, it suggests the potential of inherited story as backbone for a fragmented text in which various narrative voices emerge from and withdraw into the mysterious space of the already told. The first example of this extension of focus is *the man with seven toes.*

In the early summer of 1966, having already explored the possibilities of extending the range of the lyric in the short sequences of "Troy Town," Ondaatje was looking for a suitable subject for a new project. Given his interest in the visual arts, as the imagery and the references to Henri Rousseau, Chagall, and Epstein in *The Dainty Monsters* show, it's not surprising that the paintings of Sidney Nolan are the central "documents" from which he built his second book, the 34-poem sequence, *the man with seven toes.*[30] Nolan, one of the first Australian painters of this century to achieve an international reputation, created a series of paintings about Mrs. Eliza Fraser, who was shipwrecked off the Queensland coast in 1836, and Bracefell, the escaped convict who led her through bush and desert to a settlement only to be betrayed by the woman he had saved. Ondaatje came across the Mrs. Fraser paintings in the book that also contained the only version of the story he ever learned.[31]

The quotation from Colin MacInnes's essay, "The Search for an Australian Myth in Painting," with which Ondaatje concludes his book, appears to make an implicit claim to conventional "documentary." Instead, it serves a function similar to the original notes for T. S. Eliot's *The Waste Land:* partly parodic, partly subversive. Although Ondaatje's work continually aligns him with other makers of "documentary" poetry, novels, or films, it also signals his ironic separation from them. Just as "Peter" "forgets" its mythical original in order to construct a new story on a blank textual site, so too *the man with seven toes* dispenses with almost everything the MacInnes quotation provides for it. Ondaatje subverts the "documentary" as a form even as he makes use of the way it allows him to "novelize" the lyric sequence (Michael Holquist, Introduction to Bakhtin 1981, xxxii). Although he does not achieve the full "heteroglossia" (Bakhtin 1981, 263) of *The Collected Works of Billy the Kid* and later prose works, he at least begins to suggest the ways in which multiple voices—here, narrator, woman, and convict—must both support and contradict one another. This aspect of "novelization" ensures a formal realization of "indeterminacy" in *the man with seven toes.* A kind of rewriting, it gleefully overturns its source, putting it under erasure in order to write something new in its place. It is a palimpsest where the erasure of the earliest, now hidden layer of the "original version" of the story ensures a site for the invented one newly inscribed there.

The MacInnes quotation, coming at the end, seems to cast a "documentary" aura back over Ondaatje's book, but the two versions have too

many differences to be easily laid over one another, like transparencies.
For example, where MacInnes's commentary interprets both the incident
and Nolan's postcolonial response to it, Ondaatje eschews interpretation
entirely, especially postcolonial political interpretation of the theme of
betrayal (see Clark et al., 21–22). He alters MacInnes's commentary,
rendering it simultaneously more mythic and more contemporary. He
does keep the rigid outline of a story MacInnes characterizes as paradig-
matically Australian, but only so we may realize how far he strayed from
it in the sequence just read. As is perhaps proper for a legend, the
MacInnes version skips over any details of either the six months Mrs.
Fraser spent with the aborigines or the difficult trek back to civilization;
Ondaatje's text reverses this approach, offering no rational explanation
for her presence in the bush, but concentrating with visceral effectiveness
on the perceptual physicality of the experience. As he later wrote about a
Canadian mythic tale, he desires writing "in which the original myth is
given to us point blank," the "source is not qualified," and the "official"
story is replaced by an utterly other version, full of the "original rawness"
of immediate sensual perception.[32]

Ondaatje has always been lucky in his choice of subjects, insofar as the
documents about each of them have been few and fragmentary at the
time he was writing through, around, and beyond them. This is true not
only of Mrs. Fraser, but also of Billy the Kid (where there was a plethora
of material but almost all of it was hearsay) and Buddy Bolden. In all
three cases, works of historical scholarship appeared after his books,
possibly granting them an even greater fictional autonomy.[33] The nature
of the documents he uses ranges far wider than the term usually covers, in
this case to Nolan's paintings.[34] They are the primary documents here: as
he could only make use of the selection reproduced in *Sidney Nolan*, they
become the properly fragmented ground of his invented text. Some of his
poems specifically allude to individual paintings, but basically it is their
violent hothouse atmosphere Ondaatje renders in these poems, while
ignoring the paintings' political theme of betrayal completely. As a
"phenomenological" presentation of perception, and perception mostly
cut free from ratiocination, *the man with seven toes* refuses the kind of
political allegorization MacInnes brings to Nolan's paintings. The
woman of the poem is never named; the convict is renamed; there are
some telling anachronisms (another Ondaatje game in book after book);
she does not turn upon her benefactor, although he does disappear from
the text as soon as she leaves him; the Australia of this poem, like the land
of "Peter," is as much a wilderness of the fantasizing mind as any real

place. The poem is haunted by a 1960s spirit of revolutionary social and sexual idealism in which, to borrow a phrase from Marshall McLuhan and Wilfred Watson, psychological, social, or cultural breakdown leads to breakthrough.[35] Both the breakdown and the breakthrough can occur on many levels of experience, but one of the most effective, both imagistically and poetically, is the sexual, which ties together body and spirit, desire and denial, action and morality in a complex weaving of motive, meaning, and behavior. *The man with seven toes* is far from alone in narrating a renewing loss of civilization, a regenerative encounter with the primitive within. What marks it as colonial writing is its representation of a white, European suffering that loss in a dark new world landscape to her eventual, if also provisional, emotional and spiritual gain. Yet, set in an indeterminate place and time, it also achieves an indeterminism of personal reference that makes it resistant to interpretation, and in that accomplishment, it is an avatar of the postmodernist later works.

Chapter Three

The Collected Works of Billy the Kid

The Collected Works of Billy the Kid, winner of the Governor General's Award for 1970, is Ondaatje's first national, and international, success, "praised by critics and readers and roundly condemned—to his delight—by federal MPs for dealing with an *American* hero and outlaw" (Mandel, 276). If its use of what Annie Dillard calls "narrative collage" is the reason it is the only Canadian book mentioned in her *Living by Fiction,*[1] its utter overhauling of the given versions of the legend is what leads Stephen Tatum, in his definitive study, *Inventing Billy the Kid: Visions of the Outlaw in America, 1881–1981,* to call it "the most significant publication in the Kid's bibliography" (Tatum, 149). What the many and varied critical analyses reveal is how open to reader responses this text is, and how easily it can be turned to a particular critic's ideological needs; but they also suggest that there is a power to the book that resists analysis, something in it that seduces readers into a game of complicity with the writing and makes of them the highly active readers every writable text desires. It is, simply from the point of view of its hold over a wide-ranging readership, a highly successful work of art.

The Collected Works of Billy the Kid is one of the most interpreted texts in recent Canadian literature; and as the criticism of Canadian literature was, at the time it appeared, most given to the thematic approach,[2] it is not surprising that most of the early interpretations of the book are thematic, attempting to explicate in mythical or philosophical terms the essential opposition between Billy the Kid and Pat Garrett. Later, many critics suggest that Billy himself contains the oppositions they elicit from the text—life vs. death, energy vs. stasis, chaos vs. order, creation vs. destruction, affirmation vs. negation, visceral knowledge vs. mental obliviousness, emotional connection vs. its denial—and that these internal contradictions cause his self-destructive behavior. Such interpretations read the text as straight narrative and essentially uncomplicated representation, passing over the way the formal energies of the work overwhelm, or at least scandalously supplement, any strict thematic reading, and engage us in a powerful, if enigmatic, reading experience, a rush of surging and contradictory rhythms and images that refuse finally to submit to a neat thematic outline. In this it takes its place with others of Ondaatje's earlier and later texts as a duplicitous or doubled writing, which invites us to participate in a manner of representation (this happened to her or him, and then that did) even as various textual strategies simultaneously deny us that consolation. We are drawn on by story even if it is full of gaps that the narration can never fully cover over. The gaps are central to the reading experience.

Like *the man with seven toes, The Collected Works* evolved into a stage performance. Yet it remains a curiously static drama, full of discursive scenes that lead nowhere in terms of traditional plot, and beginning with the announcement of its protagonist's inevitable death. On the other hand, the text lends itself to dramatization precisely because its major "characters" already have a legendary existence in pulp fiction, Hollywood films, and comic books. They emerge as rounded figures not so much because the text "explains" them in realistic terms as because readers or audiences bring a sense of their personalities to them, which each scene can either substantiate or refute. In either case, the text invites active collaboration in creating a deeper sense of their verisimilitude. Billy's bibliography is so huge—"well over 800 items" by 1965 (Tatum, 5)—Ondaatje can completely alter aspects of the inherited story, knowing his readers have enough information to follow his text's transformations wherever they may lead. *The Collected Works* inserts significant gaps into a known narrative of a famous story, fills some of them with newly invented material that has its own gaps, and becomes a work that can be read in almost any order from within.

Given that "the significance of a figure as completely metamorphosed as Billy the Kid is totally international,"[3] it is hardly surprising that Ondaatje would choose him for a text exploring the black romantic theme of the artist as outlaw (see Tatum, 141–42). In the starkest terms of biographical interpretation, "[w]hat results from the title '*The Collected Works of Billy the Kid* by Michael Ondaatje' is in fact a composite figure: Billy the kid, outlaw as artist, and Michael Ondaatje, artist as outlaw, meeting in one persona, which is part history, part legend, part aesthetic image, part creator of images" (Scobie 1985c, 193). Scobie's essay, the first, and still the best, of the early interpretations of Ondaatje's book, attempts "to maintain a balance (a project which I think is typical of Ondaatje) between the two aspects of artist and outlaw" (Scobie

1985c, 207) that other critics have denied by ignoring or downplaying Garrett's role in the book.[4] But Garrett, of course, must be there, for he is part and parcel of the mythic inheritance in which, as with Robin Hood and the Sheriff of Nottingham,[5] a "symbiotic relationship between Pat Garrett and the Kid" marks the myth, whether "in basically external terms of moral values . . . [or] in psychological terms as the symbolic conflict of a divided self" (Tatum, 159).

Tatum argues that such interpretations within the versions of the Kid's life and death written and filmed during this century only occurred recently, but the basic relationship has always been there. Although their early roles were the opposite of what they would become, Garrett and the Kid are inextricably linked from the beginning in a cultural story of how civilization comes to the frontier. Tatum's study reveals how complexly layered a mythos Ondaatje found upon which to invent his own set of variations.

Ondaatje uses Walter Noble Burns's 1926 best-seller, *The Saga of Billy the Kid*, the first major publication to present the Kid as possibly heroic in his outlawry, as his basic documentary evidence.[6] Burns wrote an epic study of the Old West that foregrounds the larger conflicts, such as the 1877–1878 Lincoln County war. Full of realistic details about New Mexico society when Billy the Kid lived there, it also collects all the rumors about him, including how Garrett shot him in Pete Maxwell's bedroom. "The death of Tunstall, the reminiscences by Paulita Maxwell and Sallie Chisum on Billy, are essentially made up of statements made to Walter Noble Burns in his book," Ondaatje writes, adding what becomes his usual disclaimer, "[w]ith these basic sources I have edited, rephrased, and slightly reworked the originals."[7] In fact, he has taken more from Burns's *Saga* than he admits here, yet far less than the unwary reader might imagine. Far more important than what he puts in is what he leaves out—almost everything Burns and other such historians render as the social and historical context of Billy the Kid's story.

Far more tellingly present as subtexts are various western films. Whether or not he actually saw Lash Larue in *The Son of Billy the Kid* (1949) or Audie Murphy in *The Kid from Texas* (1950) doesn't much matter, for they are based on the same archetypal conventions as most other westerns. The subtitle of his book, "Left Handed Poems," suggests that he did see Paul Newman in Arthur Penn's *The Left-Handed Gun* (1958), based on Gore Vidal's teleplay *The Death of Billy the Kid* (1955), in which Newman also starred. He likely saw Marlon Brando's *One-Eyed Jacks* (1961). The latter two films, especially, imply an irreconcilable "conflict between the Kid's need for a violent fulfillment of his personal code of justice, and society's need for the rule of law, for restraint in the use of violence, and for commitment to democracy, family, and religion" (Tatum,132), and present that conflict in terms of mixed generic expectations. Scenes of black comedy, intense lyricism, or sudden violence, and a Billy characterized as a nineteenth-century rebel without a cause, make the clear outlines of the myth collapse. Ondaatje himself admits the power western films hold over him while explaining his love of Sergio Leone's *Once upon a Time in the West:* "Luckily I saw the film after I had finished *Billy the Kid* because here was an Italian film-maker making this western, in many ways the best western, where with *Billy the Kid* I was trying to make the film I couldn't afford to shoot, in the form of a book. All those B movies in which strange things that didn't happen but could and should have happened I explored in the book" (Solecki 1975, 20). Ondaatje also probably knew Michael McClure's poetic drama *The Beard* (1965) and Jack Spicer's *Billy the Kid* (1958).[8] Like Ondaatje's book, "these works announce the death of the Kid in the opening pages as a preliminary to the task of creating the Kid. For these writers the Kid's 'life' only begins with his death in history and in historical accounts" (Tatum, 143). The basic outline of the "historical accounts," even if only the most inventively mythical ones, cannot be changed: the Kid moves through an already given series of events to the moment when he will be killed by Pat Garrett. Ondaatje's text depends upon our knowledge of those "historical accounts," for it is because that general story is so well known, because the death has always already happened for both readers and writers, that the text can concentrate on other things, what might have occurred in the interstices of the "given" story, which myth or epic never tell.[9]

Not a story about me through their eyes then. Find the beginning, the slight silver key to unlock it, to dig it out. Here then is a maze to begin, to be in. (*CWBK*, 20)

The Collected Works of Billy the Kid is a rhythmic maze and, as the punning removal of the keylike "g" suggests, the blank spaces are as important as the full ones: " 'Be in' is 'begin' with a gap, the letter left out. As readers we are looking less for keys than keyholes, entrance not into a teleological structure that terminates in a single exit, but through and into uncertainties."[10] Moreover, our "very act of reading implicates [our] presence in the maze of discourse. Billy talks about rebeginning 'here,' on the page, in the text."[11] Once we have read the book in the usual linear fashion, we can return to almost any page and find ourselves once again in medias res, even when the fragments are prolepses to the always already given end. As soon as we enter any part we begin again: this is the meaning of collage as it operates in this text. Here, Billy appears to be the speaker, and what he says is that this version of the myth, in which we are already entangled, will not be like the other versions "through their eyes." But rather than telling us what it will be like, he simply invites us to explore the possibilities on our own, beginning with an image of him and Charlie Bowdre crisscrossing "the Canadian border. Ten miles north of it ten miles south. . . . The two of us, our criss-cross like a whip in slow motion, the ridge of action rising and falling, getting narrower in radius till it ended and we drifted down to Mexico and old heat. That there is nothing of depth, of significant accuracy, of wealth in the image, I know. It is there for a beginning" (*CWBK*, 20). Though the image may lack depth, it is nevertheless complex, for the border crossing doubles the reference for the floating pronominal "I/me" in so far as the very text we are reading, written by a Canadian, continually crosses genre borders.[12] The narrowing of radius suggests the repetitive nature of the series of events to which *The Collected Works* returns over and over again, especially Billy's own death, while "drifted" echoes significantly in the one poem in which Billy presents himself in the act of writing (*CWBK*, 72).

I keep coming back to that death because it is an unavoidable focus throughout the book. Billy the Kid is already an empty site at the very beginning of the poem, when a blank square appears above his name as a photograph manqué. This "absent portrait" is the very first inscription in *The Collected Works*, and what it "announces [is] the 'negative' of narration. It becomes, in Derrida's words, an *exergue*, what lies 'outside the work,' 'inscription,' 'epigraph.' . . . It suggests that Billy lies outside the poem, cannot be contained in a single frame" (Kamboureli 1991, 185).[13] On the following page, the text proffers a seemingly traditional epic list of "the killed . . . (By me)" and "the killed . . . (By them)" (*CWBK*, [6]). As Sheila Watson notes, the "list paradoxically includes the name of the sheriff Garrett, who survived to record the experience in print."[14] But there is a further paradox in that the "last of the killed mentioned in the list is Billy himself" (Kamboureli 1991, 189).

Although dead, Billy is the speaker of this monologue, and of all the other monologues he presumably delivers in the poem. . . . The poem's discourse, then, is largely uttered by a dead subject. It is this paradox that defies most critics' attempts to identify the narrative pattern that leads to Billy's death. Billy does not die in the poem. He is already dead when he utters his first monologue. This death is the real *exergue* in the poem. It is the 'work' that cannot be collected in *The Collected Works of Billy the Kid*. Billy's last monologue, uttered as he lies dying (95), is not a performative but a constative act of language: nothing happens under the reader's eyes but the very acting out of language. (Kamboureli 1991, 189–90)

So what are the "collected works" that make up this book? If it is a long poem, as Kamboureli reads it, they are acts of language. If it is "'modular fiction'" (Godard, 31), they are "the multiple exposures of prose, prose poems, poetry, dime novels, newspaper accounts, and interviews [which offer] the reader a number of angles from which to compose Billy's portrait" (Godard, 37). And if it is a documentary poem, they are the parts of what Manina Jones calls a "documentary collage," and the book is "a kind of 'docudrama,' a drama of documents, a play of texts . . . [with] Billy the Kid . . . [as] 'representative hero.' He is a hero of representation, for these documents are his 'collected works' not because he composed them, but because he is composed *of* them. The signifier 'Billy the Kid' becomes the shifting locus of their intersection, the place where problems of documentation become unavoidable" (Jones, 28). The text invites all these readings, and others perhaps as well. We are implicated in the text, and even in the narration, precisely because we are assumed to know the basic outline of the story.[15]

Because we know the given story so well, this text can subvert our sense of it and of its protagonist, yet because that story has such a formulaic plot, we may make the mistake of thinking that this version, too, can only follow that plot to its well-known end, with all its thematic luggage attached. This appears to be the error of those critics who insist that the whole text "points toward" Billy's death at the end of the book. But it is not the end of the book, for the "comic book legend' (*CWBK*, 110) comes after it—another intertext, another of the documents out of which Billy is composed. The argument that Billy so desires order that he forces the narrative's inevitable motion toward the final confrontation and death, forces it to follow the given plot to the end, accepts the duplicitous consolation of representation the text offers and "reads" Billy as essentially a "realistic" character.

For such readers—and all of us are invited by this text to be such readers, at least part of the time—Billy remains the collector of his own

works, and they—the various fragments gathered in this collage-text—
contribute to a multifaceted picture of a singular character. But if even
Scobie says that this "book *fixes* a certain view of the Kid into an intense,
fully realized image" (Scobie 1985c, 191), at least he does not ignore
Garrett's place in the documents, nor thereby make the error of arguing
that Billy fears and distrusts the flux of life and uses both guns and
photographs to keep the world at bay. By ignoring Garrett's place in the
story and in this text critics can accuse Billy of keeping "his emotional
distance from the violent events he is describing [so that,] paradoxically,
his dispassionate objectivity [becomes] so disproportionate that it
amounts to misrepresentation" (Nodelman, 69), or of trying "to assume
control over his world, to order the world to his liking" (Owens, 126).
But, from the beginning of the book, Billy is already out of the world,
and the documents, lyrics, memories, photographs, and other writings
which make up the collected works of, or about, him refuse to assume an
overarching narrative shape. They simply are, and each one, even in
fluctuating repetition, offers another new glimpse of the shifting sites
designated by the name "Billy the Kid."

    "Billy the Kid" cannot be "fixed," as in a photograph, which is why
the initial "photograph" is an empty space while the other
illustrations—photographs by Huffman, two modern photographs, and
even two etchings—have nothing to do with the other documents of the
poem. The *name* is legend, however much it has its basis in history. And
the "root of the word legend, *legenda*, means 'what is to be read'; Billy the
Kid is a legendary figure in the rhetorical sense, constructed in readings
and in writings. Because of the multiple, unstable, and potentially
contradictory nature of readings and writings (and readings *as* writings),
however, Billy the Kid is . . . both encoded by [the text] and refuses to
stick to script" (Jones, 28–29). No more than the documents gathered in
this text can the various essays on "Billy the Kid" or *The Collected Works
of Billy the Kid* hope to "fix" him, to place him once and for all. Already
dead, already no more than the sum of the ever growing "works of" him,
he remains beyond our grasp, defiantly and definitively indeterminate.
Yet each fragment in the collage offers another view of him or of his
world, and even in their contradictions they hint at representational
opportunities the text simultaneously proffers and refuses.

    Against narrative, Ondaatje interweaves a series of often contradictory
lyrics, dramatic monologues, and prose fragments. The "law" Billy is
really outside of is that of the mortal world, yet "his" text inhabits that
world with us, its readers. "Billy points to the radical place that is both

inside and outside, life and death, earth and the 'great stars.' This is the topos of his discourse, a place of paradox. Death does not stifle language. Instead it imports into narrative the strangeness of discourse" (Kamboureli 1991, 193), which defamiliarizes all that it touches, especially Billy's own perceptions. Billy is his own documenter in many of the segments of the poem, and "his" "speeches, head dreams, apologies" (*TK,* 46) demonstrate his difference, that he is on the other side of the border he crosses to speak. But he is not the only speaker, and the other monologues and documents both supplement and contradict what he says, so that "Billy the Kid" becomes both too fully written and somehow erased as the text proceeds, evading every attempt to capture and hold him.

Billy is not alone in being evasive. "Michael Ondaatje" manages to evade our grasp as well, for he too, the putative author of the book, is as slippery a signifier as his protagonist. And he begins to slip out of focus on the very first page, where Billy's photograph does not appear. Beneath the empty square this statement appears: "I send you a picture of Billy made with the Perry shutter as quick as it can be worked—Pyro and soda developer" (*CWBK,* [5]). The quotation[16] reveals exactly how the documentary poem works to fictionalize its materials. Once it was an uncomplicated commonsensical piece of writing, the pronouns neatly fixed, but now that it is cited it is also re-sited, slipping its moorings in history, that supposed guarantor of "reality," to float into the ocean of fiction, where it can never again be anchored in apparent referentiality. In its original text, the pronouns were specific, but now, on the first page of this new text, commenting on a photo that does not exist, and speaking for a nonreferential "I" to an equally nonreferential "you," it expands into a multiplicity of possible meanings. Where there was a single voice, there are now many. Responding to what appears to be a specific address, and looking once again to the empty space above, we find nothing there to which the words might refer. An "I" names both a "Billy" and a "you," thus linking all three at the very beginning of the reading/writing which is *The Collected Works.* A slippery rhetorical linkage of logos, topos, and ethos will hold throughout the rest of the book. "I" will slide from implied author to narrator to one of the characters as narrator; "you" will slide from implied reader to narratee to particular characters; and the name, the site of our various interests, will simply multiply into an assortment of possibilities, especially "if we decide *not* to treat the poem as a whole, but as a collection of documents—themselves neither 'univocal' nor 'autonomous'— successively 'projected' like the frames of a film, onto the blank space from which Billy as photograph and referent is absent" (Jones, 30). In other words, rather than start us or itself on a linear journey toward a given conclusion, the empty space and the re-sited quotation open up the first of a series of gaps we must fill in our own ways. This is not a map on which to follow a carefully plotted narrative but rather a thick collage painting in which to see first one thing and then another slipping into the foreground and out again. It is a maze, something like "Boot Hill," where "the path keeps to no main route for it tangles/like branches of a tree among the gravestones" (*CWBK,* 9). The image is an analogue of the reading experience the text offers.

The book as a graveyard text, tangled, following no main route, and often returning to the same gravestone, the same inscription, to view it from a different angle, just as the maze of paths, with "no main route," does in Boot Hill. By incorporating found and invented documents along with Billy's and others' monologues, *The Collected Works* keeps reinscribing central events of Billy's life "at various speeded up rhythms creating the effect of a story that goes around and around and around on itself in a/mazing spiral" (Godard, 45). Proleptic, analeptic, repetitive, and/or achronic, each segment interrupts narrative and "proclaims the triumph of the written word over the temporal order" (Godard, 54). Although the text appears to speed up toward the end, circling ever closer in on Billy's death, it does not give in to narrative necessity. Even the best-known version of his death—shot by Pat Garrett in Pete Maxwell's bedroom in Fort Sumner in the summer of 1881—is only one story, and there are other stories, including "the further possibility that the Kid did not die in Pete Maxwell's bedroom" (Tatum, 101). Thus the "comic book legend," while it does not deny history exactly, does supplement its deadly closure.

The third page of text is a story, a short narrative interpolated into the longer, fragmented and interrupted, narrative manqué of Billy's given story. Among the events Billy obsessively returns to are those mentioned in the second half of his list. While he writes a lot about "the killed . . . (By them)," he pays much less attention to "the killed . . . (By me)" (*CWBK,* [6]), preferring to present himself "as victim. There are three extended accounts of killings in the book—those of Tom O'Folliard, Charlie Bowdre, and Billy himself—and in every case the killer is Garrett" (Scobie 1985c, 203). Billy cannot be inscribed into any text without Garrett, and if he is represented as hero/victim, Garrett must appear as villain/killer, though this text is never that pure in its representations.

While *The Saga of Billy the Kid* provides a straightforward account of O'Folliard's death (Burns, 205–9), *The Collected Works* offers a very different version, the differences embedded in Billy's transforming perceptions. He begins by establishing time and place, then immediately recalls his "21st birthday, mixing red dirt and alcohol" (*CWBK,* 7) the previous month. This version seems to stick to the historical record when it says "cattle politicians like Chisum wanted the bad name out," a view of Chisum the rest of the text will strive to make us forget. The presence of this line can be read as either an error or an example of the way fragmentation works in *The Collected Works:* "the documents in *The Collected Works* both conflict with each other and gesture outward to other intertextual 'sources'" (Jones, 34), some of which are in this text. In this version, the "cattle politicians" "made Garrett sheriff and he sent me a letter saying move out or I will get you Billy. The government sent a Mr. Azariah F. Wild to help him out." Neither Burns nor Tatum even mentions Wild. This first paragraph, full of analepses, also includes a reference to one of Billy's killings: "Between November and December I killed Jim Carlyle over some mixup, he being a friend." Where Burns spends three pages on the ins and outs of this essentially accidental death, seeking to ameliorate Billy's part in it (Burns, 202–4), *The Collected Works* offers neither explanation nor description, and it is the lack of the latter which causes this death to fade before the extensive and visceral delineation of Garrett's shooting of O'Folliard.

A similar collage of analepses, the second paragraph sets Garrett and his men in Sumner and Billy, his friends, and Tom O'Folliard on their way to meet there. The third paragraph is the longest and contains the death. Its syntax slips away from rational discourse as it feels its way closer and closer to the violence it enacts. Although every sentence moves the event forward, there is a feeling of parataxis, of disconnection, as simple descriptive sentences fall into syntactical disarray under the impact of the violence they enact. O'Folliard's inability to shoot back at the man who has wounded him will become one of the texts leitmotives: Garrett's victims suffer while he watches cooly unconcerned. The final paragraph characterizes Billy's other, the opposite he can neither escape nor deny no matter how he strews the fragments of his story across the maze of the text. Having picked up the dead man, "the head broken in two, {taken} him back to the hotel room" (*CWBK,* 8), Garrett and the others "continued their poker game till six a.m. Then remembered they hadnt done anything about Wild" (*CWBK,* 8). Garrett shows no feelings about the deaths he causes. To suggest that Billy describes such scenes with "dispassionate objectivity" (Nodelman, 70) misses the point: Garrett's actions demonstrate his dispassionate objectivity; Billy's language, syntax, and rhythms demonstrate exactly the opposite.

For critics who, reading *The Collected Works* as a form of realism, see Billy and Garrett as alike, or at least Billy wanting to be like Garrett (Nodelman, 76; Blott, 193; MacLulich, 110), the plot of the given story still controls this text. Unable to accept its fragmentation and disturbance of conventional rise-and-fall action, they create a monologic character, who inevitably has to assume responsibility for his own destruction, out of the contradictory views of Billy various documents and his own shifting statements present. This Billy seeks a mechanically ordered world, one that he fully controls, and he dies because he cannot control or order his own story as he desires (Owens, 121, 139). Because this singular figure is simply a failed Garrett, the analyses "neglect or simply ignore [him, and] put Billy in his place" (Scobie 1985c, 209). A more complex argument suggests Billy's "anxious and unremitting attempts to manage life and to extricate himself from it" fail because he is too sensitive to fully emulate Garrett, a "consummate murderer" who "moves through [the] world largely undisturbed by appalling human suffering" (Cooley, 217, 230). Garrett is mentioned then only as a "complementary" figure, "inseparable"[17] from Billy. But although complementary—indeed, in the larger myth to which they belong, they are necessary to each other—they are not inseparable.

What such analyses share is a particular reading of one of the most important early lyrics in the book:

> MMMMMMMM mm thinking
> moving across the world on horses
> body split at the edge of their necks
> neck sweat eating at my jeans
> moving across the world on horses
> so if I had a newsman's brain I'd say
> well some morals are physical
> must be clear and open
> like diagram of watch or star
> one must eliminate much
> that is one turns when the bullet leaves you
> walk off see none of the thrashing
> the very eyes welling up like bad drains
> believing then the moral of newspapers or gun
> where bodies are mindless as paper flowers you dont feed
> or give to drink

> that is why I can watch the stomach of clocks
> shift their wheels and pins into each other
> and emerge living, for hours
>
> (*CWBK*, 11)

Passing over the fact that the major part of this poem is in the conditional mode, they skip over the "if" in "so if I had a newsman's brain I'd say" to argue that Billy "kills by adopting 'the moral of newspapers or gun'" (Lee, 170). If anyone has "a newsman's brain," it is Garrett: he is the "[i]deal assassin for his mind was unwarped. Had the ability to kill someone on the street walk back and finish a joke. One who had decided what was right and forgot all morals" (*CWBK*, 28). The echoes in this later description of the "moral of newspapers" line should be warning enough that at least it cannot refer to Billy alone. Insisting that Billy does think this way removes much of the complexity of the text, reducing him to a singular figure rather than the empty site in which any number of possibilities appear and disappear in the shifting inscriptions on its headstone.

Such readings miss even more than that, for most of them pay no attention to the first five lines of the poem. Like Garrett, with his stuffed birds (*CWBK*, 88), some critics seem to need to deal with dead bodies that stay in their place; the open, postmodern, indeterminate text "of a world in motion where nothing is settled, where things only approach clarity" (Cooley, 233),[18] slips away from them, and they strive to fix it and what they see as its eponymous narrator in place. But Billy is a figure in process, glimpsed in the participle, signifying his participation in the changing world. Even as he is "moving across the world on horses," and the repetition of that line feels significant, he is thinking, he is exploring possibilities. Such "thinking/moving" takes him across borders, as the next two lines imply, with their suggestions of boundaries breaking down, even the boundary of the body itself. Because he imaginatively crosses borders he can wonder about a different kind of brain, which eliminates what it cannot comprehend: this lyric demonstrates "Billy's acute apprehension (in both senses of the word) of an ideology which fascinates him only because it is his opposite, his enemy, that which will ultimately kill him" (Scobie 1985c, 209).

Billy does not possess "a newsman's brain"; he thinks with his body, through his perceptions, as the prose poem just previous reveals (*CWBK*, 10). Most importantly, he will not stay fixed in our critical gaze. The final three lines slip their moorings in the poem and float free of reference. Are they part of the long "if" clause, or are they separate? The poem deliberately refuses to provide clear demarcations. If the first five lines render Billy's experience and his being in the world while the next eleven present a supposition, do the final three reflect Billy's or his putative "newsman's" thinking? The newsman's "I" will watch differently than Billy's "I" does. And that is not even to mention the vague syntax which allows the possibility that either or both the "wheels and pins" and "I" can "emerge living, for hours." Given the various images of machinery in the book as a whole, this passage assumes some importance even as it refutes clear interpretation. But it does not simply represent Billy's character.

There is a similar slippage of referentiality in "I have seen pictures of great stars," a central poem and major thematic gesture:

> The beautiful machines pivoting on themselves
> sealing and fusing to others
> and men throwing levers like coins at them.
> And there is there the same stress as with stars,
> the one altered move that will make them maniac.
>
> (CWBK, 41)

As a poem about "energy tightly controlled by form," it self-reflexively implies that "in art the 'one altered move' will result in the dissipation of energy, a bad poem" (Scobie 1985c, 196). If Billy as outlaw-poet writes this, the self-reflexivity is his, but if Ondaatje, as poet-outlaw, also does, the self-reflexivity doubles and redoubles. The fact that the historical Billy could not have seen such "pictures of great stars" raises questions about the "I" who speaks here and whether it speaks monologically throughout. Since the "I" of the second stanza is elided, who is represented in the empty space it leaves behind? In terms of the basic opposition in the book, Garrett becomes "the one altered move" that will destroy Billy (see Scobie 1985c, 197). But this excessive lyric gestures beyond the story, overwhelming narrative as it achieves a visionary intensity (Kamboureli 1991, 192). By extravagantly transcending character and narrative, this and other lyric moments in the text bring a kind of mania to it. This poem is central, then, because it demonstrates how "the one altered move" can function as "[a] method, then, and then, and then, of composition; against the 'and then' of story" (Kroetsch, 120).

Billy and the other characters appear and reappear throughout the fragments which have been gathered into an order, but not a narrative order, in the text. But how they reappear says a lot about the book's concerns. Death is always near, if not actually occurring: the world Billy lived in is a world of violence. And violence interrupts both characterization and narration, it breaks them down. In the text as collage, events return in various forms as signs of both narrative violence and the attempts to evade it. O'Folliard's death, and the repeated versions of Charlie Bowdre's death, not to mention the numerous prolepses of Billy's death, are interrupted by memories of other times, with Charlie and his wife, Tom, Angela D., and the Chisums. These analepses—and in one sense the whole book is a complex analepsis containing more deeply embedded flashbacks and flashforwards—serve to extend the inherited characterizations of Billy by supplementing the usual documentation of his life, as it has already been written.

The killing of Charlie Bowdre is open to a variety of readings. Is it repeated because Billy is struggling to give some kind of narrative and therefore intellectual order to one more violation of his sense of the world (Owens, 122), or simply because violent death enters the imagination so utterly it cannot be sloughed off in just one statement? Does Billy's circling back upon such moments mark him as the acutely anxious photographer attempting "to freeze action in a series of still photographs" (Cooley, 217), and therefore keeping at it until he gets it right, or does it reveal him as engaged in and by "the sense of shift" (*TK*, 64) that marks him as a site of change, a figure in motion, what Robert Kroetsch once called a postmodern, fragmented, disjunctive, and open self?[19]

The first version of Charlie's death is frightening in its poetic intensity, as Billy registers his body "tossed 3 feet by bang bullets giggling/at me face tossed in a gaggle" (*CWBK*, 12). The imagery here dissolves from the visual into the aural, that very dissolution reflecting the destruction of the body Billy is witnessing. Thus "giggling" suggests the jittery motion of the many bullets and leads to "gaggle," which, although it images a flock of geese, is also a chattering sound (*OED*, 1104), here Charlie's garbled cry of pain. This garbling of sound and image leads to the further confusion of enunciation in "o my god billy I'm pissing watch/your hands/while the eyes grew all over his body," where Charlie and Billy might both be speaking in shock, except for the final line, which reiterates Billy's special perception of others (see *CWBK*, 10). A second verse registers Billy's acute feelings about the event: "Jesus I never knew that did you/the nerves shot out/the liver running around there/like a headless hen jerking." This feels right: a sense of near disbelief that cannot be maintained. In this fragment, a shocked Billy reacts with a kind of desperate flippancy. In another fragment, he will be different, as a different pretext operates in his name.

To turn directly to the repetition of Charlie's death is, of course, to revise the order of the text, something it invites upon rereading; but such revision must be self-aware in order not to impose a sense of monolithic characterization on any of the narrators. This version is a prose narrative that repeats details of the first without their almost hallucinatory immediacy. The heightened perception of minute details—the "[s]now on Charlie's left boot" (*CWBK,* 22), for example—suggests involvement rather than neutrality. A paragraph of almost all unreferenced speech, Billy convincing Charlie to "get up, go and get one," precedes the lengthy description of Charlie's dying attempt "to walk in a perfect, incredible straight line out of the door towards Pat and the others at the ridge of the arroyo about twenty yards away." A mixture of stuttering sentences and fragments renders the fear, anger, and sorrow Billy feels as he enters this scene once again. As before, Garret observes and waits but does not appear to be moved by the spectacle of someone he has shot staggering toward him while dying: "Charlie getting to the arroyo, pitching into Garrett's arms, slobbering his stomach on Garrett's gunbelt. Hello Charlie, said Pat quietly." Tonal shifts here register Billy as a personality in crisis, perhaps, but they also register the western as a form of discourse under interrogation. The sentences tend to emerge straight from the genre while the fragments interrupt generic commentary the better to subvert its ideology of heroism. Generically, Pat is the sheriff-hero of the passage, the quiet winner; but everything else in the passage, including the intertexts both within and without the book, undercut the image the generic sentences present. The final paragraph looks ahead to a later fragment that will expand it as a way of leading us toward the gang's capture and subsequent ride through the desert. The passage as a whole lacks the dramatic urgency of the earlier poem, but is still full of conflicting emotions, held in tension in the syntax as they would be in the action. Billy expresses feeling as much through form as he does through imagery and language.

Time changes things, and Billy changes time, turns it around, or reaches further back through it to moments worth registering against the pain and loss of death, from which he speaks into the text—of life and death, of change and strangeness. Immediately after a lyric outburst foreshadowing his own death, Billy recalls being with the Bowdres, drinking coffee "and with a bit the edge of my eye/[sensing] the thin white body of my friend's wife" (*CWBK,* 39). The asyntactical changes and insistence on sensual response of such passages reveal Billy as a man who lives *ostranenie,* the disruption of habitual perception, in a world continually defamiliarizing itself before him, but their tone does not suggest he finds it frightening. Billy speaks of sharing a moment of heightened perception with Charlie, intimating thereby that such moments are not his alone: "sniffing wind/wind so fine/it was like drinking ether," they take the "lover wind/in us sniffing and sniffing/getting high on the way/it crashed into our nostrils" (*CWBK,* 49). Although there is a kind of violence involved here, the tone is one of wonder and delight, perhaps because Billy is sharing the experience. All of which only demonstrates how changeable a figure he is, as each new fragment of text offers us another view of him.

One reason people read about Billy the Kid is that he is Billy the Killer; *The Collected Works* does not deny his killings, it simply understates them either by undramatic reference (*CWBK,* 86) or by dissipating the horror at his action in a black comedy of animal behavior, as in the death of Gregory (*CWBK,* 15). The horrific black humor, especially Gregory's outrageous last words, almost erases the earlier statement that Billy actually did the killing here: his action disappears before the comic onslaught of the chicken. Because the mythical pretext insists that Billy is a killer, *The Collected Works* does not deny this so much as supplement it with other views of Billy that tend to displace his violence with what might be called a pastoral vision of peace the given parabola of his life finally denies him. If he cannot escape violence, the text can at least invent its opposite, providing a balance the myth has previously denied. As left-handed gun, Billy is a destroyer, but as left-handed poet, he is a creator, most specifically of the dreams of peace and love myth and history have denied him.

Billy seeks peace, but life, and violence, will not leave him alone. In the first extended pastoral interlude in *The Collected Works,* Billy spends a week in a deserted barn to burn out a fever. "But it was the colour and light of the place that made me stay there, not my fever. It became a calm week. It was the colour and the light" (*CWBK,* 17). Billy's response is sensual and his further description of the place carefully renders his perceptions as he learns to think physically: "I began to block my mind of all thought. Just sensed the room and learnt what my body could do, what it could survive, what colours it liked best, what songs I sang best. There were animals who did not move out and accepted me as a larger breed." A kind of rite of passage, the fragment explores Billy's apprehension of what is almost a spiritual discipline, its significance implied in the attitude of the animals. "We were all aware and allowed each other" expresses a utopian ideal of community and suggests a mode of being better than the thinking he has blocked out (the thinking that marks Garrett as his enemy on a metaphysical as well as mythical level). But even in such a space and time of peace, "the one altered move" (*CWBK*, 41) infects the animals he wants to believe "never changed" (*CWBK*, 10). When fermented grain intoxicated the rats living in another part of the barn, "they abandoned the sanity of eating the food before them and turned on each other . . . [until I] filled my gun and fired again and again into their slow wheel across the room at each boommm, and reloaded and fired again and again till I went through the whole bag of bullet supplies" (*CWBK*, 18). Despite Billy's earlier protestations, "the one altered move" often appears in animals or animal imagery, which evince both the harmony and the maniac violence associated with his life. The syntax of the passage is paradigmatic in its dissolution of subject-verb-object connections and its pronominal uncertainty. Billy narrates a self he cannot hold in place: it slips from first to third person, as the peace slips into violence. A wholly invented scene inserted into an uncertain time in Billy's career, it begins in clarity and peace only to slide into smoky obscurity and disruption, a violence he cannot seem to avoid, even if he is only a "boy."

Billy does not seek violence; it seeks him. At least as he is written here. In so far as *The Collected Works* pays any attention to the social history of Burns's *Saga*, it does so in a casually dismissive manner: "A motive? some reasoning we can give to explain all this violence? Was there a source for all this? yup—" (*CWBK*, 54). What follows is a verbatim passage from the *Saga* (Burns, 48), sponsored so to speak by a committee of scholars or the voices of legend and history—"we"—who narrate almost none of this text. Of course, the question "Was there a source for all this?" is double-edged, as the quotation is precisely that—a source text, one of the many that motivate the continuing rewritings of Billy's story. In fact, *The Collected Works* invokes historical explanation only to render it impotent. It is not interested in sociological or psychological explanations; if it does provide another view of Billy the Kid, it does so by extricating him from the "sources" of history and allowing him free reign in poetry, that open book.

According to *The Collected Works*, Billy has close relationships with two women: "Miss Angela Dickinson of Tucson" (*CWBK*, 25), who appears in none of the documents about his life, but is the name of one of Ondaatje's favorite actresses,[20] and Sallie Chisum, John Chisum's sister. If Angela is an invented insertion into the received story, Sallie and John represent a wholesale rewriting of it, and such a grand revision of the given demands attention. Paulita Maxwell's denial that she was the Kid's sweetheart (*CWBK,* 96), as documented in Burns's *Saga,* serves to grant a kind of validity to the text's assertion of the other two as the important women in Billy's life. Angela D. is the sexual angel, or as some would have it, demon, while Sallie represents the caring, mothering aspects of women, which he also needs. Although both appear as essentially stereo-typed figures, they break out beyond the borders of stereotyping at certain moments of the narrative.

Sallie almost always appears with John, and they are as much a place of refuge as they are characters in a drama. By altering Burns's vision of "a home fit for a cattle king" (Burns, 10) to a small, welcoming place in the middle of the desert managed by two friendly but uninfluential people, this version removes almost all the power attached to Chisum and, rather than giving it to someone else, simply lets it disappear from the text. It also changes John and Sallie's relationship from that of uncle and niece (Burns, 11–12) to that of brother and sister. All of which further removes this Billy from the realm of petty violence and political maneuvering to a purer realm of poetic inspiration. In a sequence of brilliant and growing falsifications, the text moves through document to invention as it and Billy first approach the Chisum ranch about one-third of the way through the book. Two quotes from Burns begin the shift from "fact" to fiction: a statement by Burns about the older Sallie, whom he inter-viewed, is followed by her reminiscence, "On Her House" (*CWBK,* 30), in which a tiny narrational *mise-en-abyme,* an internal duplication, occurs as one narrator speaks from within the speech of another. The possessive pronoun in the invented title and the careful elisions and free-verse line breaks in her statement place Sallie as a center of consciousness within the poem, a voice worth listening to when she says of Billy, "I remember how frightened I was the first time he came." Yet nothing in the invented scenes between them substantiates her comment. Billy is an empty sign constantly filled with contradictory information. Next, an apparently antique full-page photo of a man and a woman in pioneer clothes invites the reader to read them as John and Sallie Chisum. As usual, appearance and reality are playfully at odds here, and although at least one critic reads this page as "Huffman photo of a man and a woman in late nineteenth century work clothes" (Godard, 59), just as the Credits

(*CWBK*, [110]) suggest, it is in fact a photo of two of the people the book is dedicated to, Stuart and Sally Mackinnon (*CWBK*, [109]). But it looks so authentic many readers probably visualize Sallie in terms of that image. The following two prose fragments contain a series of analepses, each one retreating further into the past, as Billy rides with Angela to visit and recalls both his own visits there and John and Sallie's daily routine. They set the tone for all other scenes at the ranch, and realize the paradoxical nature of this peaceful retreat in sudden images of imported violence and distortion.

The orderly yet complex syntax of memory and imagination implies a joyful nostalgia. Drawn by the peace and contentment he visualizes there, Billy draws the place and its inhabitants in just those terms. Yet the place is only wholly peaceful and gentle when they are alone there, as he imagines them. As soon as he puts himself in the scene, little, frightening changes occur. He imagines Sallie sitting in bed wrapped in her sheet, and then remembers showing her "what a mad man's skin is" (*CWBK*, 33). Set between two imagined memories of Sallie in her customary daily life, this little anecdote implies intimacy, power, and a somewhat frightening self-knowledge on Billy's part. Like most of the prose fragments, these paragraphs offer readers more traditionally representative characters than do the lyric sections, but from section to section the representation changes, the photographs alter. As his memories search further back in time, Billy recalls, often with corrections, the house's shuttered darkness in the middle of the day, and "Sallie like a ghost across the room moving in white dresses" (*CWBK*, 33). But he keeps editing his painful recollections of Sallie nursing his burned legs: "And Sallie I suppose taking the tent sheet off my legs each morning once the shutters closed. No. Again. Sallie approaching from the far end of the room like some ghost. . . . Me screaming stop stop STOP THERE you're going to *fall* on me! . . . And Sallie I suppose taking the sheet off my legs and . . . starting to rub and pour calamine like ice only it felt like the tongue of a very large animal my god I remember each swab felt like the skin and flesh had been moved off completely" (*CWBK*, 34).

In terms of the psychological reading I am resisting, this passage could explain the previous one, but in both imagery overwhelms explanation in intensely sensitive perceptions no one else can feel or understand. But even within this one repeated scene of her ministering to his pain, the mixture of fear and something like ecstacy confuses our response. Although he screams at her to stop because she is looming too close, about to break through his defenses and touch him, she does break through, in a confusion of sensual images that enact his sense impressions as she spreads salve on his legs; but these move from the roughness of an animal's tongue to a grotesquely surreal image of raw bone and nerves that nevertheless confidently holds the contradiction of "banging against each other from just her slow breath," which segues from intense violation to near erotic gentleness in a single phrase. The next two paragraphs tend to emphasize the latter in the reverse image of "her foot being soft, oiled almost so smooth, the thin blue veins wrapping themselves around the inside ankle bone and moving like paths into the toes, the brown tanned feet of Sallie Chisum resting on my chest, my hands rubbing them, pushing my hands against them like a carpenter shaving wood to find new clear pulp smelling wood beneath" (*CWBK*, 35). All three passages insist upon sensual paradox, a tension held between gentle giving and savage taking, intimacy and possible pain bound together. Moreover, both Billy's and Sallie's roles keep changing, neither one is consistently stronger or weaker than the other. Like their situations, they can be rewritten, but by whom is not clear.

The second passage goes further backward, as Billy explains how long Sallie has lived on the ranch and then recalls his first visit, the first time he saw her animal collection. But even this scene of domestic gentleness and concern for animals has its surprises, as "a huge owl . . . eyes—at least 8″ apart" turns out next morning to be "two owls, both blind in one eye" (*CWBK*, 37). In this setting, is anything what it seems? There is a peace here, but it is tentative at best, and "the one altered move" (*CWBK*, 41) seems almost part of the atmosphere. Even this new text, the invented document of another life for Billy, is full of the contradictions by which he lived and died. A kind of alienation, a sense of transgression, makes itself felt in Billy's casual defamiliarization: "The night, the dark air, made it all mad. . . . Around us total blackness, . . . and to the left, a few yards away, a house stuffed with yellow wet light where within the frame of a window we saw a woman move carrying fire in a glass funnel and container towards the window, towards the edge of the dark where we stood" (*CWBK*, 37). If the images seem casual, however, the movement of the language is not, as the careful alliteration throughout this paragraph indicates. While the narration intimates unproblematical representation, the text insists on formal complication. What distinguishes the whole sequence of memories is its poetic prose, the revelation of its narrator as, precisely, the putative author of "Left Handed Poems." More than the lyric fragments, the prose sections are the sites of genre battle, where the story appears to get its due yet is consistently over-turned, either by excision and extension or by complete revision.

Hereafter, Sallie mostly appears in scenes where Angela and others are present. The major exception to this is when John tells the story of Livingstone and his mad dogs, another narrative invented for this text. Livingstone's name, with its suggestion of powerful control—he seeks to carve his life in stone—aligns him with Garrett. But his story separates him from everyone, except Sallie, John, and Billy, who are present when it is told. It is another small narrative *mise-en-abyme,* focalization shifting throughout: Billy narrates the whole section, but immediately includes Sallie's explanation of her bassett, Henry, then John's story, which segues back in the final paragraph to Billy narrating Sallie's response to it. John says that Livingstone "seemed a pretty sane guy to me" (*CWBK,* 60), but by now we recognize the ambiguities attached to that term and are not surprised when he adds that "Livingstone had been mad apparently." The deliberately awkward placing of that "apparently" underlines the ambivalence attached to sanity throughout the text. Full of analepses and prolepses, John's story tells how Livingstone had secretly bred dogs to madness until they killed and ate him. But the telling of this story is as important as its narrative content. Its tone more mature and thoughtful than Billy's, John's narration stands out as the only specific self-revelation of his character. For a brief moment, a kind of representation foregrounds this revised figure from the given story so as to further undermine its authority, then the text slips him back into shadow.

If Sallie is quietly protective and desirable, Angela is forcefully entrancing and enigmatic. Where Sallie offers succor and a place to rest, Angela brings tension, danger, and a powerful and daunting sexuality into her relations with Billy. As a representative figure of the sexual frontier woman, she stands for a kind of outlaw freedom from every kind of social repression; but as "an allegory of the erotic" she signifies "the other desire that desire yearns for. She is an apostle of Desire itself, a desire that occurs on the edge of Billy's textual life" (Kamboureli 1991, 193). It is in Billy's representation of their erotic encounters that *The Collected Works* most fully interrogates us. In terms of reader-response criticism,[21] our personal reactions play a large part in our readings of Billy and Angela's relationship. Is the sex act between them just another "emblem of the mechanization of nature," in which "Billy articulates the contact of bodies as if they were machines tensely working against each other"?[22] Is "Angela D.'s ability to take him" so "particularly danger-ous" that he fears "that his physical contact with her leads to his loss of mental control" (Nodelman, 72)?[23] These lyrics and passages simply do not contain the fear of Angela these critics find there. Ambivalence, yes, and that is what makes it so difficult to determine their mood. Billy himself is not sure how he feels. Because Angela "is a reminder of the pleasure, fears, and violence the life of the body entails . . . the prosopopoeia of paradox itself . . . Billy both resists and adores her" (Kamboureli 1991, 193–94). Registering the resistence and the adoration equally, the lyrics work both as descriptions of desire and as poems—the inscription of desire.

The first two lyrics do not even name the other who dominates them. But although the object of desire is not named, her naming of its subject, Billy, suggests how powerfully she reflects his need and his ambiguous pleasure. Or is the ambiguity precisely that we cannot be sure who is subject, who is object, of the desiring gaze of the narrator, as his perceptions shift from her to himself, seeing both as sexual bodies, "pivoting like machines in full speed" (*CWBK*, 16). If there is a tension between delight and fear here, it is expected, though perhaps such imagery is not, in a first encounter. If she appears somewhat violent, so does he, as the "string of teeth marks" shows. The images of her are beautiful if also dramatic, and the precise description of her body in motion "natural" for a man of superior perception. That "the bright bush jumps" in the hollow of her stomach is not so much frightening as intense. In terms of tone, the two lines "Billy she says" and "this is the first time" interrupt the flow of active imagery and register a delicate hesitation that implies powerful emotion held back on both sides. Yet there is a slight comic edge to it all, as well, in the image of her orgasm causing her body to nearly break off his fingers, which are clearly doing the work required. The final quatrain, with its plural "hands," reveals that, at least when making love to Angie, Billy does use his left hand for something else besides shooting, despite the implicit pun of her clitoris as a trigger. Because lovemaking paralyzes his hands, the poem can also be read as a definitive example of making love and not war—a further little joke. The humor subverts any fear and rage. The problem of tone, important throughout the text, is especially vital here. Each reader's participatory reading will lead to a slightly different interpretation and even one that might change from one reading to another: these are the pleasures of the indeterminate text.

Each lyric has a different effect, as well. In the next one, the still unnamed woman acts decisively as Billy watches passively: she "turns toppling slow back to the pillow/Bonney Bonney//I am very still/I take in all angles of the room" (*CWBK,* 21). Again, the tone is slippery, refusing to maintain a single attitude for either writer or reader. If her assertion of body and desire is very powerful, it is also delicate and giving. Once she reaches the bed, she touches him gently and then physically demonstrates that she has fallen for him, offering herself to him in a slow and unambiguous gesture. Her name for him at this point humorously underlines her desire. And if his stillness can be read as fear it can also be read as enjoyment: as the pun on her name implies, she is "all the angles of the room" and he takes her in. This reading accepts them both as characters, but does not read them as the continuous characterizations of the critics who infer Billy's fear and hatred of Angela. Another reading argues that Angela is a rhetorical figure in a text where discourse defeats narrative. Ambiguous reference plays across the whole poem: the sheets are a bed of love and a shroud; the orange peels signify sensuality while the simile of coins alludes to pennies on a dead man's eyes; and the intimate address "Bonney Bonney" signifies both sex and death in its phonetic play on *bony* and *bonny*'(see Kamboureli 1991, 196). Such multiplicity offers grounds for both kinds of readings simultaneously.

Now that she has named "Bonney" in the dialectical terms of his paradoxical presence as the literal "ghostwriter" of his text, he can name her, and he does so in the lyric of her name. Beginning with the complete name, "Miss Angela Dickinson of Tucson" (*CWBK,* 25), it extends the naming process into one of description. At first insisting "I'm too tall for you Billy," she eventually "leans back waving feet at me/catching me like a butterfly/in the shaved legs in her Tucson room." Again, she is the sexual aggressor, the one who speaks, and then who acts. While the image of a butterfly—and is it he or she?—suggests delicacy, it also suggests beauty. Although each presentation of Angela changes the terms of the relationship somewhat, with at least one attempting to place her as a generic figure of prostitution, "Billy's discourse does not insinuate any resentment toward her" (Kamboureli 1991, 196), nor any fear.

Billy's song-and-dance routine suddenly introduces a new trope of discourse, that of the vaudeville turn. Coming right after the embedded story of Livingstone, it puts all narratives within the book back into discourse. It reminds us that every fragment is a turn, and that all the voices are performative. If the song ambiguously implies both excitement and uncertainty, delight and fear, concerning Angela D.'s sexuality, then it is up to us not to choose one response over the other. Combining fear and ecstacy in a traditonal male comic displacing of the source of emotional uncertainty, the song distorts and dismantles her body into parts, as if such fragmentation of the female body could control it (an old and conventional form of sexist inscription). But it fails: each separate part—mouth, teeth, eyes, throat, thigh, fingers, and toes—continues to exercise its power. This discourse cannot tie Angela down, partly because it keeps contradicting itself. Her mouth is both "like a bee" and "an outlaw"; "her teeth leave a sting on your very best thing," but they are also "a tunnel"; "she swallow your breath," but she also "swallow you blind" (*CWBK*, 64). She truly is "blurred in the dark," a figure whose lineaments slide beyond the male gaze, even when it seeks to fix them in a Medusan frame. This song "about the lady Miss A D," reveals more about Billy, or about us, than it does about her; she eludes us as utterly as she does him.

The next poem offers us a very different image. It not only engages her spirit and personality, precisely what the vaudeville song ignores, but also contradicts the view of another narrator, one readers have no reason to trust although he offered a different view of their relationship some pages before: Pat Garrett. At the end of his "turn," signified as such by its introductory title "Mistuh . . . patrick . . . garrett!!!" (*CWBK*, 42), he describes Billy killing the dying cat under the Chisums' house, and adds that Angie "was terrified. Simply terrified" (*CWBK*, 45). When Angela's "hand [is] shot open" by "their bullet for me" (*CWBK*, 66), her response has nothing of terror in it, but it does look to Billy's capabilities: "O Bonney you bastard Bonney/kill him Bonney kill him." Her quiet courage as she watches Billy open the skin to remove the bullet does not imply terror. As this is the only other time she uses this intimate name, and as "the use of 'Bonney' both times connects with death, we surmise that Angela mediates between Billy and death" (Kamboureli 1991, 195). If she does so mediate, it is through the body. It is as body—of desire, of the text—that she images clarity for him, and thereby for us: "look at it, I'm looking into your arm/nothing confused in there/look how clear/Yes Billy, clear" (*CWBK*, 66). This clarity occurs only at the edge, the margin between life and death. Although listed among "the killed . . . (By them)" (*CWBK*, [6]), Angela is not killed here; "blurred in the dark" (*CWBK*, 64), existing between states, at home in both, she is a part of the story and apart from it. Her body is clear but unreadable: it offers the undecidable clarity of poetry itself.

Aside from these lyric visions of her, Angela participates in two narratives. One is Garrett's first meeting with Billy, in which he tells us that he "didnt understand either of them and wanted to see how they understood each other" (*CWBK,* 44), a not unreasonable desire, since many readers share it. But his representation of her is all physical, and thus typically masculine; Billy's may be too, but at least he allows her to speak. Her other appearance is also at the Chisums' ranch, and Garrett is again present. In fact, in terms of the unwritten rules of hospitality and gregariousness there, he is the outlaw, as he falls asleep and thus misses the quiet camaraderie of talk and drink that marks the evening.

Even though "[u]sually it was three of us" (*CWBK,* 67), when the scene turns carnivalesque she fits in. Character and drama are foregrounded here, in a comedy of eros carried by their speeches: "O fooo she says . . . Her skirt over both of us and the can. Billy come on. mmm I say yes, get up first. No. Shit Angie. No" (*CWBK,* 68). Contradictions move the scene forward. The pronouns and the speeches slide into each other even as the lovers do: it is a moment of high intimacy and high comedy at once. The absence of the usual grammatical markers, especially quotation marks, causes Billy's and Angie's identities to both merge and dissipate. The undecidability of such dialogue as "Come on Angie I'm drunk'm not a trapese artist. Yes you are. No" or the shifting reference of "Youre too heavy for this I think, . . . Let me out Billy. Out Billy. Quiet she's next door. No! I know you Billy you! Youre fucking her" show how "Billy's identity swings between contradictions [until] it violates identity itself" (Jones, 35). Yet someone or some voice is speaking here as elsewhere in the text, and so paradoxically, even as identity "flickers between presence and absence" (Jones, 34), a characterization does take place. It simply does not establish itself as either "rounded" or consistent in a naturalistic sense. If, accepting inconsistency, we produce our own changing versions of the characters as they appear in each scene, we will then interpret them in terms of the formal suggestiveness of the writing.[24] Sensually registering Angela's extraordinary power, Billy segues into a comic climax that both admits that power and his delight in her: "No Angie, no, I say, honest Angie you got too much, and enter her like a whale with a hat on, my drowning woman my lady who drowns, and take my hat off."

But if the night offers drunkenness and sex and sickness—Billy out in the wind throwing up and admitting the description "is doing nothing for my image is it" (*CWBK,* 70)—in the "morning the room is white and silvery" (*CWBK,* 71), Angela D is a changing landscape, "her hip a mountain further down the bed," and Billy has new questions. Even in the peace of "[b]eautiful ladies in white rooms in the morning," Billy is a site of continuing flux and a body of sense-impressions: "My head and body open to every new wind direction, every nerve new move and smell." Blown by such wind directions, he has moved from the comedy of awkward sex in the bathroom, through the self-consciously literary (literally "ghostwritten"?) reference to his popular image, to this moment when he looks up to see that "[o]n the nail above the bed the black holster and gun is coiled like a snake, glinting also in the early morning white." This eerie image, with its allusion to the loss of the Edenic landscape Angela's body promises, matches a Huffman photo that appears twice in the text (*CWBK,* 45, 92), both times associated with Garrett. Situated between the two versions of the photo, it acts as a foreshadowing of Billy's inevitable death, harshly unsettling the pastoral mood.

In just this short span of text, let alone throughout, both Billy and Angela give closure the slip. The representation of her character changes sufficiently from fragment to fragment to assure that Angela remains an enigma, just as Billy does in the larger "collected works." Angela is as provisional as Billy: every "work" they appear in both describes and de-scripts them (Jones, 34). A mostly minor figure, she figures in a major way in the alternate scripting of Billy's life these "works" offer. To insist that, like photographs, the narrations of this text operate in an objective fashion misses how the writing works. In the passage where Billy looks at Angela's beauty, registers his body and mind's openness to "every new move and smell," and sees the gun and holster as a snake, as in the whole narrative leading up to it, objectivity is the one mood that is missing. Nuance is at a premium in this writing, every word and phrase registering the slight shifts of emotion these figures move through. Utterly *un*objective, Billy's poetic documents exist to reinvent him as lover, poet, man of feeling. The other documents, not just Burns's historical reenactments or the implied range of "comic book legends," but even the carefully excavated "statements" by the "historical" Paulita Maxwell and Sallie Chisum, reveal the ideologies that play across the story as it slowly gathers layer after layer of "new" information. In their contradictions with one another and with other intertexts, these documents operate by a "'logic of juxtaposition,' which fosters conflicting meanings" (Jones, 34) and emotions we are left to sort through to achieve our own meaning.

As Billy's narrative of his time in the barn and his repetition of the Livingstone story reveal, the animals do change on him. What doesn't change, or rather who doesn't change once he "had decided what was right and forgot all morals" (*CWBK,* 28), is Pat Garrett, Billy's opposite, the man with a "newsman's brain" (*CWBK,* 11). In an apparently neutral analysis—narrated by vox populi, it seems—of how he became "[a]n academic murderer" (*CWBK*, 28), this text's version of Garrett puts himself through a rigorous apprenticeship of alcoholism and useless learning to become the perfect lawman, static and incapable of change. In fact, it is he, much more than Billy, who fears any kind of change. Abstracted from the physical world, he lives in a world of the mind and is in fact a perfect harbinger of technological man—unlike Billy, whose every thought is rooted in bodily sensation (see Kertzer, 89–93, on this opposition). Thus "Garrett ha[s] stuffed birds" (*CWBK*, 88), preferring to deal with what is already dead and fixed, while Billy is forever noticing "flowers in the rain/ . . . /bursting the white drop of spend/out into the air at you/the smell of things dying flamboyant" (*CWBK*, 55). For Garrett, beauty is found in the static perfection of death, while for Billy beauty is transitive, the present participle of "dying" implying its opposite, living. Garrett arrives in the text already everything he will be: "body able to drink . . . mind full of French he never used, everything equipped to be that rare thing—a sane assassin sane assassin sane assassin sane assassin sane assassin sane" (*CWBK*, 29). Although this chant begins as praise, the rhythm and the repetition run the two words together until what reads as "sane" sounds as "insane," and it is in the aporia, the doubtful space of paradox, that contradiction opens up that Pat Garrett does his job.

Garrett doesn't say much in the book; usually he is waiting quietly for another man to die, as with O'Folliard or Bowdre. In this section where Billy and Angela share drinks and coffee with John and Sallie Chisum, he not only "doesnt talk much" (*CWBK*, 67), but falls asleep and misses everything. When he gets his own turn on the page, he tells of an earlier time when he came to the Chisum ranch and met Billy and Angela there. Although welcomed, as everyone is, he again remains apart. Caught in a windstorm, he arrives blinded, deafened, and "mind blasted" (*CWBK*, 42). Later, his observations form another of the various and contradictory views of Billy the text provides. A useful if untrustworthy observer, Garrett has information no other narrator can provide. We should be wary of his opinions, however. He's the one who says Billy never uses "his left hand for anything except to shoot" (*CWBK*, 43), and describes Billy's subconscious exercises to keep it supple. Like Billy, he is attracted to his opposite, and fascinated by him: "It was the most hypnotising beautiful thing I ever saw" (*CWBK*, 43).

Garrett finds Billy both attractive and undisciplined. The prosaic lawman dismisses out of hand the poetic outlaw—precisely for his poetry, the imagination confronting chaos. Because Billy's tracking and killing of the dying cat is a discipline based wholly on the senses, Garrett cannot understand it. Is it observation or projection when he says that Billy's performance "[s]imply terrified" Angie (*CWBK,* 45)? The text refuses to answer such questions, satisfied to have raised them and thus to have pushed the whole project further into indeterminacy. Billy, as the site of conflicting interpretations, thrives in the indeterminate. His death is the only thing anyone really knows about him, and the further the stories on this side of that boundary get from it the further they can explore on the other side, becoming ever more inventive and contradictory. Whatever the text implies about Billy's vacillating feelings toward Angela, they do not include fear that she is "blurred in the dark" (*CWBK,* 64), because that is his condition, too. Billy the Kid slips free of the law of closure; Pat Garrett seeks its consolation. The text is *The Collected Works of Billy the Kid* precisely in so far as it succeeds in deferring closure by refusing to allow a satisfying conclusion. Like Billy, the text escapes the confines of the law—of narrative closure (see, Jones, 35; Kamboureli 1991, 200–202). Even when Garrett captures Billy, he escapes—even when he kills him. The final passage in which Garrett speaks, taken almost verbatim from the *Saga* (Burns, 284), only serves by its very insistence to increase our general uncertainty. Which is why, no doubt, it appears after the "comic book legend."

> "*It was the Kid who came in there on to me," Garrett told Poe, "and I think I got him."*
> "*Pat," replied Poe, "I believe you have killed the wrong man."*
> "*I'm sure it was the Kid," responded Garrett, "for I knew his voice and could not have been mistaken."*
> (*CWBK,* 103)[25]

Against Garrett's assertion that he "could not have been mistaken," *The Collected Works* suggests that every version is prey to mistakes, none is free of doubt. Asserting the play of significations, the insecurity of flux, the refusal of closure, the collage text remains open, breaking out from the "frame-up" of the still photograph into a confusion of gestures that cannot be held in place.

In a way, even when Garrett has him, Billy escapes, if only into the suffering ecstasy of a "theater of cruelty" (Kamboureli 1991, 197) managed by the sun. Chained like his friends to his horse, Billy is manually "raped" by the sun, which, in a long writerly passage, dissects him, drawing up his innards into the light. Within the text, Billy's experience is brutally ecstatic; outside it, our reading is similarly complex. "The sun un-texts Billy" (Kamboureli 1991, 197); not only is there nothing in the literature of the Kid to prepare us for this, there is nothing like it in the western generally. A tour de force of lyric viscerality, the syntax breaking down in tempo with the violation of Billy's body, it appears as if from another genre, another kind of writing entirely. Its otherness signals how fully Billy has eluded the dead hand of Garrett's narrative control. And whoever returns to say "Ive been fucked Ive been fucked by Christ almighty god Ive been good and fucked by Christ" (CWBK, 78), that "I" has been altered so completely, he can give a witty interview, escape from jail, be shot by Garrett, and still ride into Mexico to save "La Princessa" (CWBK, 99). Beyond any single representation, he has become the multivalent text.

Even dying, Billy is the multivalent text: this is the formal meaning of the whole book, but especially of the proleptic series of poems and scenes leading straight to the moment when Garrett shoots him and beyond. They emerge suddenly and fade into the background all the way through the book, almost as if they were blood beads in the necklace of his text. And as they look forward to Billy's violent death, they also look back to the first example of "the one altered move that will make [things] maniac" (CWBK, 41), that is the drunken rats gone wild in the barn. The first lyric insists that the bullet entering Billy's head "was hot small bang did it/almost a pop/I didnt hear till I was red/had a rat fyt in my head" (CWBK, 38), the very spelling of "fyt" demonstrating the destructive turn of violent alteration. The next one is a repetitive gesture in the conditional mode, as Billy describes how "[o]ne dog, Garrett and two friends came down the street to the house, to me" (CWBK, 46). The past tense of this repeated remark again reveals Billy as "a dead subject" (Kamboureli 1991, 190), while the conditional mode of "[a]ll this I would have seen if I was on the roof looking" (CWBK, 46) both confirms that dead subjectivity and denies it any special ubiquity. As a character in the drama of his life, Billy cannot know this scene ahead of time; only as a subject of discourse, only as a part of the text, can his narrative voice make this doubled gesture of description and denial. Such textual moments continually confirm the antinarrative stance of the long poem as collage intertext. The intertext here is the camera-eye point of view of any number of westerns; others elsewhere include lyric moments in *The Collected Works* and various images from other retellings of the given story. Thus, another proleptic nightmare violently alters Angela D into a figure of death itself, but only after he and his readers "(watch) bullet claws coming/at me" (*CWBK,* 73) in an echo of the "rat fyt" (*CWBK,* 38) which itself echoed the horror of the rats in the barn. Once again, "the one altered move" that haunts the text explodes in his head, and as the "fire" of his passion and his imagination "pours out/red grey brain," Billy transposes Angela D's sexual power into Pat Garrett's killing power: "her eyes like a boat/on fire . . . the man in the bright tin armour star/blurred in the dark/saying stop jeesus jesus jesus JESUS" (*CWBK,* 73). Overlaid images of Angela, Sallie, Garrett, and Billy himself force a manic dissipation of syntax and reference. At the various textual moments of his death, discourse itself stumbles and falters, and through a subversive kind of imitative fallacy proves its power over narrative. However, no matter how often he repeats it, or how much new information he can interpollate into the story leading up to it, the one thing Billy cannot change is that moment of death, from the other side of which he speaks. Garrett's killing of him is what grants him the voice of this text. Its additions may transcend that death, may even on some level deny it, but they cannot erase it.

They do unsettle any sense we have of Billy or the others—except perhaps Pat Garrett—as monologic characters. However "flat" they may be, owing to the limited manner in which they are deployed in their scenes, they do achieve the opaqueness verisimilitude requires. Seen in fragments of text, each one reveals only fragments of a self. And as many of the lyrics cannot be securely attached to just one speaker, they hover at the margins of the story, modifying it, perhaps, but not in any specific way. Floating references ensure that readers cannot be certain who rides into "[a] river you could get lost in" and keeps circling "till dusk and cold and the horse shift you/and you look up and moon a frozen bird's eye" (*CWBK,* 26). Nor do they know for sure who says "[y]ou know hunters/are the gentlest/anywhere in the world" and assures us that "in the same way assassins/come to chaos neutral" (*CWBK,* 47). It is almost as if discourse itself speaks here, interrupting narrative, displacing story, and subverting interpretation. Insisting on returning us to the pleasures of the text.

Even the layered series of almost cinematic "takes" of Billy's death offers pleasure in its shifts and changes. The first one reads almost like a screenplay: "Sound up. Loud and vibrating in the room" (*CWBK,* 90). Everything is presented in terms of intense sensation: while the lack of pronominal cues and the imperative "Think" tend to implicate the reader in the scene, the final "hissssssssss ssssssssssssssss" makes it a kind of performance. Another sound—"Mммmmmmmmm"—carries the next scene into a discourse that straddles first- and third-person perspective as it dramatizes "the final minutes" (*CWBK,* 92). Although this passage owes much to the *Saga,* it alters details and adds the wholly invented and blackly comic suggestion that Billy doesn't react quickly enough because he thinks the other body in Pete Maxwell's bed is Paulita Maxwell, his sister (*CWBK,* 93).

A sudden shift into what might be seen on "the screen of a horse's eye" (*CWBK,* 94) shows a confusion of activity, Garrett running to argue with Poe, "the naked arm, the arm from the body, break[ing] through the window" (*CWBK,* 94), until finally "Guitterrez goes to hold the arm but it is manic, breaks her second finger. His veins that controlled triggers—now tearing all they touch." The sequence finally shifts back to Billy's voice rising into a manic and visionary statement that contains the imagery of his life and death while explaining nothing: "oranges reeling across the room AND I KNOW I KNOW/it is my brain coming out like red grass/this breaking where red things wade" (*CWBK,* 95). It is precisely because the lyric cannot be destroyed by narrative that the sequence moves from prose to poetry, from dramatic action to lyric intensity, finally segueing into the negation of "[a]n old story" (*CWBK,* 96) by Paulita Maxwell and then into the imagined story of Billy's remains. In death, the stories grow: "His legend a jungle sleep" (*CWBK,* 97) richly implies Rousseauian fecundity and dream. The stories that grow in the rich humus of legend following upon the subject's death include not only comic books and movies but those in *The Collected Works* itself. Writing, that "mapping [of] my thinking going its own way/like light wet glasses drifting on polished wood" (*CWBK,* 72), is what remains, and it happens no matter who appears to be doing it. What *The Collected Works of Billy the Kid* offers, finally, is the collecting an ambiguous "I" undertakes and the carefully chaotic collage text that results. Who is the subject of this effort? Finally, he is nameless, an image of transience, a man alone in a room: "It is now early morning, was a bad night. The hotel room seems large. The morning sun has concentrated all the cigarette smoke so one can see it hanging in pillars or sliding along the roof like amoeba. In the bathroom, I wash the loose nicotene [sic] out of my mouth. I smell the smoke still in my shirt" (*CWBK,* 105). When he leaves it, no one will be able to identify him.

Chapter Four

Poetry and a Maturing Poetics

An edition of selected poems, especially when published by major presses in a poet's own country, the United States, and the United Kingdom, signifies both achievement and recognition. For Ondaatje, the Governor General's Award–winning *There's a Trick with a Knife I'm Learning to Do* (1979) also provided an opportunity, again especially for the larger international audience that knew him most for *The Collected Works of Billy the Kid* and *Coming Through Slaughter,* to pare away some of the perceived chaff in his oeuvre and thus present a particular overview of the maturing of a poet. The poems dropped from *The Dainty Monsters* section appear more modernist and given to closure or too dependent upon a dictionary of mythology than his later practice allows. The selection from *Rat Jelly*[1] is larger, as befits a more mature collection, yet the poems kept, aside from the central series of poems about art and artists, tend to foreground questions of ordinary life, friendship, and family love. If, as so many critics have pointed out, Ondaatje seems obsessed with figures who violently and often self-destructively immerse themselves in the chaotic world of the senses, the choice of poems in *Trick with a Knife* reveals another and equally powerful obsession: the need and desire to "deviously [think] out plots / across the character of his friends" (*RJ,* 56; *TK,* 58). In the context of the selections from the first two books, this other obsession is best imaged in the delicate yet tough recognition of communion among friends in "We're at the Graveyard," a poem I now see as central in Ondaatje's work. The "shift" of friends' "minds and bodies . . . to each other" (*RJ,* 51; *TK,* 47), with all its implications about community, communication, and communion, is the emerging theme of Ondaatje's work as he matures from romantic young poet-hero to more complex and subtle poet-survivor. The new poems in the third part, "Pig Glass," with their increased insistence on the necessary and complex intimacy with family and friends, reveal how carefully Ondaatje has selected and reordered the earlier poems in terms of this emerging theme. Not that *Trick with a Knife* denies the other aspects of Ondaatje's work; rather, it newly contextualizes them in an emerging order that emphasizes a greater complexity of response within its various speakers and a more profound and difficult vision than that of romantic egoism.

Ondaatje wrote the poems of *Rat Jelly* "before during and after two longer works—*the man with seven toes* and *The Collected Works of Billy the Kid*—when the right hand thought it knew what the left hand was doing" (*RJ*, [72]). Many of its poems deal with the question of art's relation to life, which is why critics continue to study them as central statements on poetics and creativity. These include "Letters & Other Worlds," "Burning Hills," "The gate in his head," "Spider Blues," and "White Dwarfs," often considered among his finest poems, as well as "Dates," "Taking," and "King Kong meets Wallace Stevens." All appear in *Trick with a Knife*. This group makes up one-fifth of the titles in *Rat Jelly* and contains the only poems that stretch out to three pages in length. Although they present the best clues to his poetics at the time, I would not read them as absolutely prescriptive, except insofar as "The gate in his head" suggests a direction the later work might take: toward ever greater openness and exploration, "seeking the unrested form he requires, and the realization that it is in form that we present what we deem the real" (Bowering, 164).

Although Ondaatje's shorter poems seem to become more and more autobiographical as he matures as an artist, he actually "places himself directly before the reader as a *character* instead of an attitude" (Glickman, 73): the "I" who speaks in these seemingly "confessional" poems is purely inscribed, exists in each poem as a subject but alters his subjectivity from poem to poem. While it would be foolish to try to reconstruct the "real" Michael Ondaatje's life from the written ones of the poems, the writer has chosen, especially in the reordered selected poems, to shift the emphasis of his work away from the suffering and violent individual toward the communication and communion that are possible only in community, a community that begins in the small tribe of immediate family and close friends. Although this shift can best be seen in the works that follow *Coming Through Slaughter*, the poems on family and friends in *Rat Jelly* mark its beginning. The opening poem, "War Machine," appears later in *Trick with a Knife*, yet, despite its explicit expression of generalized hatred of the world "out there," it points to family and friends as necessary buffers against that world: "Think I dont like people NO / like some dont like many / love wife kids dogs couple of friends" (*RJ*, 11; *TK*, 48). The poem is a savage comic turn, a performance, in which the "I" expostulates at length about wanting "to live mute / all day long / not talk // just listen to the loathing," but only after telling us at great length how he hates art, likes certain sports, films, and scandalous gossip. Indeed, he represents himself as not too likable, definitely sexist, and willing to hurt to get attention. Perhaps he would like to escape into silence, but for now he sounds like a stand-up comedian desperate for one last laugh. The double edge of his rhetoric— cutting himself as much as his audience—should warn us to be very careful of whom we identify him with, or how we identify with him.

"Gold and Black," with its images of dreams and nightmares as "gold and black slashed bees come / [to] pluck my head away" (*RJ,* 12; *TK,* 37), turns to the beloved, although she, too, is presented in disturbingly ambiguous imagery: "In the black Kim is turning / a geiger counter to this pillow. / She cracks me open like a lightbulb." The lightbulb simile catches us off guard: does she break him into darkness or enter into his light? The final stanza presents an argumentative conclusion as if to a syllogism: "Love, the real, / terrifies / the dreamer in his riot cell." The turn to the third person, as it generalizes from the extremely personal imagining of the first two stanzas, suggests that this is not just "my" problem but everyone's. But is it? Some readers feel "the dream was not meant for me" (Bowering, 164). The third-person dreamer's "riot cell" implies everybody's utter lack of control in the realm of the unconscious, but the poem is not about everybody, and it has resolved nothing. That it appears to do so may be its weakness.

"Letter to Ann Landers" utterly disrupts any biographical reading we may have been constructing, as it is in the voice of a harried housewife who has found an outlet for her frustrations: "I get really / turned on by flies / crawling over my body" (*RJ,* 13). This could be one of the stories the speaker in "War Machine" tells; certainly it is a casually cruel bit of black comedy: "It *is* true Ann I *do* feel worn out / it is the flies (I mean it are the flies)." As it shifts to the necessary ending of a letter to an advice columnist—Ann's reply would help the husband "feel / not so left out of things"—it perhaps suggests just how difficult dealing with "Love, the real" can be. The cruelly accurate pastiche of the awkward style of such letters somehow invokes compassion as well as superior disdain, making us oddly complicit in this contradictory lyric joke. At any rate, entering *Rat Jelly* in an orderly fashion leads us through a misanthropic rant, a chilling dream, and a comically outrageous image of desire. Only after these three alternate visions does the book turn to its first major poem, which explores with compassion and complexity the complications of a domestic situation, "observed with the most intimate affection, out of

which the reader can reconstruct the fabric of a whole relationship"
(Scobie 1985a, 50).

The title, "Billboards," points to a central image in the poem, but one
that emerges only after a mazelike trip through anecdotal images of
"[m]y wife's problems with husbands, houses, / her children that I
meet / at stations in Kingston, in Toronto, in London Ontario" (*RJ*, 14;
TK, 34). Overlapping discourses compose the language of this poem:
there are seemingly traditional similes, witty metaphors, the occasionally pretentious diction of the high lyric, but they never quite mesh into
a conventional lyric sensibility. Or: that sensibility is corrected, dissi-
pated, as an effect of the overlapping. The first two stanzas establish the
terms of difference between these two lovers in a tone that mixes gentle
exasperation and loving humor: "All this, I was about to say, / disturbs,
invades my virgin past." This image of the speaker as a youthful tabula
rasa, his "mind a carefully empty diary" waiting to be written on by the
experienced older woman, seems unproblematic until a sudden shift of
metaphor making her a "barrier reef" opens toward subtler and more
complex possibilities. As an empty diary changes into a bright fish
among the coral, we realize that the fictional world of the poem is one of
sudden transformations, in which nothing may be what it seems. Images
associated with writing—her "anthology of kids," his "carefully empty
diary"—are continually interrupted by images of raucous, chaotic life, of
which the ocean is a major symbol (Cirlot, 241). In a poem essentially
domestic and comic, this is not too unsettling a discovery, but it provides
a sufficient reminder that the world of the shorter poems is the same as
that of the longer works.

The complications increase, for "the locusts of history— / innuendoes
she had missed / varied attempts at seduction (even rape)," etc. (*RJ*, 15;
TK, 35), seem to point to a naïveté on her part that almost equals his. The
locusts might in some way be equivalent to the bees that invade his
dreams in "Gold and Black," the dark other side of this domestic
comedy. Here sexual violence is quickly paralleled by the deaths of pets,
and all are reduced to the same level as "[n]umerous problems I was
unequal to." Although its inconsistent discourse denies it a stable lyric
sensibility, the "I" asserts primacy in "a neutrality so great / I'd have
nothing to think of, / just to sense / and kill it in the mind"; but that
primacy cannot attain lyric superiority because of the inherent dialogism
of the situation: "Nowadays I somehow get the feeling / I'm in a complex
situation, / one of several billboard posters / blending in the rain." The
lyric "I" is essentially selfish, an ego expressing only itself. Paradoxically,

however, this "I" had nothing to express to the degree it sought to "have nothing to think of." As the only referent for "it" is "nothing," the neutrality he sought is the nothing he would have killed with his mind. Solipsism like this has nowhere to go. In fact, to write at all he must be written upon. History does that as it rains experiences, his own and others', upon him. The image of the "several billboard posters / blending" overwhelms that of the empty diary, but both depend upon the concept of writing for their effect. Writing as the marking of experience upon the self is what allows the writer to focus the final stanza on the complex feelings his engagement with other complicated lives evokes. The act of writing itself becomes a sign of the communication love both allows and is: "I am writing this with a pen my wife has used / to write a letter to her first husband." Until this stanza, the poem has concentrated on memories, bits of information gathered from other sources, historical and anecdotal, moments of generalized encounters. Now the writer writing engages the physical presence-in-absence of the other, through the sense most often associated with the erotic—smell— and does so with the generosity of spirit associated most strongly with love. He does not "attempt to reconstruct" (*TK,* 17) and "freeze" the moment, as he did in "Four Eyes," but rather imagines the possible process of the actions he did not observe: "She must have placed it down between sentences / and thought, and driven her fingers round her skull / gathered the slightest smell of her head / and brought it back to the pen." Empathetically gathering her actions out of the empty air and placing them on the page, he demonstrates an antilyric dialogism by staying out of the action. The poem ends focused on her incomplete act, which we now feel touched by.

Other poems within the "Families" section move in different directions and engage different moods. The very title of "Notes for the legend of Salad Woman" (*RJ,* 18; *TK,* 38) suggests the direction much of the "autobiographical" writing takes here: toward a kind of comic myth-making, to be trusted, like autobiography, no more than a tall tale. I think it significant that the figure of "my wife" in these poems is never given a name: she is representative, not particular, another aspect of the performative orientation of these poems. "Notes" joins with "Postcard from Piccadilly Street" and "The Strange Case" to make up a delicately slapstick triptych. A line from "Postcard"—"We have moved to elaborate audiences now" (*RJ,* 19; *TK,* 39)—provides the clue to the performative nature of these poems. In them, the poet and the wife take little vaudeville turns for the entertainment of whatever "elaborate audiences" may read them.

In "Notes," the luggage "my wife" brings to the marriage expands to suggest "she must have eaten / the equivalent of two-thirds / of the original garden of Eden" (*RJ*, 18; *TK*, 38). The poem elaborates this conceit at some length, moving from images of that "eradicated" garden to "flower decorations" in their house and their own small garden, now "a dust bowl." The final stanza offers them both new roles, as Adam and Eve, and turns eviction from Eden into erotic comedy. From "Notes" to a "Postcard" is not too big a step in this comic textual world. In "Postcard," dogs, as "the unheralded voyeurs of this world" (*RJ*, 19; *TK*, 39) assume a parodic relation to the suffering animal world of his other poems: "irate phone calls from the SPCA / . . . claim we are corrupting minors / (the dog being one and a half)." The comic timing emphasizes the light tone of this poem, especially the offhand statistic of the parenthetic line. The hint of spying, in "sparrows / with infra red eyes," the importance of performance, the slight spice of danger, all combine to turn the poem just slightly aside from mere slapstick, but the basic tone is comic—as it is in "The Strange Case," where the speaker's dog is an "alter ego" displaying raw sexual desire and "nuzzling / head up skirts / while I direct my mandarin mood" (*RJ*, 20; *TK*, 40). This mood could be taken as both devious and exploitative, but the domestic comedy of father and baby-sitter in the car, with the dog in the back seat suddenly licking her ear, plays off the conventional satiric comedy of "indiscretion." The final stanza again presents the stand-up comedian: "It was only the dog I said. / Oh she said. / Me interpreting her reply all the way home." Being forced to do the interpreting breaks his "mandarin mood" and alleviates any tension we might have felt about the intentions of the poem. It remains part of the domestic comedy, after all, with no real danger in it. All three poems sustain just enough ambiguity to resist any simplistic reading. So, although "[t]heir humour is not there just for its own sake, but plays a functional role in establishing the tone and credibility of the domestic image" (Scobie 1985a, 50), part of that credibility lies in the hint of darkness that is always nearby.

A suggestion of that darkness, and of the depth of empathy parenthood confers, occurs in a poem that provides another view of the domestic scene, nearly the only one in the book with children present. "Griffin of the night" creates a *mise-en-abyme* effect as "my son in my arms" becomes "small me / sweating after nightmares" (*RJ*, 23; *TK*, 43). The poem is minimal in its gestures, which partly accounts for its power, but it is at

least as much about "me" as it is about "my son": fathers and sons slip
into one another's roles here, preparing the reader for the following
poem, in which a son attempts to slip into the nightmare his father had
come to live and die in.

"Letters & Other Worlds" has long been considered "one of Ondaatje's
finest poems: the control of tone, as the poem moves from comedy to deeply
moving simplicity, is breathtaking" (Scobie 1985a, 51). Ondaatje's first
attempt to place and placate his father's ghost (or "his" "father's" ghost—
the quotation marks signalling the essential fictionality of all autobiography, the fact that even memory is a shaping and a making, that it can never
be an innocent representation), it anticipates *Running in the Family* by almost
a decade.[2] Precisely because "My father's body was a globe of fear / His body
was a town we never knew" (*RJ,* 24; *TK,* 44), the youthful writer finds it
difficult to see his life from the inside. The poem moves from a tragic chant
to a frightening image of death, and then shifts into a kind of comic gossip
before returning to the imagery of isolation, self-destruction, and death with
which it began. The "terrifying comedy" of his father's life is represented in
fragments of narrative that look forward to the full-blown novelization of
Running in the Family, but the beginning and ending of the poem resist such
carnivalization and insist on a lyric and romantic intensity of vision in which
terror and despair overwhelm all other possibilities. The poem manages to
juxtapose farce with despair, the two modes of discourse clashing and
contradicting, acquiring a dialogic equilibrium "my father" could not
maintain, finally. Its emotional power resides in the tension between the two
moods.

While elsewhere in his first two volumes of verse, Ondaatje praises the
painter Henri Rousseau for creating "the ideals of dreams" (*TK,* 10), here
he finds in Alfred Jarry the paradigm by which to measure his father. An
infamous poet, novelist, essayist, and playwright, who seemingly de-
voted his final days to drinking himself to death, Jarry included among
his last writings "this visionary description of the hero's approaching
death: 'But soon he could drink no more, for there was no more darkness
for him and, no doubt like Adam before the fall . . . he could see in the
dark.'"[3] This quotation is the unacknowledged epigraph to the poem,
while the comment that "Jarry's death resembled nothing so much as
drowning" (Shattuck, 223) is echoed in the line, "He came to his death
with his mind drowning." The discovery of such a paradigm apparently
gave the poet metaphors by which to tentatively explore the meaning of
his father's death.

The first two stanzas of the poem form a litany set apart from the narrative that follows. Through a series of near repetitions, the poet creates a complex keen of loss on behalf of himself and his siblings, in which the use of the first-person plural pronoun implicates us in the emotional turmoil the poem enacts. The father's body is represented as "a globe of fear," "a town we never knew," and then "a town of fear." "He hid that he had been where we were going" changes into "He hid where he had been that we might lose him," while "His letters were a room he seldom lived in" becomes "His letters were a room his body scared." The total effect is unnerving, as the father becomes a kind of incredible shrinking man, retreating from world to town until, finally, he is only an inscription in the letters that are a room he seldom lives in yet which is the only small place in which "the logic of his love could grow." In this convoluted argument, the man hid the truth about himself precisely in order that his love might free his children from the troubled inheritance he brought them. Apparently he sought to become the letters, in an attempt to erase his own early behavior and write a new figure in its place. But to do so, he had to shrink his body, his physical ability to engage the world, from "globe" to "town" to "room," a final hidden and written space in which no one else could witness his "fear dance." The "logic" of his love inevitably led to a kind of lying (a rewriting of his story that *Running in the Family* will demonstrate was a behavioral pattern for his whole generation), a loss of balance he could not maintain. His body frightened the room his letters became because the truth they sought to hide was written boldly upon it. Moreover, as the poem will demonstrate, he failed in this endeavor because gossip had inscribed him in the social history of his community, and "we" had heard all the stories already.

The narrative part of the poem leaps proleptically to the climax, as "brain blood moved / to new compartments / that never knew the wash of fluid / and he died in minutes of a new equilibrium." *Equilibrium* is a key word here; but it is ambivalent in the extreme, and the mood of isolation and loss continues the lamentation of the first two stanzas. The immediate shift into anecdotal farce suggests that the father's life was continually off balance, yet he somehow kept moving, kept going, stayed alive. The "new equilibrium" is death, a stasis he fell into when he stopped moving and hid in the small room with his bottles and the duplicitous loving writing that finally failed him.

Yet writing is the only way to bring him back. The writer takes an almost possessive delight in various scenes from the "terrifying comedy" of his father's "early life," remarking ironically that "my mother divorced him again and again." The implications of his behavior are more important than the actual stories, some of which appear in *Running in the Family*. Explanations take on an almost baroque deadpan earnestness. Of the drunken halting of a "whole procession of elephants dancers / local dignitaries," the writer adds: "As a semi-official, and semi-white at that, / the act was seen as a crucial / turning point in the Home Rule Movement / and led to Ceylon's independence in 1948" (*RJ*, 25; *TK*, 45). He points out that "[m]y mother had done her share too," but the poem quickly stifles any laughter such comic stories might induce:

> And then in his last years
> he was the silent drinker,
> the man who once a week
> disappeared into his room with bottles
> and stayed there until he was drunk
> and until he was sober.
> (*RJ*, 25–26; *TK*, 45–46)

Of this period there neither are nor can be any stories: the silence swallowed them up. The room and "the gentle letters [he] composed" (*RJ*, 26; *TK*, 46) were the same; they were both a place of hiding, in which he could write with "the most complete empathy / . . . / while he himself edged / into the terrible acute hatred / of his own privacy." The syntactical ambiguity of that final phrase suggests the awful difficulty of actually explaining how and why he came to his death. He found the hatred in the hated privacy he could not escape precisely because he had created it. In the letters he achieved a kind of balance, as well as the "articulate emotion" (*RJ*, 25; *TK*, 45) he once envied his wife, but he could not maintain it; instead, even as "his heart widen[ed] and widen[ed] and widen[ed] / to all manner of change in his children and friends" (*RJ*, 26; *TK*, 46), he slowed to a stop, "balanced and fell" dead, "the blood searching in his head without metaphor." Paradoxical images, of balancing and falling as one act, and metaphors, of "blood screaming," "blood searching," an "empty reservoir" of skull, are the only means by which to argue the end of metaphor. A positive way of reading this ending suggests that, for the father "as for Jarry, the self-destruction of alcohol provided a new vision; but unlike Jarry, what he created . . . were expressions of love rather than of contempt. When Jarry died, he became completely Ubu; when Ondaatje's father died, he became completely himself" (Scobie 1985a, 58–59). We share the writer's pain because his father is, notwithstanding, dead, lost, an enigma he can never solve.

To this point, Ondaatje has seldom presented the figure of the writer in his shorter poems. In *The Dainty Monsters,* the writer appears only in "Four Eyes," where he desires to stop time, while thus far in *Rat Jelly,* he reappears, altering his stance, only in "Billboards," although he is also implied in the comic history of "Dates." There, the writer "console[s] [him]self with [his] mother's eighth month" when he lay in his mother's "significant belly" while Wallace Stevens wrote and watched "the page suddenly / becoming thought where nothing had been" (*RJ,* 21; *TK,* 41). A series of present participles invokes the process of control and balance that writing should be: "his head making his hand / move where he wanted / and he saw his hand was saying / the mind is never finished, no, never." In his "speeches, head dreams, apologies, / [and] gentle letters" (*RJ,* 26; *TK,* 46), his father too made "his hand / move where he wanted," but he apparently could not believe "the mind is never finished." The difficulty and the emotional power of "Letters & Other Worlds" derives from its inchoate recognition that the father is the kind of romantic artist Ondaatje's writing obsessively loves yet must reject in order to keep on happening. As such, he is a paradigm of all such figures one encounters in the poet's work: Peter, Billy, the "heroes" of "White Dwarfs" "who sail to that perfect edge / where there is no social fuel" (*RJ,* 70; *TK,* 68), and Buddy Bolden, for example.[4] In the figure of the father, this romantic artist appears as a writer, but it is as a writer that his son must come to terms with what he means. The paradoxical conflict is too powerful and transgressive to be contained within the limits of a single poem; it demands the space and dialectic of a novel, where other voices can provide sufficient perspective upon it. Ondaatje had not yet found the proper "architecture of tone as well as of rhythm" (Solecki 1984, 324) by which to juxtapose document and fiction, prose and poetry, into the complex "gesture" that is *Running in the Family.* With an enigmatic and contradictory central figure who transgresses every attempt at containment, "Letters & Other Worlds" at least recognizes the need to mix genres as it mixes feelings. Ondaatje's first attempt at articulating the contraditions of "other people, another age" (Solecki 1984, 331), and another place probably had to be a lyric one. Yet lyric cannot do the subject justice precisely because that subject is the lyric self. The poem is emotionally successful to the very degree that it articulates its own failure to understand, and that is what the paradox of the final metaphor denying metaphor does.

"Live Bait," with an epigraph on the self-destructive power of lying,[5] is a catchall section evoking the dangers of the jungle as a "necessary complement" (Scobie 1985a, 50) to the domestic security of "Families." "Rat Jelly," later paired with "War Machine," brings back the nasty vaudevillian of that poem. "Breaking Green," a poem about killing a snake, reveals how the destructive power of even constructive technology comes to control the actions of the human operator and influence "our" responses to them. If there is a thematic connection among the various animal poems it is only that there is no way to understand the other. The only message the "beautiful animals" (*RJ,* 35; *TK,* 23) can send is a bite, which humans can interpret as love or as attack, or "a parabola of shit" (*RJ,* 37) which puts all interpretation out of mind.

The gulf cannot be bridged—which may be why "Loop" returns to the writer only to have him insist that it is his "last dog poem" (*RJ,* 46; *TK,* 53). This opening assumes our knowledge of past poems and their possible autobiographical intent only to suggest how they could so easily slide into sentimentality: "I leave behind all social animals / including my dog who takes / 30 seconds dismounting from a chair." Against the easy humor of this too domestic image, the poem exhorts the reader to "[t]urn to the one / who appears again on roads / one eye torn out and chasing." The antisocial animal survives; "transient as shit," he cannot be fixed—in either sense of the term—for there is "magic in his act of loss" as the "missing eye travels up / in a bird's mouth, and into the sky." Like the other animals of these poems, this dog is "Live Bait" precisely because he tempts the romantic in writer and reader to join him in "[d]eparting family." As he tears "silently into garbage" the "bird lopes into the rectangle nest of images / / and parts of him move on." Parts of the dog or parts of the bird? It doesn't matter because neither is a social animal in this poem. The temptation is to escape, even if it is into a form of fragmentation. The poems of domesticity and friendship not only stand against such poems in *Rat Jelly,* but remain when those are let go in *Trick with a Knife.* The antithematic reading of Ondaatje that I am proposing here simply acknowledges the many mood swings and changes of vision any writer can go through while exploring the possibilities of the next, new, poem.

The epigraph to "White Dwarfs," like the other two, is about lying and truth telling, and the dangerous border between the two.[6] Most of the poems in "White Dwarfs" explore the problems of art's relation to life. This is true even of the lovely and moving "We're at the graveyard," which is shifted to join the other domestic poems in *Trick with a Knife,* but which also specifically alludes to the last and title poem in the section—for many readers a central statement on the temptations of one kind of art. In contrast to the other poems here, its title also acts as the first line: the poem is in process before we're fully aware of having entered it. Those old standbys "Birth and copulation and death"[7]—in reverse order, and with "love" substituting perhaps for "copulation"— are the basis of the poem's discourse. Beginning with the reference to the graveyard, the poem invokes the far reaches of the universe and the inner workings of mind and heart: "Stuart Sally Kim and I" are "watching still stars / or now and then sliding stars" (RJ, 51; TK, 47). The stars move and do not move, they are part of "clear charts, / the systems' intricate branches / which change with hours and solstices, / the bone geometry of moving from there, to there." Clarity dissipates in motion and lack of reference, which are rooted in "the bone geometry" of the human subjects. An equilibrium between stasis and change, which the poet's father could not find, exists in the universe as perceived by "friends / whose minds and bodies / shift like acrobats to each other." The next two lines deepen the necessary equivocation of the poem: "When we leave, they move / to an altitude of silence." This seems to refer to the stars, but grammatically it refers to "friends." It could be the silence each pair enters when the two pairs are not together, an implicit silence of separation. Stars and friends, the macrocosmic and the microcosmic, are suddenly equal here, where "our minds shape / and lock the transient" in an artistic process that "parallel[s] these bats / who organize the air / with thick blinks of travel." This paradoxical metaphor, where organized motion is a momentary blindness, implies the utterly exploratory nature of the act of shaping, the act of art. Finally this poem about both friendship and art returns to the first of these, yet maintains its dedication to the latter as the final three lines point back to the opening. Here everything is held in lovely tension, an equilibrium in which stillness contains the implicit movement of growth and a single human subject contains the universe the poem evokes: "Sally is like grey snow in the grass, / Sally of the beautiful bones / pregnant below stars."

"Heron Rex" offers a supplementary vision of Ondaatje's favorite bird. While "Birds for Janet—The Heron" simply insists that "Heron is the true king" (DM, 13; TK, 3) and tracks the path of one heron's suicide, "Heron Rex" sets up a series of paradoxical generalizations to create an image of a twistedly symbolic species: "Mad kings / blood lines intro-verted, strained pure / so the brain runs in the wrong direction // they are proud of their heritage of suicides" (RJ, 52; TK, 55). This heritage of self-destruction transcends mere madness—the poem revels in its contradictions—to emerge as a kind of artistry, as the lengthy anaphora suggests. At the end of the epic list of suicidal acts, the phrase "and were led away" is repeated three times to suggest that the death sought is as much of the creative mind as of the body. Indeed, "Heron Rex" antici-pates *Coming Through Slaughter* at least as much as "White Dwarfs" does, especially in its climactic fourth stanza: "There are ways of going / physically mad, physically / mad when . . . you sacrifice yourself for the race . . . celebrity a razor in the body" (*RJ,* 53; *TK,* 55–6).

The sudden shift of the pronoun here expresses the implied author's own investment in the argument. Is this "you" simply "Heron Rex" or is it (also) the artist as such? For both, the act of public display is both dangerous and tempting. Celebrity is the danger here, as it is "for people who disappear" and who "hover and hover / and die in the ether peripheries" of silence in "White Dwarfs" (*RJ,* 70; *TK,* 68), as it most certainly is for Buddy Bolden. For such people, self-destructive acts seem to be the only, if terrifyingly extreme, way out, and "Heron Rex" initiates a sequence of poems projecting images of the self-destructive artist who seeks to escape into an inviolable silence. If the poem ended at this point, it would leave its readers in an open space of speculation, wondering if or how the birds had disappeared into their meanings. The final stanza returns to the material objects of "small birds so precise . . . 15 year old boys could . . . break them . . . as easily as a long fingernail" (*RJ,* 53; *TK,* 56). This terse brush-off grounds the metaphysical symbolism of the rest of the poem at the expense of a certain seriousness of purpose. As self-destructive artist, the heron as-sumes a kind of glamour that the final stanza tries to maintain and undercut at the same time. It also strives for a sense of closure that the previous stanza resists. While the poem would feel incomplete, now, if it ended after the fourth stanza, the fifth stanza's diminution of the symbol the poem has so crazily expanded is disturbing. Perhaps this is the poet's deliberate effort to distance himself from such artists, as he begins his deepest exploration of their psychology in *Coming Through Slaughter.*

"Taking," a poem on the artist as audience, insists on "the formal need / to suck blossoms out of the flesh / in those we admire / planting them private in the brain" (*RJ,* 55; *TK,* 57). Taking paradoxically becomes a kind of giving, or rather they continually replace and replen-ish one another. "To learn to pour the exact arc / of steel still soft and crazy / before it hits the page" is an image of this process, and it is an act of the writer as reader. If having "stroked the mood and tone / of hundred year dead men and women" and "tasted their brain" smacks of taking, it is also a way to give their art its due. Although "Their idea of the immaculate moment is now" might imply that art can only "freeze this moment" (*TK,* 17), "the rumours pass on / are planted / till they become a spine" argues the other half of the paradox. A spine is both a solid object and something that grows and changes with its body, here perhaps the body of writing itself. Such poems on the nature of the work of art resist explication precisely because they are written on the margins of their own discourse, where nothing and everything makes sense simultaneously, and where the writer cannot hold to one side of the argument only and still keep writing.

With "Burning Hills," the writer turns from imagining how art works in others to registering how he works in art. A seemingly complex narrative, it continually finds ways to deny normal narrative movement by creating a palimpsest or literary archaeological dig in which to uncover remembered layers of writing that contain further "layers of civilization in his memory" (*RJ,* 57; *TK,* 59). This extremely self-conscious piece of writing first sets its narrative voice apart from its "autobiographical" subject: "So he came to write again / in the burnt hill region." Paying extraordinary attention to mundane detail, the poem plots out the "schizophrenic season change, June to September, / when he deviously thought out plots / across the character of his friends." Already the adverb begins to subvert the apparent commitment to autobiographical "truth" that the realistic details imply. Although the poem expresses the fear that some "year maybe he would come and sit / for 4 months and not write a word down," it is also the writing that fear engenders.

Readers, especially male readers, are invited to identify with the protagonist as he makes a time machine of his writing room and thinks "of pieces of history" (*RJ,* 57; *TK,* 59), especially his own teenage sexual history. The details have a marvelous nostalgic intensity, but what makes them work is the continual switching back and forth between them and the writer remembering. These shifts yield that sense of process that elsewhere the poems have desired and denied. The constant commentary of the mind remembering is what the poem's about, not the memories themselves, however evocative they are. Ambiguity remains the most powerful and seductive aspect of the process, as subject and object slide into one another. "The summers were layers of civilization in his memory / they were old photographs he didn't look at anymore / for girls in them were chubby not as perfect as in his mind." The summers in his memory become the old photographs he no longer looks at, but the old photographs are not as perfect as his mind even though the memory exists only in that mind. In fact, it seems that both photographs and memory are propelling the poem's narration along, as "he" assumes uncertain mastery over them. The games of sex, representing the chaotic changes of growth, haunt the protagonist, yet evade any summary comment. Memory and photography join in the "one picture that fuses 5 summers" (*RJ,* 58; *TK,* 60). Here "summer and friendship will last forever," although he is "eating an apple" and "oblivious to the significance of the moment." But in photographs even more than in poems, significance is what we read into them. Photograph and poem contradict each other as "[n]ow he hungers to have that arm around the next shoulder. / The wretched apple is fresh and white." Here the layering of memory mixes a present-tense "now," which is already the past of the earlier stanzas, with the deeper past tense of the picture in which, nevertheless, the apple remains in the present tense. Such a "complex tension" can be expressed only as a process, the act of remembering discovered in the act of recording.

The final stanza again insists upon the process that writing both captures and is. Yet it also acknowledges that something of life must be lost even as the writing tries to hold on to it. Present participles in the first two sentences create a contradiction, contrasting the act of writing the poem we are reading with the action of the Shell Vapona Strip mentioned at the beginning of the poem: "Since he began burning hills / the Shell strip has taken effect." Is the poem like the insecticide? The lowercase of the title phrase implies that he has perhaps been destroying rather than making, or at least in some way razing memories to make a poem. Yet the present participle suggests that doing so is an ongoing process, which never stops, never achieves a frozen stasis, perhaps because each new reading re-creates both poem and subjects. The final lines may not even be the true confession they appear to be: "He has written slowly and carefully / with great love and great coldness. / When he finishes he will go back / hunting for the lies that are obvious." To the extent that all his poems were written this way, they may contain nonobvious lies. The greatest of these may be that confession. The "hunting" is itself a continuing process, which may or may not change the poem. Although the final line appears straightforward enough on first reading, it is as indeterminate as the whole poem: a troubling yet engaging performance that insists on having its ambivalent cake and eating it, too.

If writing must take place "in the murderer's shadow" (*RJ*, 61; *TK*, 61), then it will pay that price, as "King Kong meets Wallace Stevens" intimates. Looking at photographs of the two figures, the writer asks, in parentheses, "(Is it significant that I eat bananas as I write this?)"—a comic aside loaded with implications of identity. While Kong wreaks destruction "in New York streets again," that "again" evoking the repetitive powers of art, "W. S. in his suit / is thinking chaos is thinking fences." This ambiguous creation-in-destruction, in which the "lack of punctuation equates the two activities," recalls the writer's activity in "Burning Hills" (Scobie 1985a, 56). Stevens is the exemplar here because he can write "the seeds of fresh pain . . . the bellow of locked blood" into his poems. While Kong is "at the call of Metro-Goldwyn-Mayer," "the naked brain / the thought in" Stevens exercises the control self-destructive artists repudiate.

"Spider Blues," which is moved back one to directly follow "King Kong meets Wallace Stevens" in *Trick with a Knife*, uses macabre comedy to undermine, though not utterly deny, any trust of such artists of control earlier poems might have engendered. If the writer must write and therefore cannot join his "heroes" in silence, he certainly feels too ambivalent about his art to underwrite it unequivocally. "Spider Blues" allows the subjects of such art their voice. The spider, "his control classic," is a "kind of writer I suppose" (*RJ*, 63; *TK*, 62), says this writer, the man with a wife whose "smell spiders go for." Already black comedy and speculative poetics are merging into a tall tale of *écriture*. Spider/writer is an explorer who "thinks a path and travels . . . to new regions / where the raw of feelings exist" (*RJ*, 63–64; *TK*, 62). This sounds positive, but "[s]piders like poets are obsessed with power" (*RJ*, 64; *TK*, 62) does not. Such power can "kill" the subject, as the poem demonstrates in a scene of allusive black comedy where "spider comes to fly, says / Love me I can kill you," but "fly says, O no . . . you spider poets are all the same / you in your close vanity of making" (*RJ*, 64; *TK*, 62–63). These contradictory voices provide a dialogical view of the writer's situation: the tautology that clarity only "comes when roads I make are being made" reveals the solipsism into which the artist may fall while working; "close" sounds enough like "close*d*" to suggest a making that process poetics would wish to transcend; the spider's desire to crucify "his victims in his spit / making them the art he cannot be" implies that the controlling artist hates the life he wants to turn into art (with the further implication that artists who turn to silence make their own lives into works of art, which yet must finish in their death?).

In this scene, the spider artists get no respect, but the poem isn't over, and in "[t]he ending we must arrive at . . . Nightmare for my wife and me" *(RJ,* 65; *TK,* 63), they put on a performance, the past-tense narration of which itself suggests its success, in which "they carried her up—her whole body / into the dreaming air so gently / she did not wake or scream." The writer is lost in admiration of their art, but he is not alone, and the poem concludes on a note of certainty, which only underlines the uncertainty of the whole project: "Everybody clapped, all the flies. . . . ALL / except the working black architects / and the lady locked in their dream   their theme." The flies seem to be "everybody" here, a designation of the audience that should make any reader wary. They cry and gasp, which they might also do if they were dying. The final paradox is art's central one: the artists are in process, as the present participle implies, but the firm adjectival form of "locked" equally implies the freezing of the subject of that process. It seems there is no escaping the contradiction at the heart of art, yet the essentially comic mode of this poem suggests that the paradox is, finally, acceptable—at least to the writer writing.

Artistic control is simultaneously sought and denied in "The gate in his head," which is dedicated to Victor Coleman, a poet of process, whose "shy mind / reveal[s] the faint scars / coloured strata of the brain, / not clarity but the sense of shift / / a few lines, the tracks of thought" *(RJ,* 62; *TK,* 64). The transformation from personal wounds to written trace occurs through a metaphoric "shift" that conflates reading and tracking. But, in a poem about the problem of netting chaos in language, the imagery undergoes continual metamorphosis. A tracker might move across a "[l]andscape of busted trees," but in a poem of transformations, that landscape melts surrealistically into "Stan's fishbowl / with a book inside . . . the typeface clarity / going slow blonde in the sun full water" erasing its bibliographicity.[8] Only after the first half of the poem has presented a series of rapid and confusing transformations does the writer argue its case for doing so, by enunciating what he always tries to do. The writing mind pours the inchoate materials of experience onto the page, but it must capture—net—them to do so. This contradiction manifests both the terror and the glory of art, but the glory is that the writing does come from love perceived as an act of exploration. Moreover, it can be communicated, as the "blurred photograph" of the "stunning white bird / an unclear stir" demonstrates. Writer-as-reader receives the other's "[c]aught vision" and understands the ideal he should seek in his own writing. The final stanza is necessarily paradoxical. Form is present

in chaos even as chaos is present in form: what the writer seeks to catch is
not the dead thing but the actual movement of the living, and he can do
so only by allowing words their own indeterminate ambiguity. The
poem desires clarity, but it also admits that too much clarity can stop the
necessary movement that art seeks to illuminate. What the photograph
is, and what the "writing should be," then, is a clear vision of the
"beautiful formed things" in the process of escaping closure, "shapeless,
awkward / moving to the clear."[9]

"White Dwarfs"[10] is central to Ondaatje's oeuvre precisely because it
evokes so many themes associated with his work. "Ondaatje's most
radical gesture in the direction of indicating that there are times when
'all the truth' cannot be stated, described, or re-enacted . . . [this]
variation on T. W. Adorno's 'No poetry after Auschwitz' . . . is a
profound meditation on both life and art. It is a tribute to those who have
gone beyond 'social fuel' and language" (Solecki 1985a, 106–7). A
tribute, yes, but not an uncomplicated one; if it "is for people who
disappear" and "who shave their moral so raw / they can tear themselves
through the eye of a needle" (RJ, 70; TK, 68), it not only cannot
share their silence but must speak in order to praise them. Given the
reference to Jesus' parable about the rich man and heaven,[11] "moral" has
a positive connotation, but the violence required to achieve "heaven"—
which is perhaps simply "the ether peripheries" where they "hover and
hover / and die"—savagely undercuts any sentimentalization of their
behavior.

The "heroes" of silence—a silence the poet insists he fears—"sail to
that perfect edge / where there is no social fuel / Release of sandbags / to
understand their altitude." They join the stars of "We're at the graveyard" in "an altitude of silence" (TK, 47) completely cut off from
humanity. Beyond the ordinary connections of life, they achieve a
"perfect edge," but "perfect" has the negative connotation of stasis,
completion, and implies the end of living. Like the herons of "Heron
Rex," these heroes (note the shift of only one letter between the two) have
chosen a kind of suicide, if only of their art. The poet admires them, but
he does not, finally, seek to join them; he cannot, for he still believes in
words. Their silence has an aura of romance about it, and it is based on
real pain, but someone has to speak for them if they refuse to speak for
themselves: "3rd man hung so high and lonely / we dont hear him say /
say his pain, say his unbrotherhood." But perhaps it isn't they who refuse
but we who "dont hear." The poem is riddled with ambiguity. Some
choose not to speak, like "Dashiell Hammett [who] in success / suffered

conversation and moved / to the perfect white between the words" (*RJ,* 71; *TK,* 69), and that is their privilege; others are forced into silence, and perhaps need someone else to acknowledge their suffering. It may be "Ondaatje's recognition of the adolescent fatuity of the code 'White Dwarfs' addresses, its spurious glamour, which makes him deflate it even as he continues to explore its romance" (Glickman, 79), but this is not the only contradiction at work in the poem. Of the mules with their tongues cut out, the poem asks, "after such cruelty what could they speak of anyway," and the image implies other tortures, of humans as well as animals. But mules never could speak, and always needed someone to speak on their behalf. That "perfect white" is both static, as the adjective suggests, and "can grow" into various possibilities, even into "an egg— most beautiful / when unbroken, where / what we cannot see is growing / in all the colours we cannot see." But such growth depends upon "us," who use the power of imagination to "see" the colors hidden in the white.

The whole poem maintains a delicate equilibrium, balancing silence against speech, the romantic otherness of the heroes who sail beyond society into silence against the classic responsibility of the poet as witness. There is poetry after Auschwitz because the horror had to be confronted. This poem affirms writing by denying it: that is the paradox the poems of poetics have approached over and over again. We would never "know" about "those burned out stars / who implode into silence / after parading in the sky" unless the writer told us and in telling evoked our compassion by insisting that "after such choreography what would they wish to speak of anyway." The poem honors the silenced ones by speaking. In that ambivalent balance,[12] poetry continues to explore what "writing should be then" (*RJ,* 62; *TK,* 64), as it must.

The new poems in the third section of *Trick with a Knife* were written during and after the writing of *Coming Through Slaughter.* They present themselves as more strictly autobiographical, and the "I" who speaks them seems to have much more in common with the living writer, Michael Ondaatje, than before, while the references tend to be less mythical or literary and more seemingly "real." If, previously, "[w]hat Ondaatje d[id wa]s invite the expectations of confession and the exhilarations of parable, but leave the identity of the speaker hovering between himself and another" (Chamberlin, 38), now the speaking voices of his poems still hover "between" possibilities, but they are the various possibilities of place, stance, and attitude found under the single "name" of the implied author. Poems of Canada, mostly of rural Ontario and its history, which he comes to as an immigrant, are balanced against travel poems of Egypt, India, and Sri Lanka.[13] Because the Ceylon he returns to is a place he left too young to have truly inherited a sense of his place in its history, the poems set there are as arbitrary and float as free of/from historical referentiality as the Canadian ones. The final poems return to Toronto, children, parents, and friends, and include a re-vision of Billy the Kid from the point of view of another "actor" in the story.

The apparent refusal of history and historically grounded culture that some critics find disturbing in a postcolonial writer (see Mukherjee, 33–34)[14] may equally be a choice that reflects, and reflects upon, twentieth-century rootlessness and nomadism. Moreover, the ways these poems refuse to engage with historical and social representation paradoxically call attention to it; like much postmodern writing, they accept the past as such but suggest that, "however true [the past's] independence may be, nevertheless the past exists for us—now—only as traces on and in the present. The absent past can only be inferred from circumstantial evidence" (Hutcheon 1989, 73). Even the poems that invoke history insist that it is only the invocation that can be inscribed, not the "actual" history; this is especially apparent in "Pig Glass" itself.

The epigraph to "Pig Glass," from Italo Calvino's *Invisible Cities,* says that, lacking the language, "Marco Polo could express himself only with gestures . . . or with objects."[15] It thus emphasizes the difficulties of communication, and the comedy of physical expression that arises from those difficulties. A later part of the passage, not quoted by Ondaatje, adds that, "obscure or obvious as it might be, everything Marco displayed had the power of emblems, which, once seen, cannot be forgotten or confused" (Calvino, 20–21). One way of discussing many of these poems is in terms of how they either present emblems or become them. Their power often lies in the emblematic force of their images, rather than in the argumentative force of their narratives.[16] This is certainly true of "The Agatha Christie Books by the Window" (*TK,* 72) and the beautifully indeterminate "Moon Lines, after Jiménez (*TK,* 74–75).

"Buying the Dog," "Moving Fred's Outhouse / Geriatrics of Pine," and "Buck Lake Store Auction" invoke the specific life of rural Ontario. The air of autobiography is palpable in them, and the narrative voice, studiedly realistic, "artlessly" anecdotal, seems to buttress that air of personal narrative, until the sudden illumination of poetic rhetoric just slightly undermines the apparent naturalness of the idiom. The first poem enters the world and speech of the farmer Buck McLeish only to push hard at a comic edge with the introduction of "the dog who has been / in a religious fit of silence / since birth" (*TK,* 76). Despite the attention to detail and a somewhat grandiose attempt to make the dog symbolize this world they (the "we" of the poem—speaker and family) wish to become part of—"Towns the history of his bones"—the end comically undercuts the pretensions the poem has created, as the dog "takes off JESUS / like a dolphin / over the fields for all we know / he won't be coming back." The use of the first name in "Moving Fred's Outhouse" establishes a friendly intimacy, inviting us to assume it as well. The ordinariness of the events—here moving an old outhouse across a property to make it "a room thorough with flight, noise, / and pregnant with the morning's eggs / —a perch for chickens" (*TK,* 77)—argues the autobiographical "truth" of these poems as opposed to the "mythologizing" of *The Dainty Monsters.* But if not mythical, these events are charged with something more than banal ordinariness, which is signaled once again through a comic gesture: "Fred the pragmatist—dragging the ancient comic / out of retirement and into a television series / among the charging democracy of rhode island reds." Unlike the previous poem, which ended in a question, this ends with an apparent summary statement—"All afternoon the silent space is turned"—that nevertheless turns interpretation aside. We are left with the images of dog or outhouse and chickens, not with an argument at all.

"Buck Lake Store Auction," the most socially conscious of these poems, maintains the autobiographical perspective, but only to provide a personal response within the poem to the scene of loss it witnesses. Beginning in minimal description, it soon puts a price on the items it lists. In the fifth stanza, the speaker finally identifies himself with either a family or everyone there in the "we" who "have the power to bid / on everything that is exposed" (*TK,* 78). Admitting this power over others seems to clarify his vision and move him to a kind of angry sarcasm: "I expected [the old woman] to unscrew / her left arm and donate it / to the auctioneer's excitement." This excitement is responsible for whatever is being done here, and engenders both political awareness and impotence: "In certain rituals we desire / only what we cannot have" (*TK,* 79). The false logical connection of "While for her, Mrs Germain, / this is the needle's eye / where maniacs of heaven select" only underlines that impotence. Where, in "White Dwarfs," that Biblical allusion implied reckless romantic courage among those who choose to "tear themselves through the eye of a needle" (*TK,* 68), the obvious lack of choice here suggests some reevaluation of the earlier vision. The tone here replaces the awe of the earlier poem with compassion, the uselessness of which is made clear by the subjunctive mood of the final three lines: the speaker "wanted to say" something useful, if only in a bid, but could and did not. Confronting an economic situation that is also political, this highly problematic poem can only offer the "liberal" act of witness in response. Even as it limns the liberal predicament, it also continues the autobiographical work of situating the writer in the country he has chosen to make home and whose life he seeks to enter. Its success in both endeavors reveals how postmodern Ondaatje's writing has become, in that it can self-reflexively balance these oppositions within the one text.

"Farre Off" (*TK,* 80) appears to be a traditionally lyric poem, with a self-conscious sense of beauty and personal engagement that fits the conventions of lyric utterance, even if the utterance is directed to, or through, other poems rather than a particular beloved person. But its deliberate intertextuality suggests something of its subversive nature. The lyric "I" represents himself specifically as a poet and a reader of poetry, speaking of a new discovery and translating the experience of the reading into his own rural setting. This is an engaged reader who desires what the poems of Campion and Wyatt, "who loved with the best," inscribe as desirable: "suddenly I want 16th century women / round me devious politic aware / of step ladders to the king." While the sudden rush of emotion and expression of personal desire are essentially lyric, the arresting encapsulation of the imagery of the earlier poetry is highly self-reflexive. Such narrative self-consciousness deepens in the deliberately ambiguous reference of the second stanza, which also links this poem to the previous poems of local place: "Tonight I am alone with dogs and lightning / aroused by Wyatt's talk of women who step / naked into his bedchamber." Ancient poetry is suddenly extraordinarily effective here, arousing not only the speaker but also the dogs and even the elements. But what is the nature of this highly contagious excitement? Rather than answering such a question, the poem presents a variety of illuminations and confounds any sense of literary or cultural inheritance by returning attention to the speaker. "I have on my thin blue parka / and walk behind the asses of the dogs / who slide under the gate / and sense cattle / deep in the fields." These lines veer wildly from Wyatt's traditional lyric vision to an antilyric naturalism and reinforce the syntactical ambiguity erasing the difference between dogs and speaker. Finally, the speaker seems to move toward an epiphany only to reverse the literary expectation of "illumination" from a text, and perhaps confess that opacity is all that poetry can offer: "I look out into the dark pasture / past where even the moonlight stops / / my eyes are against the ink of Campion." Literature, which is supposed to bring light, is inscribed in darkness, in ink, a material barrier to understanding, but one that readers understand in its physical presence: ink, poem, book connect, but do not explain. The mystery of the reader-writer relationship at the center of this poem is not new in Ondaatje's work, but seldom has it been presented in such a "natural" manner. The poem argues nothing; it simply demonstrates by a kind of handing on its complex sense of cultural inheritance.

The complexities both attract and repulse the poet, and "Walking to Bellrock" examines modes of escape from the responsibilities of inheritance that weigh the artist down. It presents a process, not simply a single act, over and done with. Like Depot Creek, the syntax twists and turns, pronouns slipping into each other, tenses shifting, different stories sliding over and under each other. "Two figures in deep water. / / Their frames truncated at the stomach / glide along the surface" (*TK,* 81): this is the motivating image of the poem. Two friends are taking this crazy walk, yet they are not all there; or they move along a mirror that reflects both too little and too much, and thus refutes analysis. History is present only to be ignored, yet the paradox of writing assures the affirmation and elucidation of meanings that the poem itself appears to claim are lost or tossed aside in egocentric, romantic adherence to the now of walking and talking that the poem celebrates. But even the now is lost in the welter of impressions the river, and the poem, throws up. The various images of "[l]andscapes underwater" that the "torn old Adidas tennis shoes" encounter are sharp yet indecisive, and the questions that follow cannot be answered. "Stan and I laughing joking going summer crazy / as we lived against each other" (*TK,* 82) announces the autobiographical nature of the poem and its exploration of the notion of male friendship. This companionate summer craziness might stand as an alternative to Buddy Bolden's isolated retreat into insanity, but the preposition, echoing "Farre Off," suggests how opaque the communication in even the closest friendships is. Perhaps this sense of opaqueness explains why the speaker insists "there is no history or philosophy or metaphor with us," although the rest of the poem denies this assertion with complex metaphors and historical allusions that depend upon a certain degree of documentation constantly erupting into the narrative.

The poem desires to become no more than a record of immediate perception, yet in the process of ordering experience comes up short against the questions the action raises, of which "Stan, my crazy summer friend, / why are we both going crazy?" (*TK*, 83) is only the most obvious. But "in the middle of this century / following the easy fucking stupid plot to town," there are no answers beyond the crazy act of walking the river. The poem generates excitement in its representation of the "crazy" actions of the two friends, while undercutting their romantic heroism. "Walking to Bellrock" celebrates an act of friendship but denies it any cultural viability; its insistence on denying history consistently resists the conventional attractions of tradition while failing to erase tradition itself from the text. "Walking to Bellrock" denies history and tradition only to affirm their necessity; it revels in romantic escapism only to hold it up to question.

"Pig Glass," perhaps the most stringently emblematic of the new poems, suggests their problematic relation to history and inheritance. "Bonjour. This is pig glass / a piece of cloudy sea" (*TK*, 84): while the colloquial opening addresses the reader as subject of what is said, the demonstrative pronoun points to an object that exists only in its name and in the shifting descriptions inscribed in the poem. As further transformations occur, indeterminate reference confuses "my hand," " a language," and the "pig glass" in a gesture intimating a complex intimacy, and seducing us into joining the speaker in his meditation: "the pig glass / I thought / was the buried eye of Portland Township." The line breaks imply the speaker is thinking the glass into existence as "slow faded history / waiting to be grunted up."

Only after he has allowed for such uncertainties does the speaker finally name the family who once "used this section" and describe some of the objects he has found in their "midden." Naming them places him in relation to a history, but not one he has inherited by any family right. Having said as much, he returns to the "pig glass," which the repeated demonstrative "this" self-reflexively makes identical with the text "Pig Glass" as both object and context. The next stanza shifts back to other objects in the land, and, more troublingly, to the letters and journals "I / disturbed in the room above the tractor shed" (*TK*, 85). The "I" of the poem has become his own "eye" of the township through documentary invasion of a family's privacy, and, as if recognizing the impropriety of the act, the poem leaps back to the seeming objectivity of the glass. But as glass and poem are one, there can be no objectivity, and the text implodes into the present tense of the action that broke the glass: "This green fragment has behind it / the *booomm* when glass / tears free of its smoothness." Past and present are also one in the transition to subjective perception in the final stanza, where the speaker insists on his possession of an emblem of "[D]etermined histories of glass." But we possess "indeterminate histories of the poem," for it is impossible to say who or what determined those histories, only the vaguest allusions to which the poem has provided. It is "cloudy sea" (*TK,* 84) because it allows all the possibilities of both cloud and sea to float around it: it says there is history but it cannot tell what histories there are. "Pig Glass" is the perfect emblem of the indeterminacy of knowledge that so many of these poems delineate.

The next five poems are from travels, but they neatly evade the usual problems of travel poems, where the lyric and romantic "I" reports back with a privileged commentary on the places and si[gh]t[e]s seen. The speaker of these poems performs a kind of perceiving and even meditation sometimes, but does not presume to report or comment on what he sees; he simply registers its presence in as imagistic a language as possible or allows it to tease his mind into other thoughts. The results are poems in which various forms of discourse slide over and continually interrupt one another, providing no easy place of rest or closure. "The Hour of Cowdust" opens with a "we" rather than an "I" not so much displaced as unplaced: "It is the hour we move small / in the last possibilities of light" (*TK,* 86). Still unplaced, the "we" becomes a specific "I," thinking first of his children elsewhere and then focusing on the present moment of dusk "here by the Nile," which seems to specify place and time only to let metaphors of illusion undercut any sense of "reality" that might be building up. "Everything is reducing itself to shape" seems a generalization of sense impressions, but the impression is of loss of specificity: nothing can be named. Sliding to the second-person pronoun, the poem evokes the air and the changing color of the scene only to switch suddenly in memory to "Indian miniatures" and commentaries and stories of high romance he can allude to but "cannot quite remember." The conclusion of such fallible meditation is an offhand and oxymoronic "So many / graciously humiliated / by the distance of rivers" (*TK,* 87). This returns the poem to the particular river at a particular hour, but only to introduce other questions and engender a series of syntactic ambiguities that reinforce the sense of illusion. Duplicitous, the scene becomes a dream, in which the final stanza's assertion that with no "depth of perception / it is now possible / for the outline of two boats / to collide silently" seems perfectly natural. But it is not natural, and the grammatical slippage from singular "outline" to implied plural verb self-reflexively reaffirms the textuality of the whole experience, in which the titular hour creates illusions of romance and of violence, only to prevent anything from actually happening. By inscribing its own imagining, the poem provides a sense of the mystery of the alien space that is Egypt, without resorting to commentary or egocentric "insight." Egypt remains as opaque as the "pig glass," and as beautiful.

A similar kind of defamiliarization occurs in "The Palace," which renders an Indian dawn to match the Egyptian dusk. This time "I am alone / leaning / into flying air" and "red daylight" (*TK,* 88), but this "I" is only one site of discourse among many, looking at the place and its animal life, and eventually its waking population. The stanza on the ancient king stands alone; lacking any personal introduction, it might be dreamed, heard, read. A kind of document inserted into the poem, it splits the singular voice of lyric meditation apart. Where history and myth once joined in story, now a startling image of international technology makes a strange mythic moment when "a beautiful wail / of a woman's voice rises / 300 street transistors / simultaneously playing / the one radio station of Udaipur." Contradictory political ironies suggest that multinational technology imposes alien knowledge on local or national culture, yet the use of such imperial gifts can be a form of resistance even as it is a sign of colonization. But the poem refuses to argue any case. It does not presume to speak for the people of Udaipur, only to register the moment of *ostranenie* they provided.

"Uswetakeiyawa" is a good introduction to Sri Lanka, for the very word is utterly alien, and as the first word of the poem it sets the tone of strangeness for "the dream journey / we travel most nights / returning from Colombo. / A landscape nightmare" (*TK,* 90). The poem traverses illusion and paradox, as even the senses prove untrustworthy, and "lesser" senses like smell have to make up for the failure of vision (possibly implied as a pun). The sense of transformation is central, and in the final stanzas, the poem itself turns "trickster," rendering an over-whelming sensual confusion that confounds "you" as "you" encounter "something we have never been able to recognize" (*TK,* 91). "There was then the odour we did not recognize. / The smell of a dog losing its shape" is the oxymoronic conclusion of an argument against rationality: what it recognizes as an unrecognizable odor is the final sign of a frightening transformation of something known (and in most of On-daatje's poetry, dogs are both known and loved) into the unknown. In this night journey through a nightmare landscape, what other known shapes are lost? Although he can be read as a returning prodigal of sorts, this poem establishes the writer as outsider, a tourist lost in an alien landscape who can sense its power but never know or understand it.

"The Wars" presents a series of images of natural life and death in this mysterious place that is Sri Lanka. The title suggests the violence implicit in the natural cycle the poem perceives, yet its tone is essentially light, as the image of "hundreds of unseen bats / tuning up the auditorium / in archaic Tamil" (*TK*, 92) reveals. That they sing a song of exile connects them to the speaker. The poem's quick shifts of attention reveal the outsider's inability to know what is and what is not "real" in this place of continual transformation; all he can do is render, in a series of typically sensuous images, the rich paradoxes of what he experiences: in "noon moonlight" (how the sun appears underwater?), "only [the Ray's] twin" (his shadow on the seabed?) "knows how to charm / the waters against him" (*TK*, 93). This seems a conclusive gesture, but all it manages to suggest is that nothing is quite certain in these landscape nightmares.

"Sweet like a Crow," which is dedicated "for Hetti Corea, 8 years old" (*TK*, 94) is a jeu d'esprit, all light wit and comedy, emerging from its epigraph by Paul Bowles: "'The Sinhalese are beyond a doubt one of the least musical people in the world. It would be quite impossible to have less sense of pitch, line, or rhythm." An increasingly bizarre set of similes shifts among images of odd auditory events, signs of pop culture, and specifically local references. Rhetorical overkill deliberately pushes the trope of simile beyond bounds to achieve a new comic decorum of delight and, finally, even beauty, as the final couplet returns to quotidian event by using the trope to undercut its tropicality: "like the sound I heard when having an afternoon sleep / and someone walked through my room in ankle bracelets" (*TK*, 95). To suggest that the exotic range of the similes attempts to match the exotic sensual impact of Sri Lanka itself is not, I hope, to give in to an ethnocentric blindness to the culture and people that Ondaatje, too, may be ignoring (see Mukherjee, 33), for it is precisely the chaotic combination of comparisons that marks the whole "description" as culturally contextualized by the complex juxtaposition of Sri Lankan heritage and international pop iconography. Mostly, however, the poem takes pleasure in its own fertile inventiveness.

The final poems return to Canada, but only to perceive from that perspective various aspects of the world as they impinge upon a singular individual anywhere. "Late Movies with Skyler" is precisely domestic, but insists that even in the midst of domesticity we are connected to the larger world of personal and public dreams by the media that dominate our imaginations. It can be read against "White Dwarfs" only to the extent that both visions coexist in the writerly imagination.

Skyler, the 21-year-old stepson visiting "home," has come back from an unromantic reality of "logging on Vancouver Island / with men who get rid of crabs with Raid" (*TK*, 96) to watch films of romantic escapism. But he is himself romantic and is represented as being essentially alone. When the writer joins him to watch, "*The Prisoner of Zenda* / a film I saw three times in my youth / and which no doubt influenced me morally," the young man demonstrates a desire for the aesthetic purity of craft, practicing guitar during commercials. In its apparently casual articulateness, the way it slides from one small event to another, the writing seems to deny that it is a poem, yet the careful rhythms and the jumps from stanza to stanza all contribute to a specifically poetic effect. From simply describing the situation of the two men watching, the poem slips into a kind of double commentary that envelops the mood of the film within the mood of the watchers. But the "perfect world {now} over" (*TK*, 97) cannot coexist with the mess of "the slow black rooms of the house," except in the imagination. If "Skyler is Rupert then the hero," he is also the boy-man who will shortly leave for somewhere unspecific. All the writer can realize and offer is the ironic coda that "[i]n the movies of my childhood the heroes / after skilled swordplay and moral victories / leave with absolutely nothing / to do for the rest of their lives." But the real world goes on, and although the final lines of the poem argue closure for the films, they in fact deny it for both the writer and his stepson. The writer cannot know what Skyler will do, nor even where he will go. That is an open question, as is the poem.

If "Late Movies with Skyler" undercuts the romantic vision of old adventure movies, "Sallie Chisum / Last Words on Billy the Kid. 4 a.m." does a somewhat similar job on Ondaatje's own western adventure, *The Collected Works of Billy the Kid*. Sallie's apparently random thoughts are based on memory engaging desire and its concomitant sense of loss, yet the whole process of remembering begins with a chance image of the moon as Billy's head. The tone throughout is dramatically precise as it shifts with the attention of its subject from comment to memory to comment again. There is a double sense of audience as both the moon-Billy and another "you" are addressed. She remembers that he taught her to smoke, shifts back to a moment of intense body awareness of "Billy's mouth . . . trying / to remove a splinter out of my foot" (*TK*, 98), and then converses in her mind with the moon-ghost. The memories imply a strained intimacy that remains—as it was in the book—mysteriously opaque, even to one of the participants. But the degree of her intimacy with Billy is not as important as the power he still exerts over her despite her denials of it. The poem captures her contradictory feelings as she slides from memories of his presence as an object of desire to her present-day assertions that "Billy was a fool," a comment many readers of Billy's life might agree with, but which *The Collected Works* does not support. Like "those reversible mirrors," Billy resists both Sallie's attempts at analysis and her own continuing resistance to his charm. Thus her repetitions of key images and phrases only serve to undermine their authority even as they underline her continuing obsession with him. The poem simultaneously undercuts the romance that *The Collected Works* allowed but did not exploit and adds a further glamour to it. The final stanza captures all the pent-up frustration of 37 years of remembering in a gesture of complicity and denial, as she squashes her cigarette "against the window / where the moon is. / In his stupid eyes" (*TK,* 99). The poem does not offer information so much as an opportunity to hear emotions work in memory as it works in her. Her anger reveals other, deeper, unacknowledged feelings, yet is also properly her own and completely true. Like the text it is a pendant to, "Sallie Chisum / Last Words" cannot determine a single view of its subject(s).

The ten prose fragments of "Pure Memory / Chris Dewdney" suggest that memory itself is a form of fiction making.[17] The epigraph quotes Dewdney himself, although it is not clear if it is something he wrote or something he said to the writer: "Listen, it was so savage and brutal and powerful that even though it happened out of the blue I knew there was nothing arbitrary about it" (*TK,* 100). While there is no reference for this forceful "it," we read each fragment in terms of the unnamed catastrophe it represents even as the whole poem resists dealing with it. That is why writers tell stories, sometimes, to evade the catastrophe that cannot be written.

The poem begins in a comic mode, as the writer cannot pronounce the title of one of Dewdney's books on a radio show. This comic opening shot establishes the difficulties associated with Dewdney as writer, while part 2 represents him as full of laughter and energy. With part 3, the poem turns to concentrate upon a series of stories specifically designed to put off dealing with the core experience of Dewdney's life, as the writer perceives it. Yet, paradoxically, the stories all point to the ways in which Dewdney's behavior in every situation reveals a person whose whole life is based upon an intuitive understanding of catastrophe theory. Dewdney seems to live *ostranenie,* as the stories of his childhood, or of "[h]is most embarrassing moment" (*TK,* 101), demonstrate. Although the various fragments build up a sense of Dewdney's resourcefulness in situations both ordinary and farcical, their humorous tone seems somewhat fragile beneath the weight of the epigraph. In part 7, the writer, seeing Dewdney after some time, notices the signs of a dark change: "Something has left his face. It is not that he is thinner but the face has lost something distinct and it seems like flesh" (*TK,* 102). The stuttering repetitions make palpable the writer's inability to come to terms with the change he perceives, while that vague noun *something* signals what the poem will not, cannot, tell. Although he tries to turn away from these signs of pain, the writer cannot avoid returning to what he doesn't understand, his friend's face. The fragment ends with a reiteration of Dewdney's serious interest in all "important rare information like the history of rocks," and the next fragment takes another comic turn to say "[h]is favourite movie is *Earthquake*" and describe Dewdney's apartment full of beautiful fossils and other exhibits. Part 9 then describes the writer's return to Toronto with a drawing of Dewdney by another friend. Parts 7, 8, and 9 are in fact a single story of the writer's meeting Dewdney, then visiting him in London, then returning to Toronto; they suddenly bring all the memories into a single time frame in which the catastrophe, still not spoken of, looms ever closer. In a delicate metaphor, the image of the drawing on the luggage rack above the writer suddenly metamorphoses into the person, as he says, "[w]hen the bus swerves I put my arm out into the dark aisle ready to catch him if it falls" (*TK,* 103). The "dark aisle" reinforces the disturbing undertone that the epigraph cast upon the whole poem, while the personal pronoun implies that "catching" his friend is exactly what he could not do; nor could anyone. Part 10 attempts to confront what the whole poem has evaded: "His wife's brain haemorrhage. I could not cope with that. He is 23 years old. He does. Africa Asia Australia upside down. Earthquake." What cannot be said is what turns everything upside down. As the images of previous fragments gather into a kind of litany of catastrophe, the single statement "He does" seems to suggest his ability to cope as the writer cannot. Or does it only imply the writer's hope that he can? The emotional power of the poem depends on how it both demonstrates friendship and empathy and reveals their limits.

Dedicated to the poet's mother, "Light" serves as a kind of prolegomenon to *Running in the Family,* where "the expanding stories" (*TK,* 107) implied by the photographs that are the poem's subject finally get told. The "amazing light" (*TK,* 72) of day in the first poem of "Pig Glass" now becomes a vaster, more complex series of night lights, including the lightning as well as the electric light that projects slides. Thus, the first image of "[t]rees walking off across the fields in fury / naked in the spark of lightning" (*TK,* 105) suggests movement in stillness, just as the photographs do. The writer watches the midnight storm as the "past, friends and family, drift into the rain shower." The sense of "drift" is the essence of this poem; it suggests the evanescence of both the light-projected images, and the stories conjured out of them, both of which "now stand / complex ambiguous grainy on my wall."

The long second stanza points to some of the figures in the implied gossipy tales. It further establishes the tone of casual, intimate conversation that deliberately uses the indicative pronoun to include us in the small circle listening to the writer as he points out one relative after another. But a text can only point to itself; the "pictures" exist only in the words describing them, yet the verbal gesture implicates us in the implied story of the writer's telling stories. After pointing to aunts and uncles and the gossip attached to their names, he then turns to his mother and her brother, linking a picture of their childhood to the story of their deaths. Complex narrative shifts of time occur throughout these two stanzas, as when the writer recalls his mother recalling her brother's death and her earlier memories at that time. Over and over again, he speaks in precisely personal tones about his own feelings for the people in the photographs, insisting that photographs provide a way of touching the past.

When he says "[t]hese are the fragments I have of them, tonight / in this storm" (*TK,* 106), the indicative appears to refer to the photographs, but, in the midst of the storm, it can also refer to the stories, or to the memories the photos and stories recall and create. The layers of fictional invention memory makes are implied in that single word, "these." Repeated, it emphasizes the ambiguous hold memory has on the past: "These are their fragments, all I remember, / wanting more knowledge of them" (*TK,* 107). Memory is not knowledge, yet it is all we have, and so "[w]herever we are / they parade in my brain and the expanding stories / connect to the grey grainy pictures on the wall . . . / coming through the light, the electricity, which the storm / destroyed an hour ago." That "we" once again intimately includes us in the writer's perspective, but the passage creates images only to dissipate any sense of "reality" they might create. The pictures are no longer on the wall; even they are no more than memories, part of another expanding story now being written, and read. In fact, the passage, a single, long, winding, and complex sentence, slips and slides from images and stories to the hour-old accident, to the kids playing dominoes now, and finally to the writer meditating as he smokes, watches the lightning, and returns to the image that began the poem only to deny it: "and the trees across the fields leaving me, distinct / . . . when in truth like me they haven't moved. / Haven't moved an inch from me." The play on "light" throughout the poem complicates and undercuts any symbolic meaning it might have. Yet the slides offer a peculiarly technological "illumination" in which the silent past does communicate with the present. The slippage of syntax in the final passage signals the fusion of and the fluctuation among photographs, stories, memory, imagination, and desire that the poem invokes. Neither trees nor storied memories (or remembered stories) really move away, yet this confirmation of the deception of appearances reminds us that the whole poem *may* not be what it appears to be.

"Light" is a rich collage of moments in time laid over one another in a complex metaphoric relationship. Like many of the other poems in "Pig Glass," it is deceptively anecdotal, casual in tone, and seemingly artless in narration. Here, the poet says, let me just lay out these quite ordinary random memories or impressions before you; have I told you about the time. . . . But analysis of these poems not only reveals the complicated interlocking of analepsis and prolepsis in their structures but also the subtle music of their language. Written as Ondaatje gradually involved himself in the task of writing *Running in the Family,* they provide glimpses of that larger work as well as of the other contexts of his life while he pursued it. In their more relaxed, less symbolic, approach to the idea of the lyric, itself undergoing a kind of deconstruction in both his own mind and other poets' works at the time, they also point the way toward the personal poem sequences of *Secular Love.* Certainly, as a summing up of where his writing had led him thus far, they provide a fitting and open-ended conclusion to *There's a Trick with a Knife I'm Learning to Do.*

Chapter Five
Coming Through Slaughter

Although it won the *Books in Canada* award as the best first novel by a Canadian in 1976, Michael Ondaatje is wary about calling *Coming Through Slaughter* a novel, as are the critics. "As Bolden's jazz is undefined, because it was by nature improvisational and because it was never recorded, so is the genre of the text hard to define."[1] Conventional novelistic "narrative destroys its own traditional position as somehow overseeing the text, distanced from it," to create "what Claude Levi-Strauss terms '*bricolage*,' wherein the assembler of pieces, the *bricoleur*, is both collecting heterogenous (sic) material to make a 'whole' and implicating himself in the selection of the materials chosen."[2] *Coming Through Slaughter* relies upon documentation's "thin sheaf of information,"[3] in much the same way Ondaatje's earlier long poems do. As Ondaatje tellingly comments, "I knew very little about Bolden. I'm really drawn to unfinished stories. There's all those empty spaces you can put stuff in" (Witten, 10). That "stuff" is invention, fiction. Even some of the "documents" scattered throughout the text of *Coming Through Slaughter* are fictional inventions, just as they are in *The Collected Works of Billy the Kid*. Poetic novel or long poem in prose, then, *Coming Through Slaughter* is a text that asks to be read as fiction but not wholly as a novel. Nevertheless, like the earlier long texts, it is definitely "novelized" and "dialogized," in Bakhtin's sense of the terms (Bakhtin, 324).

When Donald M. Marquis's *In Search of Buddy Bolden: First Man of Jazz* appeared, two years after *Coming Through Slaughter*, it shattered many of the legends surrounding Bolden without discovering much information to replace them. Whether in fiction or in nonfiction, Bolden remains a factually elusive figure. But Ondaatje has made the most of the relative freedom of working on his own with just the few documents and rumors he was able to track down. Although he went to some of the same documentary sources as Marquis during his research for this book, all the resultant "facts" he gathered fill just that one page of text (*CTS*, 132). He later told Stephen Scobie that he knew many of the stories about Bolden—that he worked in a barbershop, that he edited *The Cricket* (no copy of which has ever been found), and that he attacked Tom Pickett with a razor—were at best rumors, and perhaps even completely untrue (see Marquis, 6–7, 88), but went ahead and used them anyway.[4] I believe he did so because even unsubstantiated rumors exist as "historical" texts, whether oral or written, having been repeated so often, especially in various books on jazz history, that they have taken on an existence separate from, and to a writer superior to, fact.[5] Such undocumented "documents" provide a structure full of gaps, and it is the gaps that invention seeks to fill.

Ondaatje began work on his book "when he came across the cryptic newspaper reference: 'Buddy Bolden, who became a legend when he went berserk in a parade'" (Witten, 9: *CTS*, 134). Whatever the truth of Buddy's life as a player and bandleader, all the early tales agree that "while playing a parade with Henry Allen Sr.'s Brass Band, he went berserk in the street" (Williams, 14). Marquis disagrees, but in this matter, as in all else concerning Bolden, his research has led him to be tentative in the extreme (see Marquis, 117–19). He proves the rumors wrong but finds little to replace them. In all the versions, Bolden goes mad and ends up in the House of Detention and finally at the Southeast Louisiana State Hospital in Jackson. But what led him to that end remains an open book, and it is upon the many blank pages of that book that Ondaatje chooses to inscribe the various figures who meet and affect one another in *Coming Through Slaughter*.

As represented in the text, Buddy and the others tend to be figures of dramatic gesture more than consistent characters. The text does not follow the story—insofar as it is known—but rather creates narrative disconnections to highlight the antirealist, antihistorical nature of the undertaking. Buddy emerges from and fades into the background in a series of unexplained dramatic gestures—partly because he cannot understand his own behavior (e.g., *CTS*, 73) and partly because (as text) he resists any form of explanation (*CTS*, 140). The gestures are essentially images, metaphors connected throughout the text. Although there is plenty of affect, there is little or no analysis. In fact, *Coming Through Slaughter* consistently refuses to foreground psychological or sociological conditions, and this refusal is one sign of its postmodern condition. Operating by David Lodge's "five strategies (contradiction, discontinuity, randomness, excess, short circuit)" of postmodern writing (McHale, 7), Ondaatje's text deliberately sets out to create "an ontological scandal" by mixing real-world figures with purely fictional ones (McHale, 85). It is equally postmodern in its violations of "the con-

straints on 'classical' historical fiction: by visibly contradicting the
public record of 'official' history; by flaunting anachronisms; and by
integrating history and the fantastic" (McHale, 90).

The largest contradiction of the public record inserts Bellocq into
Bolden's story—because "[p]rivate and fictional magnets drew [them]
together" (*CTS*, [158]). "E. J. Bellocq was a commercial photographer
who worked in New Orleans before and after the first World War. A
plausible guess might be that his working life reached from about 1895
through the first four decades of this century. [His] portraits of Storyville
prostitutes . . . were discovered in Bellocq's desk after his death.
These negatives were made about 1912."[6] Although he worked in New
Orleans during Bolden's playing life, no information connects them, and
the photos—all of white prostitutes—are from a period some five years
after Bolden had been taken to Jackson. Since Bellocq was white,[7] it's
unlikely he befriended Bolden, a black[8] (by simply assuming color while
refusing to address its problems, the text implies that Bellocq is also
black). Finally, only in this text does Bellocq commit suicide sometime
around 1905–6. The author has taken more than a few liberties with the
public record in bringing Bellocq and Bolden together.

In his representation of Bolden's wife, Nora Bass, as an ex-prostitute,
Ondaatje follows no specific document. Williams does not mention her;
nor do Russell and Smith, although they make a point of "Buddy's
feminine admirers" (Ramsey, 15). Marquis says that she came from a
good family and that Buddy probably met her in church (Marquis,
96–97). Ondaatje's apparent decision to transform her into a prostitute is
part of a series of decisions that includes bringing Bellocq into the story,
and her small role is to love Buddy and let Bellocq photograph her, and
then to angrily despair over Bellocq's effect upon her husband.

Anachronisms proliferate throughout the text, sometimes comically,
sometimes seriously, but they all serve to remind us that the writer is
implicated in every nuance of supposed verisimilitude in the book. Some
are fairly obvious, some almost escape notice, but they all have the effect
of blurring the sense of historical distance between now and then and of
making Bolden "anachronistically, the exemplary embodiment of a tone,
an attitude, a trend in twentieth century art. By a sort of fictive *trompe
d'oeil* (sic) he is simultaneously at the beginning and the end of the
modern era."[9] Among the obvious anachronisms, Webb's use of the 14
September 1927 death of Isadora Duncan to solve the "murder" of Mrs.
Bass stands out, for the author would expect us to know that Duncan died
sometime after World War I, even if we didn't know that Mrs. Bass was

still alive when Bolden was "led away" (*TK*, 55) to Jackson in 1907. The text does alert us to the "fictional quality" of this "first death" (*CTS*, 24) but the phrasing is deliberately ambiguous. Equally, Buddy could not have listened to a radio playing the music of John Robichaux in 1906, as commercial radio did not come into use until about 1920. The historical slippage engendered by such anachronisms serves to bring Buddy more into focus as a participant in "the 20th century game of fame" (*CTS*, 134) as it has come to be understood since his time.

Ondaatje's intensely poetic language tends to push scene after scene into the margins of verisimilitude, away from the realistic documenta- tion history depends upon. Such scenes include Bolden's immobility in Shell Beach before he goes to the Brewitt's, the fight with Pickett, and the final parade. As long poem or poetic novel, the text insists upon its freedom from mere fact even as it also invites the reader's connivance in believing in the greater "truth of fiction" (*CTS*, [159]). This fictional truth appears to some critics to avoid the harsh realities of racism and poverty among blacks in the southern United States at the beginning of the century: "The anguish of [Bolden's possible consciousness of oppres- sion] is not permitted to develop into a true common ground; rather it is turned back upon ego and focused there in superficial metaphor" (Mund- wiler, 104–5).[10] By concentrating so fully on Bolden, Mundwiler ig- nores the ways in which both Webb and Bellocq act as other foci in the narrative; he reads the text as monologic rather than dialogic, and demands that the monologue be obviously political. Faulting the text for its failure to foreground Bolden's blackness and its sociopolitical effects at the time, he misses the point of the cover (or in some editions, the frontispiece), with the famous photograph of Bolden's band, a group of black men. This photographic sign says all that needs to be said. Having shown that these men are black, the text simply assumes that fact and all the cultural baggage that comes with it, and goes on from there. The whole story takes place inside the essentially separate community of black New Orleans, where everyone is black, even Bellocq in this revision of history. In a sense, no matter how impoverished and cut off from power that community was, blacks at that time had perhaps less reason to question their color because their culture and society were still separate from the larger white culture surrounding it. In that sense, the people would not be self-conscious about their color; they would not, in fact, tend to think about it.

But there is more to this problem: the "[i]nterview with Lionel Gremillion at East Louisiana State Hospital" reveals that there "[w]asn't much communication between whites and blacks and so much information is difficult to find out. No black employees here" (*CTS*, 137). This laconic comment points to a larger paucity of information, and, in a sense, to a deliberate, if possibly unconscious, white policy of ignoring such information and thus effectively denying such knowledge any outlet at the time. It is in its own way a political gesture to refuse to try to fill in a never written history of political oppression. *Coming Through Slaughter*, a paradigmatic Canadian fiction in its refusal of the European and American tradition of the novel, once again signs itself as outside, as deliberately marginal to the tradition of the historical novel, the novel *of* history, by pushing through the window of historical representation to a deeper, more personal revelation of personality in process.[11]

Many critics seek a thematic consistency in Ondaatje's writing, which is not that easily found—here the continuing examination of creativity, self-destructiveness, and the ways they intertwine in one life.[12] Such general comments are valid enough, but do not represent the emotional core of the book. Ondaatje's comment on formal change—"I think one tries to start each new book with a new vocabulary, a new set of clothes. Consciously or unconsciously we burn the previous devices which got us here but which are now only rhetoric" (Solecki 1984, 325)—applies to themes as well. Many artists prove impervious to thematic criticism precisely because they keep trying different things, and they do so because to do otherwise would prove incredibly boring. Ondaatje became obsessed with Bolden when he read one sentence in a newspaper. What counts is what he did with his sudden inspiration, and what he did was write an emotionally complex and disturbing book that calls us back to read it again and again.

Coming Through Slaughter is a highly invitational text: the explanations Buddy-in-the-text denies us (*CTS*, 140) become stories we tell as we attempt to deal with its gaps and narrative discontinuities. While possibly having difficulties with the narrative, we tend to respond powerfully to the visceral emotional currents of the text. Like Billy the Kid, Buddy Bolden is an open site—not so much for documentation (see Jones, 30) as for filling in psychological and emotional blanks. When he says "What the hell is wrong with me?" (*CTS*, 73), writer and readers feel compelled to invent stories that might provide an answer; some of these stories are called criticism. Even Bolden's long silence in the mental hospital invites speculation—the narrator's stories about those around him when he proves too resistant. But narrative does finally admit defeat before that silence, and falls into lyric despair (or rises to lyric transcendence, it is hard to tell which), at the end. The variety of contradictory critical responses suggests the depth of *Coming Through Slaughter*'s structural indeterminacy. Contradictions are built into the text, partly because the invention—of real and imagined characters in contact—can *interrupt* the given facts, opening spaces for new stories, but cannot change the endings. Endings because again there are more than one: the parade, the House of Detention, the silent life in East Louisiana State Hospital, the death (given in documents), and the discovery by Webb that that death hasn't yet happened.[13] Each is separate, and they keep slipping up and down between levels of narrative "reality,"[14] thus allowing us to imagine more stories in the blank spaces between them.

There are many ways of reading a text deliberately indeterminate in its fragmentation, yet able to evoke realistic representation even as it shatters it. While most interpretive readings tend actively to make connections across many separate pages, the first and basic reading is page by page, from the front of the book to the back. Despite theoretical dismissal of auctorial authority in these matters, Ondaatje's claim that "the editing of a manuscript . . . determine[s] the work's shape, rhythmic structures etc." (Solecki 1975, 21) cannot be ignored.[15] However much he wants to suggest a kind of chaos, the author creates an order we pretty well have to follow, at least our first time through. My reading generally follows that order while attempting to take account of how the shifts and the transpositions evoke other and even contradictory orders of story layered in the text. All three of Ondaatje's longer works to this point are full of gaps, but in *Coming Through Slaughter* the number of diegetic levels has increased as has the number of narrative voices, and no one narrator within the text has greater narrative authority than another, not even "the implied author."

Ondaatje takes the notion of epigraph to new heights in *Coming Through Slaughter,* by using two illustrations as epigraphs. On the title page, the one known photograph of his band (fictionally assigned to Bellocq later in the text) locates Bolden in history, and insists on the documentary aspect of the text to follow. It also presents an art of stillness: the musicians are caught and held out of time. Paradoxically, while a photograph is static, the act of photographing, with its jazzlike "'emphasis on intuition, spontaneity, and improvisation,'"[16] is not. The three sonographs are actually static views of a process of sounding. The relevance of the note explaining how dolphin sounds work is ambiguous, although the use of "squawk" to define elements of Bolden's playing connects him to the dolphins in terms of a visceral freedom defined by sound. Dolphins can make "two kinds of signals simultaneously" (*CTS*, 6), one of which identifies the dolphin while the other identifies its location. If Bolden's "music announces and defines location" (Kamboureli 1983, 118), his difficulties arise precisely in terms of the relation of identity to location, as the first phrase of the text proper indicates: "His geography" (*CTS*, 8). The strongest references to the second epigraph appear in the parade scene (*CTS*, 129–31), when Bolden achieves identity by losing himself in his music; but the balance he achieves there cannot be maintained, and he falls into silence and out of geography.

Beginning in the geography that once was his, a place with "little recorded history" (*CTS*, 8) because it is a few blocks away from Storyville, the text asks us to "see" this geography "today," and the imperative implicates reader with writer in the mapping and storytelling that follow, while also implying that anachrony is possible precisely because location is not locked to any specific time. Because "[t]his district, the homes and stores, are a mile or so from the streets made marble by jazz[, t]here are no songs" about it. Such songs or stories must be found—or made. As Bolden is a kind of absence in the here and now of writing, the narrator seems compelled to begin with other stories, of prostitution and gambling, of various other characters of that place, all of which have passed into legend. The tone here is humorous, but the pronominal insistence that "you" (*CTS*, 9) are somehow involved solicits our connivance in the archaeological uncovering of what went on there. Various figures are introduced, including Tom Anderson, all the information coming from such histories as *Jazz Masters of New Orleans* and *Storyville*, especially the information on Anderson's Blue Book "guide to the sporting district" (*CTS*, 9; Williams, 16–19; Rose, 136–46). The narrator's tone is coolly and wittily didactic, still using the objective "you" as he documents the ins and outs of some of the most famous houses, even one on "the street he went crazy on" (*CTS*, 9–10). Then, almost innocuously, the documentation shifts toward invention as the narrative explains that "Anderson was the closest thing to a patron that Bolden had" (*CTS*, 10). The text again invokes Bolden's "geography," "still here today, away from recorded history," by telling us to "[c]ircle and wind back and forth in your car," following a mazelike route to discover "the barber shop where Buddy Bolden worked."

That "you" is also a substitute for "I," of course. And although critics are correct to point out that the author, Ondaatje, seems to insist on being identified with the narrative voice at certain points in the text where it further identifies with Bolden (Kamboureli 1983, 117; Solecki

1985c, 254), this identification is essentially fictional, because "to reveal the author's position within the ontological structure is only to introduce the author *into the fiction;* far from abolishing the frame, this gesture merely *widens* it to include the author as a fictional character" (McHale, 197–98).[17] It is within the fictional world of the opening sequence that the narrator[18] pursues "the historian's task, as it is prescribed by Herodotus, of 'finding out for oneself'" (Kamboureli 1983, 112). Circling and winding back and forth, he enters the geography in order to find a beginning to be in, from which he can explore those possibilities about which history is silent. It's a short step and a giant leap simultaneously, crossing time while staying right in place, and it forces us "to accept a different and less tangible sense of location—one that derives from the relations between the stories."[19] Suddenly "we" are there—writer, reader, and actors—caught up in the drama of the scene. Bolden is repeating his daily round of ordinary, normal actions in the barbershop, but there are uniquely specific aspects attached to his performance, not the least of which is the fact that it is a performance, although we might not recognize this at first.

Complex and almost surreptitious shifts of focalization occur throughout these scenes, as the narration moves in for close-ups and then retreats for more generalized overviews. The tone is still that of the historian, light and ironic, but there is an edge to it that recalls "War Machine" and even suggests that Bolden could pass for the speaker of that poem. Overall, these early passages of invention show Bolden immersed in the generous and full world of his culture. There is a kind of logic to the story of how he works, drinks, plays with his children, edits *The Cricket,* gets along with Nora, and plays music at night. Yet the narrator feels compelled to respond to other views: "What he did too little of was sleep and what he did too much of was drink and many interpreted his later crack-up as a morality tale of a talent that debauched itself. But his life at this time had a fine and precise balance to it, with a careful allotment of hours" (*CTS,* 13). This "balance" is always in danger of "the one altered move that will make [him] maniac" (*CWBK,* 41), but this time the "one altered move" is Buddy's own. Although art is always a blend of energy and control, Buddy's art, jazz, is based on improvisation, on continually finding altered moves that will take both performer and audience somewhere new. The references to Buddy's mind being "as clear as an empty road" and to his teaching his kids "all he knew at the moment" or putting all the news "unedited into the broadsheet" suggest both the roots of his art and its dangers. "He was the best and the loudest and most loved jazzman of his time, but never professional in the brain," and so he "arrived amateur and accidental with the band on the stage of Masonic Hall, bursting into jazz, hurdle after hurdle" (*CTS*, 14). This language continually evokes the body. Like Billy the Kid, Buddy Bolden perceives more than most people, able to "see the air, [to] tell where it was freshest in a room by the colour," but the text at this point presents his perceptions from the safe distance of history, the third person. Although there are places in the text where Buddy speaks, he is not, like Billy, the editor of his own works. And rather than beginning in his death, the book begins in his silence, a silence now of history, then of madness, a similar but nevertheless different site in which information dissipates rather than proliferates. In death, Billy entered into the realm of explanation—all those stories. In silence, Buddy disappears from discourse, resisting both story and explanation. But stories, whether found or invented, are necessary, are all the geographer has, and so they begin. In a few pages, the narrator has taken us from a contemporary place to the less localized legend of another time, and has done so without losing our complicit accompaniment.

Bolden, who "could not put things in their place," is "almost completely governed by fears of certainty" (*CTS*, 15), yet accepts it in Nora Bass while attacking "it again and again in her, cruelly, hating it, the sure lanes of the probable. Breaking chairs and windows glass doors in fury at her certain answers" (*CTS*, 15–16). The descriptive, explanatory tone allows us to almost slide over these early signs of Bolden's violence, especially as she is "delighted by the performance" (*CTS*, 16) when he breaks the window in anger but does not cut his hand. His own surprise at both the act and its outcome reinforces the feeling that Bolden's "mind was helpless against every moment's headline" (*CTS*, 15) and that he improvises life as well as music. If Nora provides the bass line for Buddy's life as improvisation, the solid bottom from which he can take flight, she is not enough in herself, as "*Nora's Song*" seems to indicate. Its effect is ambiguous: narration stops, and lyric of a sort interposes itself, yet it also suggests a constant mood, an awareness of the way he lives, which for her, and so for us, is repetitive, a continuing activity. The repetition of "Dragging his bone over town" (*CTS*, 17) undermines the sexual innuendo of this blues for a deeper connotation of compassion and even pity. All that effort, it seems to say, and for what? In terms of the mood it reflects, it prepares us for the sudden turn to another story, of Bolden's disappearance and Webb's search. In terms of its implicit metaphor, it's a small prolepsis of Bolden's image of himself as a dog when Webb finds him (*CTS*, 83, 89) and when he is led away to Jackson (*CTS*, 139), which we may or may not recall immediately at those points in the text.

A brief excerpt from Williams, followed by a single sentence from Russell and Smith, follow. Returning to a higher level of diegesis, they reestablish the tone of documentation and oral history, so that the shift to Webb's story seems to be simply a spatial one, rather than a simultaneous drop to an embedded level of pure invention. Webb enters the text in a dramatic scene, which immediately reveals his character, especially in opposition to Buddy's and Nora's. He asks questions, makes categorical statements, and promises that Buddy will soon return. The scene ends in disorienting comic confusion: "Webb grins encouragement and walks slowly backwards down the four steps to the pavement. He has remembered the number of steps. He is wrong. Bolden will take two more years before he cruises home. . . . Spring 1906" (*CTS*, 21). The syntax suggests that Webb is wrong about the number of steps before it becomes clear that he is wrong about his friend. Or is he wrong because he is approaching the problem backwards? Even the narrator is wrong about the time, or else the date is wrong, for Bolden returns in "April 1907" (*CTS*, 108). Time is elastic when the text shifts diegetic levels from document to rumor to pure fiction, and Buddy escapes from the laws that rule the first. The problem is that the law enforcer will follow his traces through those other levels in order to bring him back to the history that has always indi(c)ted him. As will the narrator, for there is no way to escape the finality of the verdict that he went berserk in a parade.

Webb's name signifies control and relates him to the spider poets of "Spider Blues." He "is the ultimate audience, demanding that the artist perform to its liking . . . [and exerting] an almost fascist power over the artist, trapping him as a spider traps flies" (Scobie 1978, 11).[20] When Webb says "I'm very fond of him" and then adds, "He's a great artist" (*CTS*, 20), it sounds innocuous, but it also implies his demanding need of his old friend. His detective work, "trying to understand not where Buddy was but what he was doing, . . . entering the character of Bolden through every voice he spoke to" (*CTS*, 63), implicitly identifies him with the author as he represents himself near the end of the book: "Did not want to pose in your accent but think in your brain and body" (*CTS*, 134). As Webb's investigation takes on the parodic contours of pulp detective fiction,[21] the writer emerges as a kind of detective. Yet, although he writes "with great love and great coldness" (*TK*, 60), the oxymoronic aesthetic betraying a duplicity in the writing that can never be undone, the writer identifies and empathizes with his subject in ways the detective cannot imagine. The writer, for example, can imagine the final 24 pages of the text; the detective neither can nor would wish to.

While Bolden both narrates and is narrated, Webb is always represented through the eyes of the narrator. But sometimes the narrator will only show Webb's actions, while at others he will enter into Webb's thinking. One pair of sentences demonstrates the speed with which the narrative can shift from external to internal focalization: "For those who saw him it looked as if he had nothing to do. As it was he was trying to place himself casually in a mental position that was so high and irrelevant he hoped to stumble on the clues that were left by Bolden's disappearance" (*CTS*, 22). The effect is so casual here that we might miss the implications of the shift, for Webb's attempted stance parallels the position of an omniscient narrator and thus aligns writer and character. But as such transitions from outside to inside multiply, we become more and more aware of the demands the text is making upon us. "[D]isruption of the narrative process actually foregrounds the narrative process," implicating us "in the process of ordering" (Wilton, 80). Made responsible for ordering the various fragments into a coherent story of rise and fall, of escape and return, of self-destruction in pursuit of art, we piece them together in a kind of collage, "miming the activity of the *bricoleur*, miming the activity of both reader and writer of Buddy Bolden's broken book" (MacFarlane, 72).

There is an order, or rather there are orders, and so, because the fragments do connect, we tend not to notice the complexity of ordering that the text demands of us. Although, like Webb, we feel at first that all the "stories [a]re like spokes on a rimless wheel ending in air [because] Buddy had lived a different life with every one" (*CTS*, 63), we come to understand in the act of reading that, along with the implied narrator, we are the hub of the wheel where the stories join "at the level of discourse" (Wilton, 80) rather than the level of story line. The level of discourse is the level of mood, which is a key term describing Bolden's art. As Frank Lewis says (in an invented document), "[t]here was no control except the *mood* of his power . . . and it is for this reason it is good you never heard him play on recordings" (*CTS*, 37). Like Bolden, the narrator tears "apart the plot . . . [a]s if . . . lost and hunting for the right accidental notes." Because "[t]he right ending is an open door you can't see too far out of. It can mean exactly the opposite of what you are thinking" (*CTS*, 94), we can return over and over again to this text yet never feel we have finished it or the understanding of it. *We* order the anachronies, narrative pauses, and various developing stories into a larger story; the text simply provides the means. Because it is "unimportant to finish and clear everything" (*CTS*, 37), each approach to the text allows a new ordering to take place.

Webb appears to understand the man he knows from before. He realizes that Bolden "could just as easily be wiping out his past again in a casual gesture, contemptuous. Landscape suicide" (*CTS*, 22). This interesting term suggests a destruction of context rather than self, a form of escape from what surrounds and therefore controls one. If "the only clue to Bolden's body was in Webb's brain," he must think himself into that body's behavior. But the very act of doing so—like the act of writing a character into being—is ambiguous in the extreme, because the questions he asks have a way of redoubling upon him: it is not clear if Webb is asking "Whose moment of terror did he want to witness" of Bolden or of himself, and that indeterminacy suddenly applies to us as well.

The list of song titles that suddenly interrupts the narrative also points out the many ways it could be ordered. Titles about love and sexual desire, titles about going away, a final title—to be repeated in the later context of madness—insisting on personal responsibility; they reflect the harsh realities of desire, power, and loss that no one can escape while still in this life. To Webb, when Buddy begs Robin Brewitt, "Make me a pallet on your floor," he is evading the responsibility to his art summed up in "If you don't shake, don't get no cake" (*CTS*, 23). The rules appear simple from his perspective, as they would to any conventional detective. Webb expresses his basic, almost innocent single-mindedness on this matter when he confronts Bolden in the bath at the Brewitts' house, and, as he does with his magnets (*CTS*, 35–6), uses his power to "drag" Buddy back to the straight line of his story. Understanding only the material world, he cannot comprehend the spiritual malaise that drove Buddy into silence and will drive him this time into the final escape of madness. The sign of his noncomprehension is his disappearance from the text, except as the putative receiver of Bolden's notebook, until the moment when he must face the fact that Buddy is still alive in the asylum (*CTS*, 149–51). And because he is clearly incapable of understanding what Bolden has to tell him, we become his substitute, reading the notebook entries as if they were addressed to us.

The narrator reveals the abilities and limitations that lead to Webb's success and failure in the long passage describing *The Cricket*'s "excessive reference to death" (*CTS*, 24), Mrs. Bass's interpretations of "damned birds" (*CTS*, 25), her strange death, the disappearance of her body, and

Webb's solution to the mystery. Slipping into and away from Bolden's perspective, the focalization reveals that Webb is not equipped to understand, especially "his dreams of his children dying" (*CTS*, 24, 28). Webb can deal with the facts, what lies in the light of day, but Bolden's inner, night life is beyond him.

As Webb begins his questioning with Crawley, a spatial shift of narrative instance takes us simultaneously to "what Bolden sees" (*CTS*, 31). After immersing us in this other narrative, the text slides right back to Crawley's talk with Webb. Crawley speaks in the past tense, his memory of Bolden staying with the Brewitts an embedded narrative. The narrative shifts to Bolden's memory of falling under Robin Brewitt's spell, then outward to Crawley's remembered impressions, and finally back to his talking to Webb. These four separate paragraphs enact a double disappearance: as Bolden disappears into Shell Beach, the story disappears into the narrative. The invented drama of Buddy's affair with Robin unfolds in the narrative gap his disappearance opens up. But by the time it is narrated, it is over, the epistemological detective having discovered his quarry's whereabouts, brought him back in line, and gotten him to write down at least part of his story.

In a series of complex temporal shifts, Webb remembers living with Buddy until he moved to New Orleans. Two years later he "tracked Buddy for several days" (*CTS*, 36) without making contact and then watched him perform. "So hard and beautifully that Webb didn't even have to wait for the reactions of the people, he simply turned and walked till he no longer heard the music or the roar he imagined crowding round to suck that joy. Its power." Although he recognizes that the audience takes from the performer, Webb does not make the connection to himself. Back and forth the narration cuts between two pasts, Bolden's first few days at Shell Beach and Webb's memories of his and Bolden's life together. The latter is analytic, distanced and cool, the former emotional, awkward, and chaotic.

Bolden knows what he wants but cannot act on his desire. He wants Robin Brewitt, but he also wants what both she and Jaelin offer him as "[t]he silent ones. Post music. After ambition" (*CTS*, 39). Although he never becomes a "character" in the conventional "realistic" sense of the term, he is still a site for powerful emotions and sensations. We therefore tend, as we do with Billy the Kid, to read him as a character even as the text undercuts such a reading. In this suspended period before he goes and begs Robin to help him (*CTS*, 45), Buddy is "frozen," trapped between choices and incapable of making one, lacking the "fine and precise balance" he had when he was king. Balance is dynamic, but this frozen apprehension of two possible futures is static. Unable to act, he will sink even deeper into despair before he can beg for help. After "two days picking up the dirt the grime" and the "unfinished stories, badly told jokes that he sober as a spider perfected in silence" (*CTS*, 40), Buddy becomes "[a] fat full king" (*CTS*, 41). These scenes of psychological dissolution both apprehend his future silence in the asylum and contradict it, for here, however "frozen" in action he may be, he does continue to respond to the world outside him. Nevertheless, like so many other scenes in the text, the story of these two days reveals Bolden's susceptibility to loss of self-determination. Like Billy the Kid, Bolden is a bundle of contradictions, and must not be read for consistency. Suddenly a spider seeking closure, he is also the ghostly revenant traveling from one pavement grid to another to seek "the heat waves warping, disintegrating his body [while the] shady head play[s] with the perfect band." In other words, this past prologue to the present moment when he watches Robin cut carrots (*CTS*, 31) is the accidental "[l]andscape suicide" (*CTS*, 22) Webb feared.

Just as each section shifts back and forth in time and narrative level, so do the paragraphs within them. Focalization shifts continually, as well, with the narrator providing a point of view close to Webb's, then to Bolden's. The slippage of point of view increases when Webb, maintaining his isolation, goes to hear Buddy play: "The music was coarse and rough, immediate, dated in half an hour, was about bodies in the river, knives, lovepains, cockiness. Up there on stage he was showing all the possibilities in the middle of the story" (*CTS*, 43). Whether these are Webb's perceptions, the narrator's, or a combination of the two doesn't matter, except as it alerts us to the need to work as *bricoleurs* in putting all the pieces together in a satisfactory pattern. Part 1 ends with Bolden lost in uncertainty and unable even to say what he wants until Robin moves toward him: "he had to say it before she reached him or touched him or smelled him had to say it. Help me. Come in Buddy. Help me. Come in Buddy. Help me. He was shaking" (*CTS*, 45). Powerful in its representation of affect, the scene lacks conventional context and dramatic buildup, or rather it makes us supply them. The repetition at the end carries it out of narrative and into lyric intensity.

Part 2 seems essentially to be about Buddy's relations with Robin Brewitt and Bellocq, but the first section reveals another relation contained within the narration of much of it, Buddy and Webb's after Webb "came here and placed my past and future on this table like a road" (*CTS*,

86) Bolden cannot get off. Bolden's first words as narrator, signaling by their address Webb's eventual "capture" of him, recall an earlier trap, that of "the Joseph Shaving Parlor" (*CTS*, 47), presented first as a place of easy camaraderie (*CTS*, 11, 12, 42) but now as one of "my slavery here" (*CTS*, 48). The scene is the same, but the perspective has changed. Violent "[d]reams of the neck" connect vanity and slavery in Bolden's discourse here, while "power" connects both to his playing. The next passage returns Bolden to the third person as the narrator speaks of "[s]o many murders of his own body" and "[s]uicide of the hands" (*CTS*, 49), the latter recalling "[l]andscape suicide" (*CTS*, 22) as a form of escape. We are left to wonder if his attacks on his hands are one of the "many varieties of murder" (*CTS*, 49) he practices upon his own body or the way his hands escape him. Either way, the passage signals internal strife as he seeks to wend his way among his various desires.

Needing a picture, Webb reenters the detective story and finds Bellocq. But as conventional narrative does not fit easily over fragmented postmodern text, he is caught out by his quarry. As with Nora, Webb cannot understand Bellocq's refusal to seek Bolden: "Why don't you leave him, he's a good man. I know I told you he was a friend" (*CTS*, 51). Webb's possessive friendship opposes Bellocq's willingness to let Bolden go his own way. As the narrative slips easily in and out of their minds, Webb demands a print from the reluctant Bellocq and they watch "their friend float into the page smiling at them, the friend who in reality had reversed the process and gone back into white, who in this bad film seemed to have already half-receded with that smile which may not have been a smile at all, which may have been his mad dignity" (*CTS*, 52–53). It is impossible to know who thinks this, especially as the final clause heralds a possibility unknown to them as characters though known to the narrator from the beginning.

At this point the narrative drops Webb to investigate Bellocq more thoroughly than the detective can. While Webb checks Bellocq out (*CTS*, 56–57), the narrator, that superior fictionalizing detective, investigates Bellocq's art rather than his background and movements. The shifting tenses and pronouns of this investigation register not so much an action as the layers of time read into "[t]he photographs of Bellocq" (*CTS*, 54). The narrator-as-critic's imperative "[l]ook at the pictures" makes the implicit *you* explicit in a narration demanding our complicity. That the photographs exist in *Storyville, New Orleans* and *E. J. Bellocq: Storyville Portraits* raises this passage to a higher level of documentary "reality," but for many readers they will only exist as putative and therefore empty referents. In place of the photographs, the commentary becomes a form of storytelling, exploring the descriptions of them as clues to both the artist's and his sitters' lives. In this interpretation of the vagaries of Bellocq's art, these frozen images preserve an activity, the improvisation of subjectivity almost unconsciously manifested by the subjects: "she would become self-conscious towards him and the camera and her status, embarrassed at just her naked arms and neck and remembers for the first time in a long while the roads she imagined she could take as a child. And he photographed that." The various tenses here enact the viewer's, or reader's, own growing involvement in the subjective moment portrayed, and the narrator insists upon it: "What you see in his pictures is her mind jumping that far back to when she would dare to imagine the future, parading with love or money on a beautiful anonymous cloth arm. Remembering all that as she is photographed by the cripple who is hardly taller than his camera stand." The intensity of attention paid to the photographs and the stories they ignite demonstrates how important Bellocq is to the text, however marginal he appears to be to Bolden's story. Similarly, the narrator's continual reference to "you" enacts Bolden's major aesthetic imperative, which Bellocq lives in his own art and Webb resists: "Come with me Webb I want to show you something, no come with me I want to *show* you something. You come too. Put your hand through this window" (*CTS*, 91; see also 14). His pictures are windows Bellocq has put his hand through, sometimes literally, as in the scratches that "exist alongside the genuine scars mentioned before. . . . They reflect each other, the eye moves back and forth" (*CTS*, 55). The photographs thus scarred invite a further participation. "You can see that the care he took defiling the beauty he had forced in them was as precise and clean as his good hands which at night had developed the negatives." The "you" here is carefully indeterminate, but we will not easily escape its seductions. At this level of the narrative, the narrator links Bolden to Bellocq in the most basic terms of creative desire: "The making and destroying coming from the same source, same lust, same surgery his brain was capable of." The thinking Bellocq photographs is, in its own way, "all the possibilities in the middle of the story" (*CTS*, 43).

Suddenly the text shifts to Bolden's story with exterior narration and changing focalization, as he enters water to let "the dirt and the sweat melt into the heat" (*CTS*, 58). Both his entry into and his exit from the Brewitts' lives are marked by bathing, a kind of perverse baptism into one new life after another. Robin's point of view slides into his as she wakes him up. These dramatic passages insistently refuse introspection while implying its effects, at least in Robin: "I can't do things that way Buddy." When Buddy mentions Bellocq as "a photographer" whose pictures "were like . . . windows" (*CTS*, 59), an interesting and slightly comic interruption of the erotic spell returns Bellocq to the center of discourse. His presence as "the first person I met who had absolutely no interest in my music" leads Bolden to elaborate upon the way Bellocq's detachment became a window to another place, where the audience's temptation to vanity, which he has already derided in others as an implied form of slavery (*CTS*, 48), no longer exists. Now the connection between Bellocq's and Bolden's stories becomes clear, and the changes from one to the other testify to the underlying narrative decorum of the text. Bellocq, whose pictures the narrator presents as strangely honest, also offers a kind of stringent honesty in response to Bolden's music.

Robin calls Buddy back to the present, their lovemaking, and the closed room is suddenly transformed to an open field: "It could have been a sky not a ceiling above him" (*CTS*, 59). This is a new geography, of passion and escape, which complicates but does not deny the reading of Robin's and Jaelin's names as implying "a sense of enclosed space" and of Bolden being "*robbed* of his art and of his mobile state of mind" and "*jailed in* her husband's house" (Kamboureli 1983, 123). The sense of complication, of being caught between or among possibilities, is emphasized by the image placed in striking isolation on the following page: "Passing wet chicory that lies in the field like the sky" (*CTS*, 60). This sentence is consistently undecidable, conflating three elements in a form of continual exchange. The lack of a subject implicates narrator, character, and reader in the movement it registers, which for the latter could simply be the movement of the reading eye. Lacking a subject, the present progressive can also be a participle suggesting the passage of time, the inevitable destruction of natural beauty. In either case, "lies" implies both placement and deception while the syntactical connection of the final two phases could mean that the chicory mirrors the sky in the field or that the field replaces the sky as image of open space. None of these readings takes precedence over the others. The sense of metamorphosis, of transformation, in this image, which the sentence about the ceiling anticipates, is also present in the sensual confusion of "her clothes all over his naked body, as if he were wearing them" (*CTS*, 59).

An apparently irrelevant remark about his broken arm anticipates the textually later but narratively earlier fight with Pickett. Thus does the narrator shuffle his fragments yet maintain connections among them. The contradictions he cannot escape appear once more as Robin feels "his fingers had been pressing the flesh on her back as though he were plunging them into a cornet. She was sure he was quite unaware . . . [b]ut she was wrong. He had been improving on *Cakewalking Babies*." Though pleased at Bellocq's lack of interest in his music, Buddy cannot avoid making it. "[I]mproving" implies consciousness, the artist fleeing performance still creating for creation's sake. But "improving" also implies control of the chaotic materials of his art, which is contradictory at its core, as are he and his story.

Bolden as his own narrator assumes a disquieting displacement from his own story: he is both in it and beyond it, looking back. In the passage that collates all their lovemaking during his time with Robin, tenses float. The present indicative of "She. Again in the room, now in the long brown dress" (*CTS*, 61) invokes the immediate present, but auxiliaries like "[s]he will not move" and "I must get up" suggest a kind of ritual repetition in their acts, explained by reference to "the air of the room . . . [t]hick with past and the ghosts of friends who are in other rooms." Present participles and dropped verbs add to the sense of repetition: this is a scene they have enacted many times. Once again there is overlap between narrator and narratee as a verb without a subject reads as both indicative and imperative: "Step back and watch her against the corner of my room." The violence of "I attack her into the wall . . . her crazy flesh twisted into corners" proleptically anticipates their final night together, when they "tear into each other, as if to wound, as if to find the key to everything before morning" (*CTS*, 86), as this "King of Corners," "anonymous and alone in a white room with no history and no parading" bitterly recalls. Whether with Nora or with Robin, Bolden cannot escape the violence within him; it is apparently part and parcel of his creativity, and by displaying it in his sexual activity, the text underlines how for him, as for Bellocq, though in a different manner, the "making and destroying com[e] from the same source, same *lust*" (*CTS*, 55).

Orgasm empties them of passion but it also empties the room "of the other histories" (*CTS*, 62), which include all his histories of triumph in the game of fame. Yet Robin "hasn't taken one step further into my room." Contradiction strikes to the heart of this relationship supposed to save Bolden. Time slips again, as he says—at this moment remembering standing outside her door, or writing to Webb recalling their lovemaking?—"I remember when I shook against you." The final phrase floats into its own semantic open field: "A step past the territory." The terms—"step," "past," "the," "territory"—are not specific enough in their reference to the previous passage to forestall uncertainty; rather, the statement seems larger and more indefinite than its context. At such moments in the text, we perhaps feel as lost as Bolden. But Bolden, trapped as much by history as by Webb's detecting, cannot stay lost in a fictional gap, at least until he fulfills his role in the drama his legend has become.

Within the fictional gap, echoes of "White Dwarfs" in Bellocq's reponse to Bolden invoke a self-conscious intertextual level of narration: "They had talked for hours moving gradually off the edge of the social world" (*CTS*, 64). Bellocq is the more typical "White Dwarf" type, which leads to an ironic reversal of roles: "As Bellocq lived at the edge in any case he was at ease there and as Buddy did not he moved on past him like a naive explorer looking for footholds. Bellocq did not expect that." The subliminal image of "White Dwarfs" carries over into the scene of Jaelin and Bolden connected by their love for Robin: "There was this story between them" (*CTS*, 65). While the "silence of Jaelin Brewitt understood them all," his story of the Wolf Ryat star[22] demonstrates how: "There were two people who found it. Someone called Wolf and someone called Ryat. . . . There was that story between them." Although Jaelin remains a background figure of little depth, he has a specific weight in the story of Bolden and Robin, and here is even able to assess it. The deliberate indeterminacy of reference—each name is just a "someone"—in his story suggests how far Bolden has traveled from "reputation" to "anonymity" with them. The shift from the personal and close "this story" of their own names to the more distanced and cosmic "that story" of the two astronomers marks the kind of imaginative expansion the text continually demands.

The description of the "one photograph that exists today of Bolden and the band" (*CTS*, 66) inscribes a double absence: names replace the picture at the front,[23] but the picture is of a group already disbanded in terms of the complex time scheme of the text. The narrator's insistence that the photograph is not "precise" acts as a warning about all forms of documentation, including those in this text. After the absence of a photograph, the sudden absence of a photographer: the formality of Bellocq's preparations for his carefully planned and awkwardly executed suicide matches that of his photography, but where acid only etches slowly into being what he knows will be there, fire is the element of absolute change and removes all certainty. Throwing himself at "a fire curtain" where the wall used to be, "he falls, dissolving out of his pose. Everything has gone wrong. . . . Nothing is there to clasp him into a certainty" (*CTS*, 67). Bellocq has sought in certain death the certainty Bolden hates, yet even that has failed. Are we invited to wonder if death is indeed the logical escape from art and fame? Are we invited to speculate about madness as an alternative? At least one critic has done so, and concluded that Bolden's choice is in fact a positive one.[24] The text gives nothing away.

When the embedded memory of Bolden's violent and unthinking reaction to an argument with Robin in front of Jaelin and her friends slides into a present-tense scene of reconciliation, the man who once showed "all the possibilities in the middle of the story" (*CTS*, 43) finds these emotional complexities beyond him. The scene ends in a paradoxical image of swimming, which should suggest cleansing and new beginnings, but appears instead to herald endings and loss: "Below our heads all the evil dark swimming creatures are waiting to brush us into nightmare into heart attack to suck us under into the darkness into the complications. Her loon laugh. The dull star of white water under each of us. Swimming towards the sound of madness" (*CTS*, 69). Another of the star images that float in and out of this text evokes the sense of an ending associated with white dwarfs. With its poetic evocation of darkness and imagined monsters, this passage sinks powerful emotional hooks into us. Has even Robin become a sign of the madness he is moving to embrace, or are they both swimming toward that sound? It is impossible to decide.

The narrative leaps back in time to the fight with Tom Pickett, a sign of one kind of madness he swims toward. The longest passage in the book, it initiates a narrative sequence that would have led up to Bolden's disappearance but instead leads to Webb's discovery of him. Just tracing the temporal shifts of this part of the text reveals how complexly ordered it is, and how difficult it is to find any single narrative level on which the rest depends. Its movement mirrors in miniature the sudden shifts of narrator and focalization throughout. The effect is paradoxical in that it confirms Bolden's tendency toward violence already seen in other scenes, yet it does not seem as shockingly violent as it might, because those other scenes have prepared readers for this one. From a purely dramatic dialogue with Cornish, the narration takes Webb to Pickett and more dialogue with the once beautiful man; then when Webb asks, "How did it happen?" (*CTS*, 71), it shifts to Bolden as narrator. For the rest of the scene, the narrative shifts back and forth between Pickett recalling for Webb and Bolden narrating in the present tense. This overlapping of time schemes and narrators mimes the violence described, violating the realistic surface of the text itself. The extended scene elaborates upon images floating through the rest of the text: mirrors, windows to go through, even spider webs. Buddy initiates the fight although Pickett's talk appears to be the spark that sets him off, according to Pickett's narration. But as quickly as he blows all the news through his horn he expels all his anger. Caught in the middle of an action he no longer wants and cannot control, he is more accidental than ever. Although he cannot move when Pickett throws slivers of mirror at him, Nora's appearance forces him to act, seeking a "[b]alance. His strop and my chair" (*CTS*, 74), and then pushing Pickett through the window. This time the other pulls him through the window, too, and they end up on Liberty street in the rain, its name an ironic contrast to the prison their fight has become. When Nora supports Bolden, Pickett escapes. Despite the visceral verisimilitude of his description of the fight, Bolden does not understand it, and the conclusion to the scene is strangely opaque. Buddy's glib assessment that others now see him as mad contradicts the emotional honesty of his sense of complete isolation found in the complex image of the "rain like so many little windows going down around us" (*CTS*, 75). These "little windows" separate him from Nora, and there seems to be no way to break through them.

The invented document of Brock Mumford's comments—that Buddy "didn't leave at the peak of his glory you know. No one does" (*CTS*, 76)—adds another voice but fails to clarify anything. His is a musician's standard explanation of the inevitable loss of ability, but the imagery of Bolden entering and leaving by windows no one else will go through suggests a deeper malaise than that, which the fight also implies. The text represents that malaise in Bolden's terrible exploration of jealousy: "If Nora had been with Pickett. . . . Then the certainties he loathed and needed were liquid at the root" (*CTS*, 78). It does not question the paradox that the loathing and the needing already place those certainties in flux. Nor the further paradox that Bolden's belief in "the wet deceit" because "Tom Pickett didn't have the brain to have fantasies" is a form of certainty. In his jealous rage, he can no longer perceive "all the possibilities in the middle of [his own] story" (*CTS*, 43). Yet, unable to entertain the certainty Bellocq will rush to embrace, he cannot commit suicide. Entering too fully into the raw emotion of now, he forgets then, so what seem like certainties change as he does. Death would stop that process, so instead of biting open his wrist, he stops and goes "to sleep while feeling his vein tingling at the near chance it had of almost going free. Ecstacy before death. It marched through him while he slept" (*CTS*, 79). While Bolden's personality seems to alter from one fragment to another, the unifying thread is the intensity of perception and of articulation attached to his name in every scene up to the final parade.

History interrupts fiction at this point, supporting even as it supplements it. Dude Botley's monologue of hearing Bolden play "hymns and blues cooked up together" in "a battle between the Good Lord and the Devil" (*CTS*, 81), comes from Martin Williams's *Jazz Masters of New Orleans* (13–14), but as in *The Collected Works of Billy the Kid*, some creative editing, rephrasing, and reworking have occurred. Just another rumor, a story like all the others collected within the text, but on a higher level of narrative "reality," it simultaneously underwrites and short-circuits our sense of the verisimilitude of the previous scenes. When the narrator shifts from Botley's historical present tense to the historical past tense to describe Webb finding Bolden at the Brewitts', it's hard to know at first which of the two descriptions is more "real." Caught in the bath, Bolden once again cannot take death as a way of escape. Trying to behave like the Anhinga Mrs. Bass described (*CTS*, 25), he fails, becoming instead Webb's dog in an image that recalls *"Nora's Song"* (*CTS*, 17) and predicts later images of being controlled by others: "Webb was releasing the rabbit he had to run after, because the cage was open now and there would always be the worthless taste of worthless rabbit when he finished" (*CTS*, 83–84). The effectiveness of the image lies in a complex connection between its innate power and its attachment to Bolden's life as entertainer.

As with *"Nora's Song,"* *"Train Song"* creates a lyric invasion of narrative. The repetitive image riff looks back to its first appearance as a single line (*CTS*, 60) and forward to its final appearance as an embedded narrative description (*CTS*, 139) where various image clusters conjoin in a moment of final insight or abdication. In *"Train Song,"* the rhythmic near-repetition of fragments of the original phrase emphasizes its duplicitous punning nature and achieves a lyric purity that slips free of narrative meaning.[25] The change of "field" to "fields" may at first escape notice, but it points to the continuing movement of a train over long distances and suggestively evokes continual transformation, which Bolden eventually seeks to escape. Recalling the song when we read the phrase in its final appearance, we may read it as a sign that he has eluded change only by denying his own potential multiplicity. If this is the case, his madness is in essence a retreat from "all the possibilities" (*CTS*, 43) to just one, one that isolates him from everyone else as well as everything else. The phrase's repeated eruption into the text near Bolden's narration invites us to think our own stories about his actions back and forth across its appearances. Interfering with conventional representation, it nevertheless creates connections in the text that support an always tentative reading of Bolden as realistic character. Its indeterminacy is part of the larger, structural indeterminacy of the whole text.

The deeper into the text we go, the more connections we are invited to make. Part of the emotional power of Bolden's narrative of his and Robin's last night together rests in its allusions to other moments of the text. "[T]he wall of barrier glass [that] went up between me and Robin" (*CTS*, 86) recalls the "rain like so many little windows going down around" (*CTS*, 75) Bolden and Nora as well as Bolden's attempts to get people to "put [their] hands through the window" (*CTS*, 14). With Robin now, as with Nora, however, even Buddy fails to break through, and his sense of their new isolation from each other is emphasized when he says "[t]his last night we tear into each other, *as if* to wound, *as if* to find the key to everything before morning" (*CTS*, 86, emphasis added). It doesn't matter that they "give each other a performance, the wound of ice" (*CTS*, 87), because no matter how hard they push, the "as if" denies the possibilities they desire. "We follow each other into the future, as if now, at the last moment we try to memorize the face a movement we will never want to forget. As if everything in the world is the history of ice." This last sentence recalls the transformative power of ice as it "changed shape all day before your eyes" (*CTS*, 47), but the only transformation here is loss.

Other images and phrases—"King of Corners" (*CTS*, 86); Robin, "who drained my body of its fame when I wanted to find that fear of certainties I had when I first began to play, back when I was unaware that reputation made the room narrower and narrower"; "[b]lue cloud light in the room" (*CTS*, 87)—echo backward and forward in a similar fashion. Almost every paragraph rhymes with other parts of the text. Even Buddy's last despairing violent gesture of crashing his hand down onto the bed echoes and denies the time he broke the window with Nora (*CTS*, 16). The echoes signal this scene's centrality while its paratactic rhythms and tonal subtleties add to the effect of emotional destruction it achieves.

External narration and internal focalization separate the trip to Webb's cottage from the seemingly straightforward development of Bolden's story. The "cruel, pure relationship" Bolden imagines with the anonymous woman is a sign of what Webb has taken from him while leaving him with only a "dead brain" (*CTS*, 88). The image of the brain resurfaces now to parade its contradictions. The brain is responsible for Bellocq's double-bladed art of "making and destroying" (*CTS*, 55), but when he "pushed his imagination into Buddy's brain" (*CTS*, 64), it replaced his intuition. It is the brain that writes to and thinks through the arguments with Webb, that recognizes his power and his failure: "All you've done is cut me in half, pointing me here. Where I don't want these answers" (*CTS*, 89). Writing from a single point of time—his time at Webb's cottage—Bolden-as-narrator continues to shift back and forth in time, connecting with the other stories through his own acts of memory. Analepsis and prolepsis interpenetrate each other as the echoes accumulate.

When Buddy explains how he copied a stray dog's pissing habit and the dog "must have felt there had been a major breakthrough in the spread of hound civilization," he adds, in a blatant comment that expands from Webb to include us as well, "How about that Webb, a little sensa humour to show you" (*CTS*, 90). Self-reflexively reminiscent of Billy's "[t]his is doing nothing for my image is it" (*CWBK*, 70), it depends upon the text it's in rather than exterior ones. It also complicates the growing image catalog of Bolden as a carefully bred dog (*CTS*, 17, 83, 89). But bred to what? Buddy's continuing failure to answer the questions his own narration raises emphasizes the central contradictions of his personality and his legend. This sequence of short narrative takes—held together like a serial poem by the tone of their "author" rather than by any consistency of thought—is as close to explanation as he (or the text) gets, but explanation falters before the contradictions of temporal and psychological discontinuity. All Buddy can do is remember and argue, carrying on an insistent dialogue with the other, trying to get things as clear as possible before returning to make his final break for freedom. Lost in paradox and paradoxically able to discover nothing but loss in his past, he achieves only the oxymoronic suspension of "this awful and stupid clarity," which he is always "[t]rying to overcome" (*CTS*, 100). It is another form of balance he cannot sustain. Nor does he wish to, and the mood of his denial prepares us for the manner of his escape from "the world of audiences" into the "mole comfort, mole deceit" (*CTS*, 91) that Bellocq offered him.

In a way, Bolden recognizes the problem: "All the time I hate what I am doing and want the other" (*CTS*, 89), he writes, but is he talking about how he feels now or about what he has always felt? The only escape from his fear of not finding the "one person who will be the right audience" is to break through the moment and never return. His desire for that other led him to Bellocq, who, cynical and romantic, "wanted me to become blind to everything but the owned pain in myself" (*CTS*, 91). Bellocq's "scorned all the giraffes of fame" and wanted Buddy "to step back into my body as if into a black room and stumble against whatever was there" (*CTS*, 91). Bellocq's "black empty spaces" recall "the white privacy" (*CTS*, 68) Bolden found with the Brewitts. Since Webb has torn him away from Robin, he turns back to Bellocq's example, in order "to come home Webb with that casual desert blackness" (*CTS*, 91). Bellocq's suicide becomes a kind of avatar of Bolden's intent, a preparing of the way.

If Bellocq tempts Bolden toward an art of pain and love, Jaelin Brewitt actually creates it. Staying downstairs when Buddy and Robin went to bed, he "remove[d] the anger and stuff[ed] it down the piano fresh every night" (*CTS*, 92). He would wait for half an hour as dogs wait for masters to go to sleep before they move into the garage of the kitchen. To Buddy, "[t]he music was so uncertain it was heartbreaking and beautiful. . . . lost anger . . . Bullets of music delivered onto the bed we were on." In this lovely passage full of reversals, Jaelin becomes a dog, while Bolden usurps the place of master, yet he manages to master himself. Creating his music in the midst of pain and loss, he improvises a form of beauty in which both pain and loss are lost: "Everybody's love in the air." Here the paradox of art relieves the man of the paradoxes of life, so he stays, and stays alive. No matter how much he and the central narrator argue that "the making and destroying com[e] from the same source" in Bolden, the text provides in Jaelin at least one example of how the making might destroy the destroying, and thus allows for a wider range of possibilities than Bolden recognizes.

When Bolden listens to John Robichaux on the radio, he fully understands what Robichaux's other kind of music represents—a "mechanistic pleasure" that comes when a musician "put[s] his emotions into patterns which a listening crowd ha[s] to follow" (*CTS*, 93). Desiring an audience that would improvise its responses as much as he improvised his music, Bolden "loathe[s]" Robichaux's "utensil" music. Caught between the Robichaux music he rejects and the Jaelin music he loves but cannot accept as a possibility for himself, he recalls the earlier players "who put their bodies over barbed wire. For me" (*CTS*, 95). They too, like Robichaux, are opposites, but opposites he could learn from, teaching "not craft but to play a mood of sound I would recognize and remember. Every note new and raw and chance." The language here pretends to analysis but is actually doing something else, creating metaphors, making stories. Bolden sees them, and by extension himself, as "[d]rawn to opposites, even in the music we play. In terror we lean in the direction that is most unlike us. Running past your own character into pain" (*CTS*, 96). Once again, even as he attempts an explanation, he is lost in contradiction. No common concept connects these fragmentary comments on music beyond Bolden's unstated insistence that he is different from or has surpassed all his "fathers" (*CTS*, 95).

From music and its emotional potential, Bolden turns back to the dog and his identification with it. This leads to a meditation on the frightening power of passion, that it "could twist around and choose someone else just like that" (*CTS*, 99). Whether Nora turns from him, or Robin turns from Jaelin to him, his stance is one of absolute passivity: "There was nothing I could do." Bolden's abdication of will here is fascinating, especially when he makes it a basis of his art: "We had no order among ourselves. I wouldn't let myself control the world of my music because I had no power over anything else that went on around me, in or around my body. My wife loved Pickett, I think. I loved Robin Brewitt, I think. We were all exhausted." Buddy knows passion's power, knows his own inability to do anything about it, but does not know his own feelings. Somehow, this *cri de coeur* increases our emotional commitment to Buddy while forcing our intellectual detachment from and skepticism about his motives (whether conscious or unconscious). The competing discourses of the text are more complex than its narrators realize.

Locked into the exhaustion both the passion and its loss have created, Bolden writes to the audience he knows and fears, telling Webb only that he knows the loss and seeks a way out. He trains but refuses to have anything to do with "[a]ll that music. I don't want that way any more. There is this other path I beat the bushes away from with exercise so I can walk down it knowing it is just stone" (*CTS*, 101). This stone path is empty—of other people, art and audience, complications. All that is too difficult, and with Robin "become anonymous as cloud" (*CTS*, 100), there is nothing left of passion anyway in "this awful and stupid clarity" Webb has dragged him to. Unable even to pretend an interest in music, he can still cruelly want his "old friend's girl. What have you brought me back to Webb?" (*CTS*, 101). Bolden's sarcasm and irony in the scene with Crawley and his girlfriend are dramatically acute, but do they also reveal his continuing unwillingness to take any responsibility for his own acts and feelings? The text invites us to ask such a question, but it resolutely refuses to provide a single simple answer for it. The syntax in this section deliberately lays speech over writing so that it is difficult to know if Bolden is saying certain things to Crawley or writing them to

Webb (and us). This doubled narration underlines the undecidabiltiy of what he says. Finally, as Bolden insists on his stance as a writer who has finished writing, his imagery insists that what he has written has come as fully from his body as his music ever did: "Alcohol sweat on these pages. I am tired Webb. . . . don't want to get up. When I lift my head up the paper will be damp, the ink spread. The lake and sky will be light blue. Not even her cloud" (*CTS,* 102).

But if Buddy no longer writes, he still narrates part of the final few days before the parade and a small part of what comes after it. As part 3 begins, there can be no escape from the imperatives of the given story, at least in terms of the narration, which moves relentlessly to the climax of the parade. But the text can still interrupt narration, and embed other narratives within it. Thus the interview with John Joseph that opens part 3 testifies to the uncertainty surrounding that climax. It shatters the narrative momentum of the story by erupting into it from its future and the writer's and our past. A document with no documentation, it floats in a historical limbo in which nothing is fixed and rumor is all that is left. The sardonic comedy, as the interviewer says he "heard" Bolden "lost his mind" and Joseph agrees, further undermines the authority of the story, especially as Joseph is talking about Bolden's death "in the bug house" (*CTS,* 105) and not his famous breakdown in the parade.

After that comedy of misinterpretation, Bolden speaks again, but it is a speech not of explanation but of preparation. "Home to nightmare" (*CTS,* 106), he says, seeing himself as "a parcel on a bus," nothing more than "labels. The labels are coming home." His sense of alienation is complete here, for he cannot find a person beneath the labels, and we are invited to wonder if he ever could. In the middle of this fragment, indented, there is an odd imperative: "Come. We must go deeper with no justice and no jokes." It is not clear who says this, Bolden or the narrator; nor is it clear who the "we" it is addressed to is. But writer and readers both are implicated in its demands. The list of band names insists the labels are already there, and everybody has to live with them. Another document of sorts, it suggests the ubiquity of street bands and parades.

"So in the public parade he went mad into silence" (*CTS,* 108). With this the narrative jumps forward to the parade, begins to describe it and then embeds stories of the four days leading up to it in which past and present overlap, as do narrative voices. But this first version, even that first sentence, already says everything. All the rest—the description of the parade, Bolden's own narration of his performance, the increasingly awkward attempts to bring the story and the text to a halt—is an attempt to supplement what is contained within that one sentence. First an exterior narration renders how Bolden appeared to his audience: "After about half a mile his music separates from the band, and though the whole procession is still together Bolden is now stained untouchable, powerful, an 8 ball in their midst. Till he is spinning round and round, crazy, at the Liberty-Iberville connect." Then it begins to slip backward, to the beginning of the parade, and then through the speculations of the crowd, back to Bolden's arrival back in New Orleans. The narrative perspective remains distant as Buddy comes to his old house and then deliberately fails to discriminate between his and Cornish's feelings as they meet. Focalization attaches to Cornish as he notes a new silence and stillness in Bolden. Nora accepts Bolden's return easily because, as the narrator carefully explains, "[s]he had never been a shadow" and had "at times cleared away the chaos he embraced" (*CTS,* 110). That tone of explanation places the scene in history, something already decided; it is the tone of a finished story, and it alerts us to how the narrative is becoming almost conventionally chronological.[26] Yet the continual shifts from Buddy to the narrator and back keep it from becoming too transparent, especially as both Buddy and the other characters become the focus of emotion and thought in the narrator's sections. Imagery also interrupts the inevitability of the story, as it begins once more to overflow the constraints of narrative. When Buddy lies on the floor with Nora, the description of his kissing her body "as if placing mines on her with his mouth" (*CTS,* 111) recalls Robin's behavior with him (*CTS,* 58). When they decide that "it was friendship that had to be guarded, that they both wanted" (*CTS,* 111), the narration is realistic, but the next sentence slips into metaphoric surreality: "The diamond had to love the earth it passed along the way, every speck and angle of the other's history, for the diamond had been earth too." If he is the diamond, is it his attitude that is expressed here? If so, it seems he must see himself as beautiful, hard, and far beyond any potential for further change.

Nora and Willy "are complete and exact and final" (*CTS,* 112) to him because he sees them that way through his "one-dimensional eye. I left the other in the other home, Robin flying off with it into her cloud." The image precisely suggests the complex interaction of passion and music that he has lost; no longer bifocal, he can see Willy and Nora only in the stasis he projects upon them. But that stillness he desires is paradoxically "the one altered move" manifested inside his brain, for, like "great stars" and "beautiful machines" (*CWBK,* 41), he has become "[l]ocked inside the frame, boiled down in love and anger into dynamo that cannot move except on itself." The past perfect of "I had wanted to be the reservoir where engines and people drank, blood sperm music pouring out and getting hooked in someone's ear" confirms Buddy's loss. Yet simple as he believes himself to be, he is an untrustworthy narrator here, for even as he accuses them of wanting "nothing to have changed" (*CTS*, 113), he seeks his unchanged past in the pages of *The Cricket* and wonders why "people forget hate so easily." Contradiction continues to haunt him even as he tries to slip out from under it. His description of *The Cricket* matches the descriptions of his playing, yet all he can say now is "I suppose that was the crazyness [sic] I left. Cricket noises and Cricket music for that is what we are when watched by people bigger than us" (*CTS*, 113–14). The disturbing paranoia implicit in this comment, like the equally disturbing reprise of the diamond image, raises more questions about his emotional state.

As much as the labels have come home, then, so have the images. A series of jazzlike reprises moves the text inexorably toward the parade. Yet shifts of scene and tone continue to delay and even undercut the sense of doom associated with Bolden's descending mood. The shift into future event and back to the present keeps us on our toes, the vaudevillian scene at the school in which he is an absent provocation occurring as Bolden inquires after Pickett. He appears to be trying to connect the different stories about himself *in* himself through his actions. Yet when he behaves like a detective, the narrator displays a sudden uncertainty about "the facts," saying only that he "perhaps" spent the "late morning" with Pickett as he had "probably" been in Chinatown before with Bellocq (*CTS*, 117). "Second Evening" switches to Bolden's narration and shows no doubt about its reality, only about his own place in the world he has returned to. The savage yet compassionate vision of the "gypsy foot" whores (*CTS*, 119) implies a system of exploitation the text has not really addressed. Buddy feels for them, but is it only in self-pitying terms? For some critics, this passage reveals only his self-absorption and signifies the book's failure to come to grips with social realities (Mundwiler, 104–6; Mukherjee, 35–37). But the question to ask is whether this exploration of the trials of the romantic, self-absorbed artist idolizes him. Bolden's thinking doubly identifies him with both the victims and their exploiters, but his descriptions also implicate commerce in their ruin, and if they are "[t]he sum of the city," he has added to that sum. Yet he partly understands their situation, to be able to identity with it, because of Bellocq's photographs. Although his thought of "[t]heir bodies murdered and my brain suicided" may be too egotistic to develop the anguish of the whores' situation "into a true common ground" (Mundwiler, 105), the complexly woven language of the whole passage refuses to let anyone—Bolden, writer, or readers—off that easily. We discover another aspect of Bolden here, and insofar as he notices these suffering beings, we recognize his continuing ability to empathize, but insofar as he merely uses them as a metaphor for his own despair, we acknowledge the failure of the romantic imagination. Again, we have to respond to both possibilities simultaneously.

"Third Day & Third Evening" returns to exterior narration, but the focalization slides around, into Buddy's or Nora's mind, or just overseeing the activity of all those who visit him. Although he intellectually strives to be cruel and hard, untouched by others' feelings, even Nora's, Buddy remains a character in flux, despite himself: "One of the kids cried and *without thinking* he went into their room and lay on the edge of the bed his arm around the child. Act from the past" (*CTS*, 121, emphasis added). Here he somehow slips the guard of the suiciding brain and acts intuitively, and for another. In the aftermath of this act, he and Nora communicate more than before, although he does not (cannot?) tell her what he feels or why. At this point he is trapped, or has trapped himself, in the motions of escape, an inevitable slide to self-destruction begun when Webb forced him back from exile.

Being with Nora sparks a recollection of bringing Bellocq to photograph the whores, when Nora was still working. By connecting Bellocq to the mattress whores through the description of his camera as a "metal animal grown into his back" (*CTS*, 123), this retrospection ties Bolden to both. The story has its own grotesque comedy, but it also recalls Buddy as intuitive man of the body before Bellocq and then Webb tempted and forced him into thinking. At the end of this passage, next to the fight with Pickett the longest in the book, the narrative returns to Bolden and Nora on "this last night" (*CTS*, 126). Seeing Bellocq as a "harmless," "lonely man" whose pictures were "beautiful" and "gentle" (*CTS*, 127), he asks, "Why do you hate him?" Her reply brings the scene to a dramatic and appalling close: *"Look at you. Look at what he did to you. Look at you. Look at you. Goddamit. Look at you."* Dialogically, her answer forces us to pay attention to its implications, not only in terms of what is to follow but also in the light of all we have read to this point. The other voices do have their place in the text, and hers here points to the darkness and utter isolation of those who "die in the ether peripheries" (*TK*, 68), undermining their romantic glamour. His daughter's dream represents another such voice, as it comically disrupts the descent, once more registering domestic reality against the dream of artistic transcendence.

In the tour de force of "Parade (5th Morning)," Bolden narrates his own breakdown—or is it breakthrough?—in a rush of images and dissipating syntax. Contradictions erupt in the rapid movement of the prose, and although there is a strict logic to the destructive creativity he enunciates, everything ends in incoherence and the silence of empty space on the page. It begins in vanity, apart from and against the band and the music, as Bolden admits that what he is doing is "[p]arade of ego, cakewalk, strut, every fucking dance and walk I remember" (*CTS*, 129). But then the image of his desire, the audience he feared and sought, appears: "She's Robin, Nora, Crawley's girl's tongue" (*CTS*, 129–30). From this composite identity, who may or may not exist, there can be no retreat now; this dancing woman can only pull him toward the climax he seeks: "Get there before it ends, but it's nearly over, approach Liberty" (*CTS*, 129). If it is freedom he seeks, it will have to include freedom from the very audience he so loves. In the silence of the band, and then of his own broken body, he can no longer hear the music he plays nor the people on the street, only the dancer "hitting each note with her body before it is even out so I know what I do through her" (*CTS*, 130). A kind of tunnel vision sets in, as the language begins to stretch beyond normality: "God this is what I wanted to play for, if no one else I always guessed there would be this, this mirror somewhere." The "this" suggests how he is already moving beyond humanity to some other realm, yet he comes back to the woman, anonymous but vital, and he reverts to seeing her "testing me taunting me to make it past her, old hero, old ego tested against one as cold and pure as himself."

Until the very end, his old ego keeps subverting his new selfless self, but as the pace of syntactic and imagistic breakdown increases and his body also breaks down, he does get beyond the old ego's needs. The perfect audience is a cold, pure mirror he cannot touch but can see his music in, and he insists "this is what I wanted, always, loss of privacy in the playing, . . . this hearer who can throw me in the direction and the speed she wishes like an angry shadow." Although the perfect audience is a tyrant, as audiences have always been in his eyes, he now happily abdicates his own will to her. While the only way to express his transcendence is through the metaphors of bodily desire, he finally begins to lose the ego he has so often denied he had. The text signals this loss through the growing abandonment of the first-person pronoun in a systematic derangement of sense perceptions, as "my heart . . . at my throat hitting slow pure notes" (*CTS*, 131) shifts to "the long last squawk," and then to "the stomach, feel[ing] the blood that is real move up bringing fresh energy in its suitcase." Fear and ecstasy mix in "god can't stop god can't stop it can't stop the air the red force coming up . . . watch it *listen* it *listen* it, can't see I CAN'T SEE. Air floating through the blood to the girl red hitting the blind spot I can feel others turning, the silence of the crowd, can't see." As he moves to "victory," is it his or hers? By the end the "I" has disappeared into and the inner eye is blind before this ambiguity. The narration shifts outside to describe Cornish catching him and suddenly seeing "*the blood spill out from* [the horn] *as he finally lifts the metal from that hard kiss of the mouth*." The paradox of Bolden's situation is caught in the oxymoronic image of blood and metal mixed in the "*hard kiss*." The blank space suggests the silence in which he now finds himself, beyond the complications the oxymoron invokes. The final "What I wanted" returns the "I" but in such a fashion as to put all inquiry off.[27]

And what can inquiry reveal anyway? A turn of the page brings only the "single page summary" (Witten, 9) of facts, a paratactic document so barren it almost demands artistic expansion. A leap upward through diegetic levels, it is followed by a further step upward as the narrator— here represented as "the author"[28]—returns as a speaking "I" to play a variation on the opening fragment of the text. Mixing second- and first-person pronouns, the narrator enters the scene and comments on his response to it: "The place of his music is totally silent" (*CTS*, 133). As he slowly admits the personal stake he has in discovering Bolden's story, he also recognizes how fully that silence hides the "truth." In a change from the beginning, he now talks of photographing "the barber shop he *probably* worked in" (*CTS*, 133, emphasis added). All the text has accomplished, in other words, is to render Bolden more uncertain as a figure of knowledge. The image of "his skeleton . . . disintegrated, and . . . lost in the water under the earth of Holtz Cemetary" emphasizes the vacancy where his story should be; yet the narrator throws himself into that very emptiness as if it were a mirror: "When he went mad he was the same age as I am now." In this moment of pure *frisson* we "naturally" identify this "I" as Michael Ondaatje, the author of the book. Nevertheless, because it is a book, it is only the inscribed figure, "Michael Ondaatje," who identifies with Bolden, seeing his photograph as a mirror.

Mirrors form a complex system of imagery in *Coming Through Slaughter*, but that Bolden saw the dancer in the parade as a mirror should warn us of the dangers as well as the seductiveness of the mirror-image the narrating "I" finds in Bolden. His statement that he was already mirroring Bolden's actions by cutting his face with a razor before he ever heard of him leaves open the question as to where the narrator "read he stood in front of the mirrors and attacked himself," as that particular piece of information appears in none of the documented sources referred to in the acknowledgments. If Bolden's story has come to some kind of climax, the text's invention has not yet ceased; rather, it has transferred to the narrator as subject of the storytelling, which is itself a story. The narrator has always been present in the story of the telling of Bolden's story, but he has remained in the background. In foregrounding himself as subject, he disrupts Bolden's story but not the larger story of the artist's dilemma in an age of demanding audiences. Of course, this narrating "I" is also complex and even contradictory: he insists that he did "push my arm forward and spill it through the front of your mirror and clutch myself" (*CTS,* 134), thus obeying Bolden's injunction to "[p]ut your hand through this window" (*CTS,* 91); yet he also insists that he "did not want to pose in your accent but think in your brain and body" (*CTS,* 134), a comment that connects him to Webb, "entering the character of Bolden through every voice he spoke to" (*CTS,* 63). If, as we are invited to do, we attempt to read this section as autobiography, these contradictory echoes thoroughly problematize the identification of "Ondaatje" with Bolden.[29]

What is left, then? Reviewing the rumors that appeared after Bolden was "dropped into amber in the East Louisiana State Hospital," the narrator realizes that "[t]he excesses cloud up the page. There was the climax of the parade and then you removed yourself from the 20th century game of fame, the rest of your life a desert of facts. Cut them open and spread them out like garbage" (*CTS,* 134). Here the argument from fame is the argument against the whole text. Recall that one excess must be the (wholly invented) story of Robin, who became a cloud once her story lost touch with Bolden's. Note that "the rest of your life" could refer to everything except "the climax of the parade," which puts the whole text, not just the final 22 pages, under suspicion. And who is the final imperative addressed to: "I," "you," or a "we" that includes writer and readers both? Appearing to answer questions, this fragment has only opened more of them. Indeterminacy reigns supreme: "The sun has swallowed the colour of the street. It is a black and white photograph, part of a history book" (*CTS,* 134); and it explains nothing.

Critics are divided about the conclusion of *Coming Through Slaughter.* Scobie thinks Bolden "is destroyed. Ondaatje reduces the years in the. asylum to flat, prosaic statements, lists of dates and interview transcripts in which Bolden is scarcely mentioned" (Scobie 1978, 20). But the fact that he "is scarcely mentioned" could be read as a sign that he has succeeded in removing himself from the "game of fame," that he has made his escape, no matter the cost. One version of this argument sees Bolden's "breakthrough" at the end as an affirmation of extremist art, because "Bolden the extremist knows what Ondaatje knows: that the need to break through 'certainties,' to find new ways of thinking and seeing and being, is the very essence of creativity. Extremist art is that which in its style and subject matter takes that 'breaking through' somehow more literally than the normal artist may do" (Rooke, 269).[30] The text, however, refuses to be pinned down, even to the affirmatives of breaking through "certainties." It is possible to argue that Bolden is happy in his extremely reduced circumstances precisely because the reduction—he has no more choices to make—is so extreme. The world of the asylum, especially the rituals he has created for "his friend" (*CTS*, 148) the sun, is a world of certainties, not of breakthroughs. Having lived his art of improvisation as fully as possible until he could no longer manage it, Bolden has taken it one step further and then stepped away from it and from everything and everyone else. As novelistic character, he invites such speculation; as textual figure he simply continues to confound it.

More than just lists, these final pages include further narration by Buddy, a strange breaking of the silence he entered, in which he makes demands—"Everyone who touches me must be beautiful" (*CTS*, 135)—that can be met only within his psychological geography; walled within his "paranoia" (*CTS*, 137), he sees what he wants to see. His passivity before his treatment and before the attempts by people like Lord to reach him (*CTS*, 141, 148) is his method of evading explanation, and in the end it works. In a sense, there are too many implied explanations, and they erase one another. Does he choose his fate or not? Webb forces him back to New Orleans, but he joins the parade of his own free will. The image of "Bolden's hand going up into the air / in agony. / His brain driving it up into the / path of the circling fan" (*CTS*, 136) captures the mixture of passivity and willfulness in the act. The first sentence suggests a lack of control, while the second says he willed the act. The separated sentence on the same page is equally equivocal: "This last movement happens forever and ever in his memory." Because of the open space between it and the previous sentences, we cannot be sure who "his" refers to, Bolden in the asylum or the narrator who has followed his story to this conclusion. After all, in that story Bolden has both chosen to act and been forced by others, like Webb, to act. The image only confirms a dichotomy the text has consistently insisted upon.

Between the lists, which appear to be there only to emphasize their irrelevance, textual uncertainties continue to proliferate, as do images connecting Bolden to his pre-parade self. As images, especially the by-now familiar "[p]assing wet chicory that lies in the field like the sky" (*CTS,* 139), fall into place in the narrative act of "coming through Slaughter" on the way to the asylum, the voice loses any sense of discrimination. A gruesome comedy results, in which transcendence and slapstick collide. Bolden now accepts his position as a dog "[g]oing to a pound," yet sees the "operation on my throat" as "a salvation on my throat." He describes being raped in the same tone he tells the comic story of the food climbing over the "[b]oot in my throat"; every incident now has equal weight in the telling. His serenity is indiscriminate, and everything in his experience is the same—a kind of transcendental certainty that only madness can bring.

Bolden describes his ritual of string and sun in what is almost a parody of scientific objectivity, and then adds, as if to mock precisely the scientific attitude his previous words have parodied: "Laughing in my room. As you try to explain me I will spit you, yellow, out of my mouth" (*CTS,* 140). This is perhaps the greatest moment of reversal in the whole text, for it operates on a formal level. Suddenly the communication model of "author / implied author / narrator // narratee / implied reader / reader" (see Rimmon-Kenan, 86) is overturned, for the "you" here applies as much to the "implied author" as to us. If Buddy is the narrator here, he is denying the author-as-narrator the identification he has sought, forcing him across the borderline in the center of the diagram to join narratee, implied reader, and perhaps even the "real" readers. So, if we have allowed ourselves to believe that "Michael Ondaatje" is, as "he" asserts, uniquely qualified to identify with Buddy Bolden, we are now forced to question that possibility. The utter refusal of explanation paradoxically denies what the text has affirmed through its entering of Bolden's "voice." In making that "you" suddenly contain both writer and readers, the text divides the writer from himself and renders every figure in the communication model indeterminate, capable of becoming something else. Yet the rest of the text is there, and we have already made and acted upon the very assumptions this passage calls into question. Unable to deny that experience, we are, perhaps, forced to reevaluate it.

This is the last clear instance of Buddy narrating, although there are two short fragments that might be in his voice before the end. The extradiegetic narrator now tells the stories and gathers the documents that paratactically add to the historical narrative but fail to give it any satisfying shape. The scene between Webb and Bella Cornish, for example, is both dialogic and disruptive: Webb has disappeared from the text since he found Buddy, partly because he has disappeared from Bolden's mind, but also because Nora put him out, just as she tried to do at the very beginning of his search. Now this entirely fictional figure returns only to hear Bella's stories of Bolden, which are secondhand and, like all rumors, full of errors that the narrator must correct (*CTS,* 150). Webb's response suggests his guilt, but the reason for it remains unclear: does he feel guilty for having failed to be a proper "master" to his "dog" Bolden, or for having believed Nora's lies, or for never having understood his friend at all? Such questions assume his presence as a realistic character, yet from a formal point of view he is nothing more than an engine to propel this text's narrative, and now both disappear, leaving only the empty trace of his sweat on the wall, fading fast (*CTS,* 151).

Fascinating documents in themselves, the "Frank Amacker Interviews" demonstrate both how lost to history Bolden has become how the Amackers of this world have lost much more than he did. In his willingness to provide a song for "a really good singer, like Perry Como" (*CTS,* 154), a "song, furthermore, [that] gives a precise summary of the world that revealed its full horror to Buddy Bolden" in both its "compulsion of the audience's love [and its] sexual violence" (Rooke, 291), Amacker becomes an emblem of the "game of fame" Bolden escaped. That is one way of reading the interviews, but Amacker's cheerful survivalism, however ignoble, suggests an alternate reading is always possible.

There are two fragments in the final pages that resist interpretation even more than the rest. As indeterminacy of identification is central to their effect, it is difficult to say who is speaking in them. Perhaps Buddy says "[i]n the room there is the air / and there is the corner / and there is the corner and there is the corner / and there is the corner" (*CTS,* 146), for he has earlier described himself as a "King of Corners" (*CTS,* 86); but this could also be the narrator describing his or any room from the outside. Similarly, "[i]f you don't shake, don't get no cake" (*CTS,* 146, 23) floats apart from any particular voice as song title, admission, and final evaluation simultaneously. It is document, Bolden's confession of what he has given up, the narrator's opinion of Bolden's withdrawal from performing, and the author's awareness of the stakes involved in every artistic endeavor. Something similar happens on the final page of narrative text, in which "Michael Ondaatje" and "Buddy Bolden" seem inextricably intertwined in one "I" only to dissipate into a cloudy, fluctuating syntax. The indeterminacy of subject matches that of image and statement: "I sit with this room. With the grey walls that darken into corner. And one window with teeth in it. Sit so still you can hear your hair rustle in your shirt. Look away from the window when clouds and other things go by. Thirty-one years old. There are no prizes" (*CTS*, 156).

Even the preposition extends the gap between description and understanding, for sitting *with* a room is not the same as sitting *in* one. The "with" implies an imaginative act of creation. The parataxis in this fragment is extreme, yet the mood, though hard to pin down, holds throughout. I am not sure that the images of the passage "no longer threaten" and that "there seems no need to look out the windows for 'clouds and other things,' as everything is there in the grey room already" (Rooke, 291), but neither does the passage leave "a flat sour taste in the mouth" (Scobie 1978, 21). My reading of this segment, like my reading of the whole, depends on my mood as much as on the implications of the text. But it remains opaque. Are those verbs simply the active present tense of a dropped first-person singular, or are they imperative? Do they address character, author, or us? To what and whom does "Thirty-one years old" refer? What does the final sentence really mean? It is so large and general a statement that it can be made to mean anything: there are no prizes for losers, for winners; prizes do not matter, only the act of art; if you take yourself out of the game there is nothing to win; perhaps there is no award for just living to a certain age, etc.

Throughout *Coming Through Slaughter,* the dialogism implicit in the various narrative voices on various diegetic levels refuses any single reading and invites a continual return to other readings. Yes, Buddy Bolden went mad and destroyed a great talent; no, Buddy Bolden managed to escape the horrors of fame in the twentieth century. Yes, art is great; no, madness is never really an escape. The various voices make sure that no single meaning gains supremacy. Meaning is not the point; writing is. Finally, what I come back to, again and again, is the ever-changing yet always engaging energy of the writing itself, and the fact that because I can't fix either the characters or the text within a single generic focus or a particular kind of reading, they remain in flux, evading explanation, yes, but singing a siren song of empathy I cannot resist.

Chapter Six
Running in the Family

When *Running in the Family* appeared in 1982, it met with almost universal acclaim, although—or perhaps even because—it evaded easy generic categorization. Whether autobiography, biography, historiographic metafiction, personal history, oral history, collection of anecdotes, or memoir, its textuality "keeps its final intelligibility forever at bay by practicing a deferral of meaning and of generic definition related to the autobiographical elements of the book."[1] Apparently contradictory, these terms all describe aspects of "one of the most complex of Ondaatje's postmodern challenges to boundaries" (Hutcheon 1988, 82). Unlike many such challenging texts, however, which attempt to reject traditional notions of representation and human intentionality, *Running in the Family,* like other Ondaatje texts, simultaneously allows and denies conventional readings, drawing us in to its apparent representation even as it reveals the deeply fictional agenda of all writing. Memory is a form of fiction, and in this text memories are the basic documents the writer has to work with. All are of equal value, including his own, and in their juxtaposition he creates a deeply dialogic text in which every voice—his own; those of family, friends and relations; those inscribed on a tombstone, in a church ledger, and in ancient or new graffiti; and those he invents—emerges into fragmentary foreground to contribute to the bio- or historiographic metafictional process that writer and reader share.[2] The intense immediacy of the language of *Running in the Family*'s collage text holds out the temptation of gossip while pushing beyond gossip's limitations at every turn.

As in *The Collected Works of Billy the Kid* and *Coming Through Slaughter,* Ondaatje's "Acknowledgments" (outside the text proper) both clarify and undermine the documentary process in the text, this time with an added suggestion of collaboration. "A literary work is a communal act. And this book could not have been *imagined,* let alone conceived,[3] without the help of many people" (*RF,* 205), says the writer, indicating that "[t]he book is a composite of two return journeys to Sri Lanka" and that "[r]aw material came from many sources," a list of whom he thanks.

But his final comment undercuts the conventional responses we might bring to documentary writing: "While all these names may give an air of authenticity, I must confess that the book is not a history but a portrait or 'gesture.' And if those listed above disapprove of the fictional air I apologize and can only say that in Sri Lanka a well-told lie is worth a thousand facts" (*RF*, 206). "Gesture" is a key word here, for gestures can either signify or point, and sometimes do both; a gesture can signify something else, or it can merely signify itself, the act of gesturing, of pointing toward that which cannot be named. In a book full of naming, full of stories, full of both the writer's family and his own life as a writer, great mysteries remain, and all the text can do is point them out. It does so with such intensity and emotional clarity that we sometimes think we understand what we (and the writer) only perceive and feel. But rather than explanation, Ondaatje's texts seek to create a sensual and emotional awareness of the other's living, in the midst of his or her experience. To slip into the other body and feel what it's like to live there, even if the living is chaotic—that is the gift they offer. And of course, there are many different others to engage, many different lives, including the writer's own, to explore. The gestures are linguistic; they are inscribed in the text and can be found nowhere else.

The first gesture is of writing itself, which also deflects the autobiographical into the novelistic while setting up the first of many intertexts. Separated from the rest of the book, and not even listed in the table of contents, a half-page of writing serves as a kind of authorial epigraph, an exergue, both outside the text and part of it (Kamboureli 1988, 82). Although the name of the author has led us to expect autobiography, the use of the third-person pronoun undercuts that expectation here, while the juxtaposition of ice, a dream, and time recalls the opening of that central text of postcolonial postmodernism, Gabriel García Márquez's *One Hundred Years of Solitude* (see Hutcheon 1988, 88), and thereby throws us further off the traces of autobiography. Like García Márquez's novel, Ondaatje's book is a self-consciously written text based on oral tradition; however, after presenting the subject of discourse in the alien landscape to which he has returned, responding to the image of men rolling ice carts, the nightmare, the room, and the clarity of a brief morning moment, all in the third person, the text returns to the possibility of autobiography in a gesture that acknowledges a different sense of time than narrative or analepsis provide: "*Half a page—and the morning is already ancient*" (*RF*, 17). This "ancient" morning is both that of the time passed in writing the half-page we have just read and any

morning in an ahistorical space seemingly outside of time, which is how
Sri Lanka appears to the newly returned alien. The act of writing, and the
time it takes, situates the subject of autobiography in the process of
inscribing the stories rather than simply inscribing him in them. But
what kind of autobiographical subject emerges in the process rather than
the "content" of a text? Perhaps one for whom the act of writing is part
of the act of remembering, which is what this book is "about." While the
various fragmentary tales of past and present Ondaatjes appear to represent familial and personal histories, there are sudden moments of textual
mise-en-abyme that call us back to the book in our hands and our reading
of it as the activity of discovery parallel to its writing.

Having created an exergue that disrupts autobiography through its
use of the third-person pronoun and then returns us to a different sense of
the genre as process, the writer does enter the text as a subject of story. As
"I," he dangles a fragment of autobiographical story before us in "Asian
Rumours," the first section of the book: "What began it all was the
bright bone of a dream I could hardly hold onto. . . . my father,
chaotic, surrounded by dogs" (*RF*, 21). Dreams are always potentially
predictive, and in the heart of a Canadian winter this one clearly points
the way back to Asia. Soon, "in the midst of [a] farewell party" (*RF*, 22),
he drunkenly acknowledges that he "was already running . . . back to
the family I had grown from—those relations . . . who stood in my
memory like frozen opera. I wanted to touch them into words." The
image is apt, for opera is the spectacle in which large gestures seem most
at home. The writer desires to connect with that spectacle through the
act of writing, to touch them, but to touch them *into words*. A reminder,
if any is needed, that we are engaged in a textual endeavor. The chapter
titled "Asia" takes place in Canada, and it ends, appropriately enough, in
the image of a grand drunken party for the child of the people whose
grand drunken parties and their aftermaths he will chart in the chapters
to follow. Currents of imagery, nets of metaphor, will carry him, and us,
deeper into the network of relations and relationships the text will slowly
construct but not necessarily resolve.

That he has found his way into a maze of stories comes clear in the
second fragment, "Jaffna Afternoons," where copious description of the
interior of the governor's home, a "labyrinth of 18th-century Dutch
defense" (*RF*, 25) segues into a story of spending the morning "with my
sister and my Aunt Phyllis trying to trace the maze of relationships in our
ancestry." Aunt Phyllis, "the minotaur of this long journey back," can
lead him, and us, back and forth within the maze, showing off more and

more of its unique architecture in each passage: "No story is ever told just once. Whether a memory or funny hideous scandal, we will return to it an hour later and retell the story with additions and this time a few judgements thrown in. In this way history is organized" (*RF,* 26). Such organization is the method of this book and continually disrupts any singular reading habit in its slippage from genre to genre. There are mirrors in the labyrinth of stories but there are also windows onto other sites of narrative. The writer will see others more often than he sees himself.

The image of the maze reappears when the text approaches the life of Ondaatje's wild grandmother, Lalla, in a fragment paying homage to García Márquez and the magical realist mode, but it takes on an aura of danger, of fear, that underlines the risks the writing has engaged. "This overbearing charmed flower" (*RF,* 125) is a woman who loved the company of children yet diverted grandchildren "into the entrance of the frightening maze in the Nuwara Eliya Park and le[ft] them there, lost" (*RF,* 119). In "her last perfect journey," she "floated over the intricate fir tree hedges of the maze—which would always continue to terrify her grandchildren [of whom the writer is one]—its secret spread out naked as a skeleton for her" (*RF,* 128)—but not for the writer, nor for us. The secret, the mystery, is what the text desires to preserve and embellish. Like the grandchildren, we are left in the maze of stories to figure our own way out.

The mystery of story and of dream mix and enter into each other. The dream of father and dogs will return as a story later in the book (*RF,* 181–82), while the 20-foot-high doors of the governor's home become "not so much a dream as an image that repeats itself" (*RF,* 27) that very night. Seeing himself perched near the top of a family pyramid, the writer casually notes how "[w]ithout discussing it the whole family ignores the opening and walks slowly through the pale pink rose-coloured walls into the next room." This passage gestures proleptically toward the stories to follow, of the reckless lawlessness of the whole family, its willingness to ignore the conventions of "normal" life.

The writer insists, self-consciously, on reminding us that the translation of oral stories into written ones is the focal autobiographical action of this text: "The air reaches me unevenly with its gusts against my arms, face, *and this paper*" (*RF,* 24; emphasis added). As writer, he is also reader, gathering and inscribing, finally, *a* version of the stories he has heard and now interprets, if only by the way he "re-writes" them. The stories he now proceeds to tell—of both the past and the present, and of the telling itself—compose the writer in the act of writing the text we read; but they discompose the author as a subject of autobiography, and thus he flickers in and out of focus as a presence seeking to make the past present to us in a writing that continually shifts among genres.

Although *Running in the Family* deals with the lives of both his mother's and his father's family, it is his father the writer seeks most to comprehend, and so "the history of good and bad Ondaatjes and the people they came in contact with" (*RF,* 26), the story of his patronymic, fascinates the writer. Yet, since the people they came in contact with include his mother's family, they, too, play their part. And although the book is a collage of fragments, some deeply private, some extravagantly public, the labyrinth does seem to turn inward toward the father's final silence near the end of the book. But it begins in the gossipy history of the whole generation of mixed-race Burghers who lived high and flighty in the 1920s and 1930s.[4]

"A Fine Romance" offers various glimpses of that gossipy history, beginning with "The Courtship," a highly ironic title for a series of episodes that demonstrate Ondaatje's father's "technique of trying to solve one problem by creating another" (*RF,* 33) rather than any pro- longed romantic pursuit of a beloved. This first chapter speaks always of "my father" (*RF,* 31), clearly identifying the writer's involvement in the stories he discovers. Combining a brittle tone of social comedy with an elegiac awareness of lost youth and missed opportunities—implied intertexts include Noël Coward, P. G. Wodehouse, and F. Scott Fitzgerald—it condenses a great deal of information into sentences that convey both the comedy of a situation and its ethical uncertainties: "He had rented extravagant rooms in Cambridge and simply eliminated the academic element of university, making close friends among the stu- dents, reading contemporary novels, boating, and making a name for himself as someone who knew exactly what was valuable and interesting in the Cambridge circles of the 1920s" (*RF,* 31–32). The final clause exemplifies the ambiguity of his situation: was he recognized within those circles as someone who knew what counted or was he recognized only as someone who knew what counted in those circles? The question implies much about race, caste, and culture both in England and in Ceylon. A single paragraph covers his parents' "hearing the distressing news" (*RF,* 32) (and how ambiguously shaded is that adjective), their travel to England to confront him, his retreat into silence and then into an engagement with Kaye Roseleap, who "leapt from the notable Rose- leaps of Dorset" (*RF,* 33), and how that pleased his parents and his sister.

Again, puns, ambiguities, and elisions realize both surface comedy and an underlying somewhat dark code of colonial behavior.[5]

The autobiographical writing "I" is especially present in this first chapter, wondering, questioning, admitting he is "not sure" (*RF,* 33) about various events even as he describes them. Although he uses documents like "Rex Daniels' journals" for an impression of his mother and her friend dancing, the basic "documentation" comes from that minotaur, or possibly Ariadne (Kamboureli 1988, 85), Aunt Phyllis, who "was always close to my father" (*RF,* 25) and who provides with her linked stories the thread that allows the Theseus poet to track his way through the labyrinthine past. Still, if he passes on tales of comic disasters and social scandal, what he leaves out is as interesting as what he actually tells; there are certain walls he cannot penetrate, stories he can never discern, as the final two sentences of the chapter intimate: "The next day the problems were solved and the engagement was established once more. They were married a year later" (*RF,* 35). The nuances of love and its difficulties are utterly excluded from the narrative at this point.

"Historical Relations" maintains the "objective," "historical" tone of documentary except for the giveaway possessive pronoun "my," which admits the narrator's relation to these people, and by extension, his obligation to their stories. Yet he is absent in the stories, present only as their teller, now. Moreover, he "engages in a paradoxically and seemingly redundant activity, for what he discloses about his father [and the others] is already public property, has already been read. Autobiography and biography here overlap in ways that cancel out each other's generic distinctiveness" (Kamboureli 1988, 86).

Aside from its ironic allusion to Robert Knox's *An Historical Relation,* referred to later in the text, "Historical Relations" punningly constructs its own ironies. Thus, while "my grandparents" (*RF,* 39) are relations in history, historical relations have also made them and their families part of a small social circle: "Everyone was vaguely related and had Sinhalese, Tamil, Dutch, British and Burgher blood in them going back many generations" (*RF,* 41). Moreover, their summer retreat of Nuwara Eliya was also fertile ground for a never-ending series of relationships, summed up in a pair of sentences that gesture perfectly to the code "I still cannot break" (*RF,* 53): "It seems that most of my relatives at some time were attracted to somebody they shouldn't have been. Love affairs rainbowed over marriages and lasted forever—so it often seemed that marriage was the greater infidelity." In "Flaming Youth," a series of quick takes about "my father's generation" (*RF,* 44), the tone remains playful and generous, yet always capable of allowing darkness its place. There are quick shifts between a distant historicity and an immediate memory like that of his mother singing an old song in the kitchen. The apparent authenticity of the latter validates the former, and all the stories, however the writer came to learn them, assume the same weight in the text. "The Babylon Stakes," with its evocation of the horse races and betting and the parties far into the night, might seem to romanticize "this charmed group [that] was part of another lost world" (RF, 51) if the barbed implications of the word "Babylon," however authentically documented, did not already hold their behavior up to potential political analysis. The text most reveals itself as postmodern in such richly doubled textual moments (see Hutcheon 1989, 14–15). But if "[t]he only occupation that could hope to avert one from drink and romance was gambling" (RF, 48), the descriptions of "devil dances" where "the gramophone accompanied a seduction or an arousal" (RF, 52) reveal that dancing and swimming nude, all in anonymity, were really just another form of gambling, perhaps for higher emotional stakes.

But across the distance of time, the writer cannot "break the code of how 'interested in' or 'attracted' they were to each other. Truth disappears with history and gossip tells us in the end nothing of personal relationships" (RF, 53). Gossip is precisely what he seeks to transcend, but his desire for "the intimate and truthful in all this" (RF, 54) is frustrated because he can't "sit down with someone and . . . talk to all the lost history like [a] deserving lover." If history fails, he will have to invent, and that is what he does as the text accumulates. "Kegalle (i)" returns to the family place itself, the home the ancient patriarch built to found a dynasty. This traditional trope begins to crumble in the text as quickly as its referent did in life: people remember the great uncle rather than the grandfather, who ignored them, too. After his chaotic and farcical funeral, the family neglects the mansion. Within this history, the narrative shifts into the future (now past to the writer) when his father returns with his second family to the inheritence he is drinking and selling away. The text records the father's death long before it inscribes the stories of his life, and then records the writer's visit with his half-sister to a place large in memory but "now small and dark, fading into the landscape" (RF, 59). But memory suddenly takes the foreground, as he remembers the tree he played in, and someone provides the remembered images of the drunken father, engaging an equally drunk polecat, and singing his songs. This unsubstantiated "memory" slips into fiction, an anecdote from the father's point of view, of finding the polecat walking on the piano and "finally walking up to the kerosene lamp hanging in the centre of the room at head level, and draining *that* liquid into his mouth. He and his polecat" (*RF,* 60). The tone here appears transparent, but it is a transparency laced with mixed admiration and disgust, a kind of limpid pain of implied judgments created by the larger context. The final paragraph returns to the writing present, as the writer's sister gestures toward some of the places their father hid bottles in the now overrun garden: "Whatever 'empire' my grandfather had fought for had to all purposes disappeared" (*RF,* 60).

That key term *empire* is itself a gesture, toward the next section of the book, which explores the history of Ceylon as a colony, in relation to the history of the family. In the punningly titled "Tabula Asiae," with its implications of European visualized emptiness to be written upon by the pens (or rather the swords) of empire, the writer describes a series of "false maps. Old portraits of Ceylon" (*RF,* 63).[6] Even the maps are fictions, implied narratives of discovery and conquest, revealing "rumours of topography, the routes for invasion and trade, and the dark mad mind of travellers' tales" (*RF,* 64). Its changing shapes, like its many names, mark Ceylon as a sliding signified, an aesthetic construct that "became a mirror . . . pretend[ing] to reflect each European power till newer ships arrived and spilled their nationalities." Having created a cinematic image of imperial inscription upon this "tabula asiae," the writer shows his ancestor being inscribed into the Dutch imperial plan some 380 years ago, "rewarded with land, a foreign wife, and a new name which was a Dutch spelling of his own. Ondaatje." But patriarchy worked, even for those who served imperial power: "when his Dutch wife died, marrying a Sinhalese woman, having nine children, and remaining. Here. At the centre of the rumour. At this point on the map" (*RF,* 64). The center of a rumor is only another location of story, and all the writer can do is find traces of earlier stories in the various documents he uncovers.

Both the place and the chapter titled "St. Thomas' Church" can provide only the barest clues to the past. The narrator slides from first-person plural to second person to first-person singular, as he represents his family, himself, and the generalized possibility of his actions in attempting to trace genealogical history in a country where even the insects join in the general destruction of historical inscription. When the "I" says that to "see *your* name chiseled in large letters . . . in some strange way removes vanity, eliminates the personal. It makes *your* own story a lyric" (*RF,* 65–66; emphasis added), the very shift into the second person signals the elimination of the personal at that point, and also reminds us that autobiography is occurring in the act of writing itself. Despite elisions "caused by silverfish, scars among the immaculate recordings of local history" (*RF,* 66) "the stones and pages are full of" Ondaatjes' names. The chapter illustrates the method of the book: at the beginning the writer knows nothing about either the names or the people they refer to, yet out of this barest documentary evidence he conjures, in an apparently "objective" tone, a tale decidedly domestic and surely private, an act that once again calls attention to the story-making process at work in this text; as does the final image of his writing and then washing his hands and seeing "the deep grey colour of old paper dust going down the drain" (*RF,* 68).

The "Monsoon Notebook" chapters, the first of which immediately follows, argue the writer's engagement with the immediate present, although it begins with "[r]eading torn 100-year-old newspaper clippings that come apart in your hands like wet sand, information tough as plastic dolls" (*RF,* 69). The pop sensibility of the simile, while hinting at cultural imperialism, suggests the opaqueness of whatever information he can uncover. The paratactic sentences that follow evoke the rush of experiences overwhelming him and argue a representational immediacy; yet if they come directly from the notebook he kept while in Sri Lanka, they imply the alterations and revisions of the rest of the text. As soon as they do, they also imply the same possibility for themselves: there is no such thing as unmediated inscription of the sensed world. The writer can witness, but as *a* witness he must and will give shape to what he writes.

How he does so appears immediately in the next chapter, "Tongue." It begins with both the Canadian and the Ceylonese Ondaatje children walking with the writer on a beach. The discovery of a body leads to identification, which leads to zoological information, the legendary writings of Sir John Maundeville and Robert Knox,[7] and finally the "myth that if a child is given thalagoya tongue to eat he will become brilliantly articulate, will always speak beautifully, and in his speech be able to 'catch' and collect wonderful, humorous information" (*RF,* 73). More information follows, on how to eat the tongue, plus a possible side effect—"the burning of furniture, etc." (*RF,* 74)—mentioned almost as an afterthought. But when the writer then points out that his Uncle Noel became "a brilliant lawyer and a great storyteller, from eating just *part* of" a thalagoya tongue, the afterthought recalls "The Courtship," with its reference to Noel's bad behavior at Oxford. By asking us if we have been paying attention, the writing calls attention to the way it works, as writing. The final paragraph of the chapter deliberately "makes strange" what we normally think of as a commonsensical act: "About six months before I was born my mother observed a pair of kabaragoyas 'in copula' at Pelmadulla. A reference is made to this sighting in *A Coloured Atlas of Some Vertebrates from Ceylon, Vol. 2*, a National Museum publication. It is my first *memory*" (*RF*, 75; emphasis added). Ondaatje has not eaten even part of a thalagoya tongue, yet his writing, if not his speech, does catch and collect wonderful and humorous information, including this new definition of memory as a written story concerning people he knows that occurred while he was present but unable to perceive the occurrence. The slippages, from thalagoya to kabaragoya, from seeing to reading, all render our sense of this writing's secure fix on "facts" extremely problematic.

Only now does the writer introduce his schizophrenic sense of simultaneously belonging and not belonging to this magical place. "The Karapothas"—a personification of "the beetles with white spots who never grew ancient here, who stepped in and admired the landscape, disliked the 'inquisitive natives' and left" (*RF*, 80), by which his niece names all foreigners—opens with a series of quotations from British travelers who did not come to love the riotous fecundity of Ceylon. Admitting that "I am the foreigner. I am the prodigal who hates the foreigner" (*RF*, 79), the writer revels in the heat of Colombo and points out that that heat disgraces Englishmen like D. H. Lawrence and even his own Canadian-born children. Yet, dangerous aliens "overpowered the land obsessive for something as delicate as the smell of cinnamon. Becoming wealthy with spices," (*RF*, 80). This statement of cinnamon's relation to power appears before the poem "The Cinnamon Peeler" attempts to enter the place not by forceful aggrandizement but by imaginative identification.

From something like analysis, the writer slips to further stories, documented in journals, histories, and even dramas. Robert Knox is invoked once more for his self-pity, while the first specific reference to a Shakespeare play is to *Othello*, a drama of *mis*understanding, in which Desdemona, not Othello, represents the failure of the imagination to leap across the gap that separates self from the other, whether it be lover or country. The journals of an ancestor who delighted in noting the vast variety of poisons to be found in the flora of Ceylon give way to Knox's memoir, *An Historical Relation*, which served Defoe as a source for *Robinson Crusoe*. When he concludes that "[a]part from Knox, and later Leonard Woolf . . . , very few foreigners truly knew where they were" (*RF*, 83), what are we to infer about the writer?

After a typographical break, the writer celebrates the Sinhalese "curving alphabet . . . Moon coconut. The bones of a lover's spine" he learned as a child. In his perception, the letters are images of "the small bones in the body," the alphabet a deeply sensuous inscription even before it shaped any meaning. From meditative memory of learning this alphabet, he turns to the more profound and lasting inscriptions of fifth-century graffiti poems honoring the "mythological women who consumed and overcame mundane lives" (*RF*, 84). The writer implies but deliberately does not draw a fine distinction here by translating the romantic self-pitying images of these "first folk poems of the country" without comment. The comment comes in the next paragraph, reporting the students' graffiti written during the "insurgency of 1971." These "[q]uatrains and free verse about the struggle, tortures, the unbroken spirit, love of friends who had died for the cause" covered the walls of the Vidyalankara campus and, after the police had broken the rebellion, "students went around for days transcribing them into their notebooks before they were covered with whitewash and lye." The "lie" in "lye" is emphasized by its position at the very end of the paragraph.

After another typographical break, the writer meets a historian who tells him of the insurgence and of Lakdasa Wikkramasinha, a political poet who had died recently. The historian "is a man who knows history is always present, . . . is the burned down wall that held those charcoal drawings whose passionate conscience should have been cut into rock. The voices I didn't know. The visions which are anonymous. And secret" (*RF*, 85). This powerful passage simultaneously admits that its writer is Karpotha and takes out citizenship papers. The writer writing in Ceylon then adds that "[t]his morning . . . I read the poetry of Lakdasa Wikkramasinha" (*RF*, 85) and quotes "Don't talk to me about Matisse," which provides the title for this section of the book. This is another document whose presence signs the carefully written nature of the text we are reading. A defiantly postcolonial rejection of "the European style," with a single-minded political agenda, it is too monologic for this text, yet its presence in it adds another voice to the dialogic collage it is becoming.[8] The four poems that follow, the last to appear in *Running in the Family*, attempt in differing ways to enter imaginatively, if also privately and personally, into the life of the county. Juxtaposed to the other voice of Wikkramasinha, they provide a variety of views of "[t]he woman my ancestors ignored" (*RF*, 87), her husband "the toddy tapper" (*RF*, 88), the people of the villages, the "brown men / who rise knee deep like the earth / out of the earth" (*RF*, 90), the writers of "the communal poem—Sigiri Graffiti, 5th century" (*RF,* 92), and the cinnamon peeler and his wife (*RF,* 95–97). They cannot, as Wikkramasinha demands, talk "of the culture generally" (*RF,* 86), but they do, in a lyric leap of identification, at least acknowledge some of the complex choirings of individual voices within the general culture, which has survived and changed throughout the centuries.

Ondaatje's poetic of the physical image, the gesture of perception, creates images implying much more than they state, but at least some of the implications have a political overtone. In the first two, the writer can only humbly descry (and describe) the others of this place from a distance, refusing any temptation to do more than name them as images in the distance. But they are named, and so become a part of the text, if only on the margins of the stories he can tell (because he has been told them; they are family property, so to speak). "Women Like You" speaks both of and for the women and the men who wrote graffiti about them. If it luxuriates in the romanticism of these ancient gestures of allegiance and loss, it does so by poetic identification. Refusing to make fun of them, it can acknowledge the power that "carved an alphabet / whose motive was perfect desire" (*RF,* 93) and even enter into it. The "I" of the poem is both observer and participant, the writer now, and then, engaging new love.[9] He creates his own addition to the graffiti in "The Cinnamon Peeler," where the subjunctive establishes the conditional state of a poem of romantic yearning and triumphant desire. In its successful dreaming it moves beyond the liturgy of loss inscribed on Siguri rock walls, yet it does so in images of local pride, utterly at home in the land. The poem begins in conditional desire: "If I were a cinnamon peeler / I would ride your bed / and leave the yellow bark dust / on your pillow" (*RF,* 95). A kind of writer, the cinnamon peeler would inscribe his love upon the body of his beloved in the odor of his calling. As he describes how her body would carry his cinnamon smell, he leaves the conditional behind. Now inhabiting that persona, he recalls how he "could hardly glance at you / before marriage / never touch you" (*RF,* 96), and then recalls another time when she accused him of infidelity in jest and then acknowledged her own desire for him by touching him and thus taking his smell upon her own body as a kind of treasured marking. By the end of the poem, the original conditional mood has disappeared, yet the whole poem depends upon it. The four poems together map a distance the writer had traveled in empathetic identification with the people of this place. If such identification remains possible only in the private terms of sexual desire, it at least argues the possibility of seeing beyond the glittery confines of family history to other social worlds surrounding that of his parents and their friends.

"Kegalle (ii)" concludes this section with a series of stories about the writer's father and his other family. These anecdotes move from his successful use of Ping-Pong balls against snakes through his less successful attempts to shoot the snakes that broke into the house, to his own reappearance after his death as "a grey cobra . . . come to protect his family" (*RF*, 99). The calm acceptance of family legend (or superstition) in the telling signals the magic realist fictional mode at work here. The final story returns to the insurgence of 1971, the event the writer has said he cannot know at all. This comic pastoral vignette, in which the young insurgents end up asking the writer's sister to join them in a game of cricket on the lawn, may also be the writer's one possible gesture of solidarity with them, at however great a distance, for it is in some way his family they played with.

"Don't talk to me about Matisse" establishes, however surreptitiously, a larger historical and social context within which the stories of Ondaatje's family can be measured. *Running in the Family* is not about their failure of social imagination; it is a much more personal and private rumination upon a past that affected the writer if only by its loss. But the accusation that Ondaatje simply ignores the social and political misses the point. The early allusion to *One Hundred Years of Solitude* prepares us for a magic realist myth of origins, an invention of self and others in a brightly fictional setting: the "scenes from the book that come alive in fantastic, unreal, poetic imagination convey . . . the real fact of the lives of these people, the spirit in which they *should* have lived, if they had extended their situation to its logical conclusion" (MacIntyre, 317).

From a present context in which the political and social realities of Sri Lanka must be acknowledged, the writer turns to the texts of his family members' lives. They live, now, for him and for us, in the stories told about them, as the first chapter of "Eclipse Plumage," "Lunch Conversation," makes clear. Essentially a dramatic scene, it is in fact a carefully written passage, in which the shift from speech to writing is blurred as much as possible. None of the common indicators of speech appear, so that a shift from paragraphs of conversation to one of description passes almost unnoticed. The writer, as almost passive listener, stands in for us as he tries to follow not one but three separate episodes in the lives of his mother and her mother. Names that he is supposed to recognize (we, too?) flash by, only later provided with necessary background information, as he requests it. The sense of communal enjoyment of a tale many times told is palpable, but in fact all the information is new—to both writer and reader. The whole sequence of conversation conveys the collective complexity and delight of such family tales, and, because with every retelling something new emerges, there is always the delight of new discoveries for both tellers and listeners. As the linked stories return to the primary narrative of Lalla floating out to sea when her daughter was nine, the writer shifts into pure fictional textuality, shaping the rest of the story into a narrative not heard but imagined. A harsh comedy plays across the surface of this anecdotal conclusion to the tall tale of Lalla's trip about the harbor, the humor working to keep death at a distance precisely as it does in the Noël Coward plays these people likely all enjoyed. Told to tell her sister of her husband's death, Lalla waits for her to wake up: "Dickie stirs. Lalla is holding her hand. She looks up and her first words are, 'How is David? Is he alright?' 'Quite well, darling,' Lalla says. 'He is in the next room having a cup of tea'" (*RF,* 109). Full stop, no explanation, this is the end of that tale. The next page returns to the present and to the writer's problematic relationship with his aunts, from whom he has received such stories with which to build his book.

Because one of the genres interlaced in *Running in the Family* is autobiography, this text tends more than others to display its methods. When the writer says of his aunts, "How I have used them" (*RF,* 110), he is acknowledging the attitude toward documentation that propels all his larger works. Documents, the given stories, are but springboards from which invention leaps into the ocean of story. He "would love to photograph this," because photographs would hold everything in place, while their telling, and now his, keeps displacing the "facts" further and further into fictional constructs. Having indicated how the writing works, this chapter stays with the present encounter with his aunt Dolly, especially the photograph of her younger self and Lalla and other friends, which she can describe even though she can no longer see it. This is the way it is, the writing seems to say, this is the pure fact of reportage. But the similes of the final sentence put this possibility in question while once again reminding us of the fictional quality of all stories. The photograph "has moved tangible, palpable, into her brain, the way memory invades the present in those who are old, the way gardens invade houses here, the way her tiny body steps into mine as intimate as anything I have witnessed and I have to force myself to be gentle with this frailty in the midst of my embrace" (*RF,* 112). The contradictions insist on the paradoxes writing always confronts. Is memory really tangible when it invades the present? Gardens invade houses, as the descriptions of Kegalle reveal, only to speed up the process of disintegration; are memory and story examples of such disintegration in the house of "fact" or "truth"? How does the way she steps into his embrace match the way memory and gardens "invade"? If all three acts are parallel, what does that say about the frailty of memory, for example? What kind of gentleness does the writer bring to his embrace of her memories? The tropes reinforce the sense of metamorphosis attached to the whole remembering/storytelling process in this book.

No story within the book is more full of magical metamorphosis than "The Passions of Lalla." It begins with her death because that is the apotheosis of the way she lived her life—as a grand, dramatic gesture: "My Grandmother died in the blue arms of a jacaranda tree. She could read thunder" (RF, 113). Purporting to tell her life story, it in fact immediately apologizes for not being able to do so. There are claims, there are rumors, but "[t]here is no information about Lalla growing up." When she is old enough to marry, there is information, and the representation appears to hold to the decorum of factual reportage but quickly descends to the farce of gossip. As she adjusts to life as a widow with young children, the narrative voice maintains a documentary distance, yet the stories keep slipping into tall tales. A single sentence during one story about the death of the husband of Lalla's best friend indicates the oral tradition from which they all derive: "It is believed he was the victim of someone's charm" (RF, 115). The present tense implies that those who told the writer the story still speculate about what really happened. No story can be free of revision based on such speculation; all the stories are part of an ever-changing, ever-expanding, shared oral "text."

The chapter is full of comic tales of Lalla's increasingly eccentric behavior, as she took care of her dairy work by early morning and spent the rest of the day "gallivanting" while "she *also* brought up her two children" (RF, 116; emphasis added). The time schemes are complex, sliding back and forth over a large period of years, highlighting Lalla's "casual and irresponsible" (RF, 117) behavior by showing how "being used as part of [her] daily theatre" (RF, 118) affected her growing children. Lalla's ironically shocked announcement that "my mother" was "'going to marry a *Tamil!'*" anticipates the mother's similar announcement, even to "exactly the same tone and phrasing" (RF, 119), that "'Michael has become a *poet!'*" Having thus introduced himself into this story from the past, Ondaatje remarks how a person capable of generating a mass of wonderful stories can be terribly irritating to live with. Again, the syntax of a sentence undoes its apparent logic in the context of the whole narrative: "My mother, for instance, strangely, *never* spoke of Lalla to me." The force of that "strangely" itself sounds strange in the context of all the descriptions of what Lalla put her daughter through. This section of the chapter concludes with Lalla again abandoning children—now her grandchildren—in the maze because she refused "to be 'pinned down.'"

The next section deals with her meddling in the lives of her siblings, except for Evan, who "manages to escape family memory" (*RF*, 121), and therefore remains absent from stories, outside the telling of the family. A narrative shift to Lalla's later years informs us that "*We* now enter the phase when Lalla is best remembered" (emphasis added). But who does that "we" refer to? Possibly a kind of historical grouping of all the family, it also implicates us, who have been allowed to share the discoveries and delights of this singular comic narrative, and acknowledged as intimates in so far as the gossip is, precisely, intimate, of the family. Truly caught as voyeurs, gossip lovers, we can only go on reading by admitting our complicity with the writer in his unearthing of the whole story. Lalla stands beside Joyce Cary's Gully Jimson as a great comic figure, but, like Jimson, the more detail that attaches to her the more "written" she becomes. Whether all the tales are "true" or not, they assume a fictional propriety that cannot be denied, as in the case of her famous false breast, which assumes a character of its own in its wanderings.

It is her "chameleon nature" (*RF*, 124) that the collage of contradictory images seeks to create, and accomplishes precisely insofar as its various fragments do not fully add up to a singular portrait. This quality of continual metamorphosis is also present in her daughter, the writer's mother, and once he acknowledges this—"Maybe they were too similar to even recognize much of a problem, both having huge compassionate hearts that never even considered revenge or small-mindedness, both howling or wheezing with laughter over the frailest joke, both carrying their own theatre on their backs" (*RF*, 124–25)—he is able to take the final transformative step into pure invention. No longer translating stories he has been given, he instead gives back the necessary final story of her grandiose mythic death, "the great death" (*RF*, 125) she spent her final years searching for. He can conjure up her final days with her brother, oblivious to the growing flood surrounding their house. Without telling us what they actually say, he suggests with deep compassion how "they talked as they never had about husbands, lovers, his various possible marriages" (*RF*, 127), and the implications are far more moving than any listing of facts would be. When she steps outside and into the flood she didn't know was there, the narrative flows with her into "her last perfect journey" (*RF*, 128). The sentences expand, gather in a mass of details just as the flood gathers in everything it passes. Repetition and syntatic parallelism reinforce the sense of inevitability as she rushes to her apotheosis in the trees. The sentences enact the movement of the flood in terms of perception, so that although the narration is outside her, the focalization is within. Thus, in the image of her floating over the maze, "its secret spread out naked as a skeleton for her," the analogy appears to be hers while the comment on its continuing terror for her grandchildren is his. Similarly, in the final long sentence both the similes and the shortening phrases map her loss of consciousness, and when she stops, the narration stops, too: "The water here was rougher and she went under for longer and longer moments coming up with a gasp and then pulled down like bait, pulled under by something not comfortable any more, and then there was the great blue ahead of her, like a sheaf of blue wheat, like a large eye that peered towards her, and she hit it and was dead" (*RF*, 129). The sentence, indeed the whole passage, like that of Bolden's last performance, is closer to a prose poem than to conventional narrative, yet it also fulfills all the requirements of narrative, including psychological closure at the end of a chapter.

"The Prodigal" begins in the present, and seems once more to concern the writer's return. It begins with an image of the harbor as a container of contradictions. Ondaatje says he loves it because, although not wise, "it is real life. It is as sincere as a Singapore cassette" (*RF*, 133). Although the oxymoron implicit in the simile may seem a deliberate insult to both writer and reader, the analogy between the general image of the harbor as container of everything and this text cannot be ignored. And however much a Singapore cassette may be a counterfeit, the moods and emotions recorded in the counterfeit construct have their own truth. If this text is counterfeit, it is so only in terms of any single generic definition; once again, by calling itself in question it has paradoxically asserted its transgeneric "sincerity" as a comprehensive form. "Monsoon Notebook (ii)" again presents the writer writing, but the present of that writing proves as indeterminate as what is written. At first, it seems clear that the "notebook" records events in Sri Lanka, but the final paragraph slides from the "now" when the writer records (on a Singapore cassette?) the night sounds of Ceylon to "[n]ow, and here, Canadian February, I write this in the kitchen and play that section of cassette to hear not just peacocks but all the noises of the night behind them" (*RF*, 136), and then, in describing those noises and what they represent, slides back to the "now" (now past) of making the recording.

"How I Was Bathed" suddenly places the narrator in a story as another about whom stories are told. A complex subject, he both tells the story being retold, and tells the story of its telling; he is there listening to others telling of him elsewhere and elsewhen. The chapter, by calling attention to the storytelling and story-making processes, calls attention to the processes by which the whole book is being made. And it does so precisely to remind us of the complexities of narration at work in the previous stories of Lalla and the upcoming ones of the writer's father. But before he turns to the grand black farce of his father's life, he offers another glimpse of his experiences "now." "Wilpattu," with its nicely judged comedy of tourist tribulations, demonstrates how far Ondaatje has traveled from his original home even as it also reveals his sympathetic perceptions of that now-alien place. His and his family's behavior at the wildlife sanctuary marks them as foreigners, and this is confirmed when his soap disappears and the cook and tracker both tell him that the "wild pig has taken it" (*RF*, 143). It is a moment of high comedy, in which the locals play a trick on the outsider, and yet, by taking their fantasy and extending it in the same manner as his narration has extended the stories of his family, he returns to the realm of story and, within the text, transcends their contempt.

Having asserted his traces of citizenship and lulled us into a receptive mood for his own travels in Ceylon, Ondaatje turns in the chapter of that title to his father's tragicomic trips about the country. Like the stories of Lalla, the stories of Mervyn Ondaatje are as delightful to read as they would be appalling to experience. He is given to the same grand gestures as his mother-in-law, and it is suggested that he made them partly in competition with her. The writer neatly places his father in the larger history of Ceylon's railways through a falsely syllogistic connection to the nineteenth-century officer who obsessively oversaw the construction of a major road. He then retells a series of stories about his father's outrageous behavior on the trains. Every episode involves at least one other member of his family, even his wife in the infamous case of hiding naked in a tunnel; this explains why the stories are available within the family. But since they all take place in public, they scandalously enter public discourse, as well, which means they are not purely biographical but also historical. This scandal in behavior can stand as partial explanation for the scandal in literary form that the writer has perpetrated in *Running in the Family,* a book that breaks literary codes the way the father's behavior broke social ones. "In a filial gesture, the writer's language makes itself part of what it refers to, it speaks of the scandalous, of the slippages from genre to genre, from subject to subject" (Kamboureli 1988, 87).

The question of writing comes to the foreground in this chapter, for Mervyn Ondaatje not only created havoc in his drunken riots aboard trains, but also engaged in a famous feud in the visitors' books of various rest houses throughout the country. This story comes immediately after the writer notes how his mother's writing changed after she rescued her husband from the tunnel in "[a] moment only Conrad could have interpreted" (*RF,* 149), as Ondaatje so carefully puts it, allowing all the resonances of Conrad's name to play across the scene. If she seemed to have "lost the use of a habitual style and forced herself to cope with a new dark unknown alphabet" (*RF,* 150), he retained a mastery of invective that could only lead to more trouble. The literary war between Mervyn Ondaatje and Sammy Dias "broke so many codes that for the first time in Ceylon history pages had to be ripped out of visitors' books. . . . Pages continued to be torn out, ruining a good archival history of two semi-prominent Ceylon families" (*RF,* 152). The text asserts this loss of "history" in the very act of (re)creating it (where are the quotations from the first encounter? how were they preserved, if they were?). The scandal here is one of writing, of exceeding the limits of social discourse, yet it is precisely its scandalous nature that grants it a place in this text of generic excess.

The black comic fabulation of Mervyn's last train ride, accompanied by the man who would one day be prime minister, lifts the narrative up beside the story of Lalla's death, as it dramatizes both Mervyn's alcoholic paranoid fantasizing and the "rational" measures both he and everyone else aboard the train took to make sure the one car full of British officers never found out what was going on. "They slept on serenely with their rage for order in the tropics, while the train shunted and reversed into the night and there was chaos and hilarity in the parentheses around them" (*RF,* 154). But "the parentheses" are where the scandalous stories occur, and this sentence stands as a further warning of what this text is about. The climax of the story acknowledges the power of his father's imagination as he tosses all the pots of curd he believes to be bombs "into the river below, witnessing huge explosions as they smashed into the water" (*RF,* 155).

In pointing out that his father made this trip the year he was born, Ondaatje once again inserts himself as a writing subject into the story. In the next chapter, "Sir John," he and his sister visit the retired prime minister only to ask him about their father, certainly no more than a small parenthesis in his life. Yet magic accompanies him, too, as he feeds his peacocks and other pets, and adds another version of the story to the collection, another voice to the chorus. At his "legendary" breakfast, the writer barely escapes having his toe cut off by a fan, and then hears another story, this time about a truly historical figure, Sir John, which demonstrates that "scandal" can be found as easily in public life as in private. As gossip erases the boundaries of both genre and class, Ceylon emerges as a country in which all boundaries are blurred.

From the "blatantly sexual" (*RF*, 160) photograph of Sir John's story, Ondaatje turns to "the photograph I have been waiting for all my life. My father and mother together. May 1932" (*RF*, 161). A perfect image precisely because it, too, scandalizes by crossing social codes, this honeymoon photo gone astray, showing them making grotesque faces, assures the writer "that they were absolutely perfect for each other. My father's tanned skin, my mother's milk paleness, and this theatre of their own making" (*RF*, 162).[10] The photograph appears on the following page, after we have read Ondaatje's description of it, and the power of language is manifest to the extent that we "read" it in terms of that description. As "the only photograph I have found of the two of them together," it is important for the clues it offers to their behavior, their theatrical approach to life. As one of a series of photographs in the text, it testifies further to the way the book "playfully runs from one genre to another [and] deliberately postpones the naming of its genre" (Kamboureli 1988, 79). It also signals the further collapse of generic boundaries in the collation of others' stories in the final two sections. More and more, as these other voices clamor to be heard, the writer allows them their own space, to stand beside the rest, leaving him and us to pick among them, become *bricoleurs* striving to build some kind of structure that contains, that is made from, them all.

Titled after the perfect photograph, "What We Think of Married Life" scandalizes the reader by shifting its gaze to the other marriage. "Tea Country" begins with an unattributed quotation we only later discover is spoken by Ondaatje's half-sister. The "Mum" she refers to is Mervyn Ondaatje's second wife, and not the writer's mother at all. Confusion of reference reinforces the sense of familial and ontological instability in the text. Visiting with his half-sister and her husband, the writer experiences both the dangers and the overwhelming fertility of the natural surroundings, and then imaginatively reaches back to his own parents' lives in the same place: "This is the colour of landscape, this is the silence, that surrounded my parents' marriage" (*RF,* 167). But the title chapter begins again in the present, seeking to engage the dynamics of that marriage by contrast. Out of the contrast between the "calmness and quietness" of his half-sister and "the anger and argument which I see in myself, my brother, and two sisters" (*RF,* 168), he begins to construct an inheritance, recognizing that "it is from my mother's side that we got a sense of the dramatic, the . . . ham in us. While from my father, in spite of his temporary manic public behaviour, we got our sense of secrecy, the desire to be reclusive."

From this double inheritance, Ondaatje constructs two opposed traditions of reading and behavior that find contradictory expression in both him and his book. If much of the entertainment in this text owes its existence to those Gratiaen women who "would take the minutest reaction from another and blow it up into a tremendously exciting tale, then later use it as an example of someone's strain of character" (*RF,* 169), its sudden ellipses and autobiographical silence come from the father's devious secrecy. Yet, as the analysis continues, we realize that the writer is offering, through examples of both parents' behavior, a kind of insight into his own actions *in both the narrative and the narrating of this text.* By dramatically describing how his mother used the children to shame his father and how his father used charm and humor to repair the social damage caused by his drinking bouts, Ondaatje reproduces these two models of writing as an act of generic slippage in the site of the open text. But he also points out the price both his parents paid for living so fully the roles they had chosen, for they had lost all the wealth and prestige attached to their families' names by the time they were divorced. Ondaatje concludes his tale of family disintegration with the fortune-teller's prediction that his mother would never see all of her children together again, which turned out to be true. The explanation offered is simultaneously a rebuke and a boast: "Magnetic fields would go crazy in the presence of more than three Ondaatjes. And my father. Always separate until he died, away from us. The north pole" (*RF,* 172). The final comment is a confession of loss.

"Dialogues" contains eleven recorded statements about the writer's mother and father. With its various voices and stories it neatly models the dialogic structure of the whole text, as various unidentified "I"s step into the foreground just long enough to provide another view of the protagonists. Like the writer, each of these speakers is given to gesture, but as all these separate gestures accumulate, it becomes less and less possible to assign any single meaning to them. The book continues to evade generic generalization, as they register a sense of compassion and love for both parents, revealing each one's ability to elicit love from friends and family.

"Blind Faith" opens with an inclusive "we" that implicates us in the text's attempts at interpretation. Not just his but "our job becomes to keep peace with enemy camps, eliminate the chaos at the end of Jacobean tragedies, and with 'the mercy of distance' write the histories" (*RF*, 179). Perhaps. But the next paragraph retreats to the personal as the "I" makes an ambiguous list connecting Shakespeare's tragic studies of father and son disunions with himself and his siblings. *King Lear* raises the most troubling question: "why of Shakespeare's cast of characters do I remain most curious about Edgar? Who if I look deeper into the metaphor, torments his father over an imaginary cliff." Suddenly, in a text that has continually called the representational powers of memory, fact, fiction, writing, and language itself into question, the writer points to the emptiness of conceptual words "such as *love, passion, duty*" and acknowledges that he "never knew what my father felt of these 'things.' My loss was that I never spoke to him as an adult." But fiction may allow what fact denies. Dreaming of "the moment in the play where Edgar reveals himself to Gloucester [, a moment that] never happens," he seems to write what Edgar would say, but is he Edgar, or is Edgar he, speaking directly to his father, wanting "to say I am writing this book about you at a time when I am least sure about such words. . . . Give me your arm. Let go my hand. Give me your arm. Give the word. 'Sweet Marjoram' . . . a tender herb" (*RF,* 180).[11] The slippage here between autobiographical and dramatic identification creates a moment of intense compassion and desire, a moment only possible in this text, as he writes it.

Shifting from Lear's heath to a similar landscape of dream or fiction, "The Bone" recalls the dream from the first page of the text proper, but now it is "a story about my father I cannot come to terms with," another "one of the versions of his train escapade" (*RF,* 181). As "story," "versions," and "dream" collide, they lose all documentary validity in the midst of hallucination. Is it invention or fact? We are left to decide, and I suspect we change our minds with each reading, depending upon what other parts of the text have stuck in our minds. Presenting the dramatically terrible figure of "the naked man who held [the dogs] at arm's length, towards whom they swung like large dark magnets" (*RF,* 182), it points away from the inadvertent farceur of the earlier train comedies toward the silent solitary the son will identify with in the act of composition.

The final section begins in loss and depression but does not end there. "Thanikama" is all invention, for there can be no stories about the solitary despair Mervyn Ondaatje lived through after the divorce. With subtle understatement, the writing represents the father in the third person, drinking, wondering what to do, remembering fragments of the stories inscribed in earlier sections of the text, driving back from Colombo to Kegalle, picking up a cinnamon peeler—in "a scene that had inspired (or been inspired by) a poem that the son had written and that we had read over ninety pages earlier" (Hutcheon 1988, 92)—and finally returning to his empty home to lie, sleepless and despairing, looking for the book he had been reading. The *mise-en-abyme* here unites writing son and written father in a self-reflexive loop of psychological identification. First, in a startling shift of pronouns, the "he" of the father remembering old friends from the earlier gossip becomes for one sentence the "I" sitting "on the bed like a lost ship on a white sea" (*RF*, 188). Then, as he looks for "his book . . . not Shakespeare, not those plays of love he wept over too easily," he finds "the novel" (i.e., the fiction) attacked by ants, a "whole battalion" of which are "carrying one page away from its source, carrying the intimate print as if rolling a tablet away from him" (*RF*, 189). If the son sought Shakespeare to help explain his complex connection to his father, now the father avoids Shakespeare in order not to confront the utter separation he has achieved. Instead, he finds another sign of separation, which he accepts with the same fatalism with which he accepted the failure of his wife to meet him earlier in the day: "He knelt down on the red tile, slowly, not wishing to disturb their work. It was page *189*. He had not got that far in the book yet but he surrendered it to them. . . . The white rectangle moved with the busy arduous ants. Duty, he thought. But that was just a fragment gazed at by the bottom of his eye." "Duty" recalls the writer's difficulty in believing such words only ten pages back while the disappearing page of the book within the text is the very page—"189"—we are reading. A wholly invented identification and displacement occur simultaneously in a gap between document and gossip, where only fictive imagination can operate.

Turning the page, we find "Monsoon Notebook (iii), "in which the writer writing assures himself of the materiality of his endeavor and the world in which he pursues it. But like the written father, the writing son is situated in "dry black night. 'Thanikama.' 'Aloneness'" (*RF*, 190).

The difference is that he is writing: "At midnight this hand is the only thing moving. . . . Watch the hand move." The imperative implicates us with the writer as subjects of the writing process, subject to it as it happens.

"Final Days / Father Tongue" returns to other voices, this time carefully identified, the "truth" of documentation implied. Jennifer, another half-sister, speaks directly to the writer. The intimacy of her address achieves a precariously balanced evaluation of their father's generous love in his later years: "He missed you all terribly, he longed for you, but with us—his second family—he was just as loving" (*RF*, 194). The portrait that emerges from her, and his friends', last memories is of a man fighting the demons that destroyed his earlier life and winning just enough to carry on. These other stories have less of the quality of caricature about them than the anecdotes of the aunts, and thus they add touches of chiaroscuro to the final, complex, portrait of the man about whom the whole book has continually circled.

Given the wide range of evidence, the writer cannot easily sum up his father, and the fragmentary collage structure of the book attests to his refusal to do so. Yet, he seeks something like an explanation, and finds it in the words of another poet: "I keep thinking of the lines from Goethe . . . 'Oh, who will heal the sufferings / Of the man whose balm turned poison?' I can only clarify this range in him by focussing on this metamorphosis" (*RF*, 198). As he recognizes how well his father could fool his children, Ondaatje extends the imagery of "Letters and Other Worlds" into narrative, finding the human and even tragicomic narrative that transcends the earlier poem's despair. Yet narrative or lyric can only go so far: "There is so much to know and we can only guess. Guess around him" (*RF*, 200). Once again that "we" implicates us with the writer in the endeavor, and if we have stayed with the text this far we cannot refuse the appeal. The continual pronominal slippage from "I" to "you" to "we" to another "you" in the final paragraph indicates that "the book is again incomplete" (*RF*, 201). Its undecidability rests in the inability of anyone to know another fully, and in the writer's recognition that the only perspectives he can offer are partial, fragments of various genres jostling one another for preeminence and all equally incapable of rendering "the truth."

"Last Morning" conjures a moment of infinite possibility, before the writing and shaping begin (and end). "My body must remember everything" (*RF*, 202), the writer thinks, but also "I want this emptiness of a dark room where I listen and wait" (*RF*, 202–3). Past and present mingle in the moment between night and day, in the moment of transition: "There is nothing in this view that could not be a hundred years old, that might not have been here when I left Ceylon at the age of eleven" (*RF,* 203. In the eternal present of writing, mother and father continue to live *now,* and in that now, memory and creation become one. Images of poison and music mix in the final paragraph of the text to remind us that it could finally make no demarcation between them in the life stories it gathered, in an order but not necessarily the only order to grant some understanding of their relationships.[12] The congested vitality of "all this Beethoven and rain" implies that the end of writing is just the beginning of reading, again.

Chapter Seven
Secular Love

Ondaatje's acknowledgments page to *Secular Love,* with its laconic "Thanks to friends in the clutch" and "Bellrock-Toronto-Honolulu-Colombo-Blyth-Collingwood-Madoc 1978–1983,"[1] reveals that its poems and poem sequences were a major part of his writing life while he worked on *Running in the Family.* It also invites speculation about their autobiographical content, which the individual poems also feed. Nevertheless, the subject of all these speculations is a written one, and to that extent a creature of invention. This is not to deny that there are strong autobiographical elements in these poems; it is to argue that they succeed or fail as poems and not as gossip.

Ondaatje sees *Secular Love* as "'a novel.' . . . its structure and plot are novelistic . . . [yet its figures] are drawn in a lyric, perceived by a lyric eye" (Solecki 1984, 324). Patricia J. Eberle argues that *Secular Love* seeks "a new kind of coherence as it follows the course of the current of feelings involved in a personal breakdown and the end of a marriage."[2] The "novelistic" structure and plot do render a complex story of the destruction of a marriage and the rediscovery of love with another, but the assumption that the first section "describes *Ondaatje's* feelings during a party at his house one evening when everything seemed to be 'slipping away' " (Eberle, 75; emphasis added) seems a bit simplistic. In fact, in all the sections of the book, the writer is very careful not to name any of the central actors in the drama,[3] granting them the fictional freedom implied by his choice of the term *novel.*

Secular Love is divided into four sections. "Claude Glass" and "Tin Roof" are single medium-length poems; "Rock Bottom" is a sequence of linked lyrics; and "Skin Boat" is a collection of separately titled poems that are nevertheless carefully ordered into a larger unit that brings the collection as a whole to a satisfying, if open, conclusion. The main sequence of narrative events is carefully kept at the level of implication while other, smaller, narratives occupy the foreground and complicate the obvious "plot" with implied connections among characters and their changing environments. Even as a novel, the book fragments and deconstructs conventional narrative, substituting intense lyric moments of perception for the gradual construction of insight that story allows and seeks. As in all his other longer works, Ondaatje invokes generic distinctions here only to confuse them in the actual writing. The borders are blurred, as usual.

I always read the title "Claude Glass" as an odd name.[4] But no, the epigraph explains that it's a special kind of dark mirror "used to concentrate the features of the landscape in subdued tones" (SL, [11]). The third-person protagonist of the poem is himself a kind of dark mirror, reflecting and distorting the features of his personal surroundings, including both landscape and people. Immediately establishing a distance between narrator and narratee reinforces the generic breakdown between fiction and autobiography that will be maintained in various ways throughout the book. The poem begins after its action is complete, setting up the rest of it as a complex series of analepses: "He is told about / the previous evening's behaviour" (SL, 13). This sounds like a singular situation, but the series of present participles suggests that neither the party nor the behavior are one-time-only events. The behavior is drunken, mean, excited, possibly desperate, certainly angry, and also blackly comic at times. Throughout, the syntax creates ambiguities that raise questions without answering them and make it quite unclear at times who is doing what.

Even if we read the first verse paragraph as referring to a single night, within that time there are other conditional possibilities, and the tense shifts mime a drunken slipperiness of focus as they move from "he has always loved that ancient darkness . . . where he can remove clothes" to "as he moves in back fields . . . and then stands to watch the house" (SL, 14). Beyond the ambiguity of tense there are other syntactical slippages, as in the image of him lying "with moonlight on the day's heat / hardened in stone, drowning / in this star blanket this sky / like a giant trout" (SL, 14). The modulations of the text here—in which moonlight or heat or "he" could be "hardened in stone," while all three or the stone could be drowning, and then whoever is drowning or the sky might be "like a giant trout"—thoroughly dissipate any possibility of a single meaning. The text resists interpretive analysis, as such.

It also continually sets up echoes and reiterations that maintain a sense of narrative, however dislocated. Yet the sense of disintegration exceeds the poem's power to hold things together: "And he knows something is happening there to him / solitary while he spreads his arms / and holds everything that is slipping away together" (SL, 14). Is he holding everything together as he desires or only holding on to everything that together is slipping away? The apparent statement of power dissolves into an admission of none. A similar attempt at bravado falls apart in the following stanza, where he once again enters the continuing world of the present participle, "slouching towards women, revolving / round one unhappy shadow,"[5] which may be his or that of the friend waving from "the darkest place." Again, the insistence that "[h]e is not a lost drunk / like his father or his friend, can, / he says, stop on a dime, and he can / he could" stumbles on that slip from "can" to "could," implying at least the possibility that the "could" of the past is no longer the asserted "can" of the present.

For readers of *Running in the Family,* the references to son and daughter, to a drunken father, imply that the "he" is an autobiographical subject. But the writing subject is displaying the written subject as a figure of invention as much as of memory. The linguistic echoes, the sudden shifts of point of view and tone, and the various intertexts, including Salinger's Glass family stories, Yeats's poem, and Phyllis Webb's "Naked Poems,"[6] as well as the darker tales in *Running in the Family,* all recall us to the poem as written performance rather than transparent rendering of a given autobiographical history.

The poem is something of an emotional roller coaster, leaping up to highs as soon as it hits lows. In "this brilliant darkness," at least the protagonist knows "the hour of magic / which no matter what sadness / leaves him grinning." The world refuses to let anyone with perception escape fully into depression or self-pity. Yet within that magic, the animal night of species warfare continues while his desires go unassuaged. Returning to narrative, the poem presents more images of self-destructive behavior at the party and further examples of what he lacks and wants (*SL,* 15). The tone keeps sliding from humor to anger to pain, with no single emotion allowed to dominate, as the man keeps struggling over and over again out of the house and into nature. But he cannot escape the human and technological, no matter where he goes or what he desires, as the simile of "blood like a cassette through the body" (*SL,* 16) suggests. He may remove his clothes, but the inner man is implicated in civilization even to the way he images the circulation of his blood.

In a parallel action, his "desire to be riverman," makes him remember "his drunk invitation to the river," an invitation only made possible because he "steered the awesome car" to its banks. A contained flashback, this stanza makes the by-now expected gesture of escaping the party only to return. A complex image of an outdoor slide show follows, but the sheet collapses and the "pictures fly without target / and howl their colours over Southern Ontario" (SL, 17), giving him the slip, like everything else in his purview. Despite his loss of coherence, the exhilaration of "[l]andscapes and stories / flung into branches" and across animals and birds has a transformative energy. By its shifts of tone and image, the poem continues to invoke contradictory feelings from stanza to stanza, line to line. Bleak desperation is not allowed to be the only, and somehow "true," mood of the poem.

"Rivers of the world meet" and local waters become foreign when Asia is projected onto them. The poem shifts direction once again, to deal with a specific time, as "he wakes in the sheet / that earlier held tropics in its whiteness" (SL, 18). By metaphoric overlap, the sheet and the invited river have become one, and when that river "flows through the house" and "he awakens" again "and moves within it," the second waking renders moot any judgment as to whether the vision is "real" or a dream. It is textual, and recalls earlier texts (the "river he has walked elsewhere" is the Depot Creek of "Walking to Bellrock," as the list of places where the poems of *Secular Love* were written implies). The image of the river washes everything in the house clean, but even inside the image "he" can only *wish* "to swim / to each of his family and gaze / at their underwater dreaming." The desire expressed in "wants" and "wishes" negates itself, but even if he got his wish he would remain apart from those he loves, because "for hours / there has been no conversation" (SL, 19), no connection with them.

Read that way, the poem seems once again to present a figure cut off from friends and family, in fact "a lost drunk" (SL, 14). But imagination refused defeat, and the text insists he is "the sentinel, / shambling back and forth, his anger / and desire against the dark" (SL, 19). This image of the undaunted warrior, the protector of the hearth, cannot sustain itself, possibly because anger and desire mix contradictorily in the effort that contains its own defeat: he has closed his eyes, and, given one waking within another, how are we to know that he is awake, eyes open, even now? Each sentence within the text makes sense, but together they create contradictions and enigmas. Even in its final few lines, the poem continues to alter all it touches, gathering an image of its own process into the aural pun of "[c]reak and echo"[7] as it moves to an apparent conclusion that resolves nothing: "With absolute clarity / he knows where he is." But the only clarity of this poem is that of its fragmented vision, not of its overall insight, and we cannot decide even if he is awake or asleep, let alone where precisely he might be.

As the title's dictionary meaning suggests, "Claude Glass" offers a richly chiaroscuro vision, full of contrasts, dark brooding, crazy laughter, and, more than likely, distortions. Its subject is not so much lost as at a loss, cut off from former connections, however much he desires to maintain them, yet without any new ones to hold on to. This poem leaves him in limbo, but it is only the first of four parts; later ones will take him out of that lonely place in one direction or another. Despite its period, the ending is an open door.

Ondaatje reveals his gift for finding exactly the right epigraph throughout *Secular Love*. A wryly comic quotation from Elmore Leonard prepares us for the homage to and subversion of romantic tough guys in "Tin Roof," while suggesting that it will *try* "to tell you how I feel without exposing myself" (*SL,* 21). Feelings will be important here, but also ploys of self-protection; and the first of these is once again to project subjectivity onto some other pronoun than the first person: "You stand still for three days / for a piece of wisdom / and everything falls to the right place // or wrong place" (*SL,* 23). This "you" appears to represent the "I" who appears later, but it is also the generalized "one" who is everybody, and it might even be the other whom the poem comes to address more and more as it proceeds. Neither figure nor ground is fixed in this passage, which thus pulls the rug out from under the final assertion of "Claude Glass." Both the identity of the subject and "where he is" are suddenly unclear, and as the next stanza emphasizes, "you" may speak, but you "don't know" anything, let alone "whether / seraph or bitch / flutters at your heart." The poem begins in complete uncertainty.

Parataxis interrupts rather than adds to any sense of unified flow, while the sudden intrusion of the first person underlines the sense of interruption and fragmentation, even as it offers an apparently sincere confession: "This last year I was sure / I was going to die." We can but do not have to read this final couplet as a comment on the previous poem. Connections are hinted at but never made absolute. Parataxis becomes the operating mode of the whole sequence, each section fragmenting narrative and pronominal reference, although some tentative connections of image and mood emerge by implication.

The second section is a first-person description of the writer's cabin at night, but the third section throws the subject into the third person. These continual pronominal shifts signal a profound uncertainty in the text as to the autobiographical agenda of the poem. Equally indetermi-

nate is the way the poem attends with great care to the specifics of
perception and action in each small fragment while refusing to tie them
up in a single narrative knot. Questions go unanswered, deictic pointers
fail to clarify the situations they apparently point to, everything remains
in flux like the ocean, which figures throughout as a kind of symbol of
uncontrollable change, "the unknown magic he loves / throws himself
into // the blue heart" (*SL*, 25).

Each section seems self-sufficient and works as a separate gesture, yet
none can really stand alone. "Tin Roof" comes closer to matching the
definition of a serial poem than anything else Ondaatje has written,[8] for
its unity depends upon an implicit narrative of the writing rather than
any explicit narrative, which is at best only hinted at, of the written story
of some part of one person's "life." And perhaps the pronominal shifts are
one way it seeks to avoid the conventional egotism of the speaker in
traditional lyrics. As in his earlier long poems about other figures,
Ondaatje has created a forum for various voices in "Tin Roof," achieving
a dialogic heteroglossia that is "novelized" in the Bakhtinian sense
(Bakhtin, 324–31). The various deliberately prosaic passages, let alone
the tone of questions like "Do you want / to be happy and write?" (*SL*,
27), implicate language "as a social phenomenon that is becoming in
history, socially stratified and weathered in this process of becoming"
(Bakhtin, 326).

If each section seems unconnected to the others, sometimes the lines
and stanzas within the sections break apart as well. The slippage from the
almost Japanese images of "[i]llicit pockets of / the kimono" and "[h]eart
like a sleeve"[9] to the image of "[t]he cabin / its tin roof / a wind run
radio / [that] catches the nose of the world" (*SL*, 28) suggests both the
diversity and the unity of the poem. Like a radio, its subject focuses many
different voices and points of view into one ongoing discourse. Whether
"I" or "you" or "he," this subject swerves among possibilities, and keeps
finding reasons to keep functioning.

The ocean offers both life and death, but the possibility of love keeps
leading him back to the former: "What protects him / is the warmth in
the sleeve." But if love protects the subject *in* the text, the refusal of
the confessional mode protects the subject *of* the text, as he slips once
more into another pronominal presence, slips away from our regard even
in the act of making moral pronouncements: "We go to the stark places
of the earth / and find moral questions everywhere" (*SL*, 29). There we are
with him and all we find is the movie on tv we could have watched at
home. Is the reference to *Red River* serious or comic? It's impossible to

decide, just as it's impossible to know if the later couplet, "[t]here are those who are in / and there are those who look in" refers to the moral questions of the film, to the "I" and the geckos, or to the writer and his readers.

The text creates linkages in the allusions to old movies, the self-reflexive comments on writing and other writers, and the increasingly specific references to the presence of the new beloved. The first two join when the text shifts from *Red River* to *Casablanca,* presenting both as examples of moral behavior in a tone neither ironic nor simply straightforward. Yet if the heroes of these films are one kind of exemplar, so too is the poet Rilke, not referred to specifically until the final section, yet first hinted at in "the bird whistling *duino* / duino, words and music / entangled in pebble / ocean static" (*SL,* 31). This passage actually manages to connect three aspects of the text in one metaphor of the world radio, the destructive ocean, and the commitment to writing.

Only in section 10, more than halfway through the poem, does the writer abruptly introduce the physical presence of the lover, first in the third person and in a gesture that signals both eroticism and strength: "her feet braced / on the ceiling / sea in the eye" (*SL,* 32). One sign of Ondaatje's growing antilyric stance in these poems is the minimal manner in which he presents complex systems of perception. The image of "sea in the eye" suggests both a reflection and an inner energy and power, which later sections of the poem will emphasize. One of Ondaatje's typical subjectless sentences, this one concerning an ancient report on gout that "speaks / of 'vain efforts / and deceitful promises,' " could refer to the behavior of the subject of "Claude Glass" as much as to the fears of the subject of "Tin Roof." But the potential for problems enunciated in the quotation is forgotten in the sudden shift to direct address to the lover's body. The ribald good humor of "Good / morning to your body" soon gives way to more serious analogies in which that body becomes the world itself. (*SL,* 33).

Now the subject assumes the first person to talk of her and of their passion, which he cannot know will last but which he accepts "precarious in all our fury" (*SL,* 34). The plain style of this section argues its sincerity, but like all literary sincerity, it is carefully crafted, and nowhere can the craft be seen more clearly than in the spaces between stanzas, the luminous silences they imply. Although the lover still barely exists as a character since she is present only in his perceptions of her, the openings where she does not speak but can be imagined tend to novelize the text. It invokes our active imaginative invention precisely by what it leaves out, and by its continuing appeal to us when the "I" includes her in his "we." The self-reflexive reference to "maps now whose portraits / have nothing to do with surface," that is "bathymetric maps" (*SL,* 36) of ocean depths, finally offers a guide to its own reading. It insists that a "you" who could be either the lover or the reader remember images we know only because the text inscribes them. This uncertainty of reference is central to the poem's effect. For example, some of the lines address not the lover but the writer, such as "(Ah you should be happy and write)," and who then speaks them (*SL,* 37)? "His" answer to both the order and the question—"No I am not happy // lucky though"—is proof that he is writing, yet what he writes keeps arguing against what he appears to be writing. The voices are too mixed, as well as mixed up, to fit any conventional definition of lyric speech, just as the shocking contradiction of his desire for "the passion / which puts your feet on the ceiling / this fist / to smash forward" takes the text "out of the rooms of poetry."

The series of toasts to nipples, kneecaps, and long legs are another kind of discourse, contradicted immediately by the "slam [of] her car door" and the transition into the too lyric cry of "wrote my hunger out, the balcony / like an entrance / to a city of suicides" (*SL,* 38). But no longer able to believe that language, he offers another somewhat comic toast and simply acknowledges by continuing the poem that he will never go beyond "the edge / of the trough of this city" (*SL,* 39). The form of "Tin Roof" denies traditional lyric subjectivity even as it continues to explore traditional lyric themes. In the penultimate section, the conditionality of "I could write my suite of poems / for Bogart drunk / six months after the departure at Casablanca" (*SL,* 40) confirms the fictional drive of the whole. The pronominal slippage in the savagely comic fantasy from third to first person and then from character to writer reinforces the narrative uncertainty that has been active throughout the poem. Although it sees *Casablanca* and *Trapese* ironically, the text suggests their emotional validity, thereby harnessing popular culture and its discourse to its own complex emotional project. The final lines (in which we are implicated, but which clearly address the lover within the text), with their references to "complexities / and commandments" (*SL,* 41), move to a more profound awareness than the endings of either movie addressed.

Having appealed to popular film, the text finally appeals to the great wise poetry of Rilke's *Duino Elegies* and of Phyllis Webb.[10] The tenses argue a complicated renunciation, as "I want" retreats to "I always wanted poetry to be that / but this solitude brings no wisdom / just two day old food in the fridge, / certain habits you would not approve of" (*SL,*

42). Desiring identity with Rilke, his grand romanticism, he only discovers difference: "I want / the line to move slowly now, slow- / ly like a careful drunk across the street / no cars in the vicinity / but in his fearful imagination." Having to address Rilke as "you," as other, he can still imagine "the machinery of the night / . . . sweeping *our* determination / away with its tail. *Us* and the coffee, / all the small charms *we* invade it with" (*SL*, 43; emphasis added). If the two poets join to "remember the colour / of the dogwood flower growing / like a woman's sex outside the window," the erotic charge of that image drives the writer back into the singular self that "wanted poetry to be walnuts" but finds "it is the sea / and we let it drown us, / and we fly to it released / by giant catapults / of pain loneliness deceit and vanity." This last "we" may include Rilke, but it certainly includes the lovers, and may even allow us to identify with its assessment if we wish to. The poem as performative statement insists upon its chaotic and open nature. It is not a small closed world, but rather a large and welcoming one, as the ambiguities of the final lines reveal: the catapults may be made of "pain loneliness deceit and vanity" or may release us from them, but either way they send us back into poetry, back into this poem, even. It surges and changes like the sea, but it offers a kind of release that the closure of lyric would deny. In this book, it also opens a gate to what follows.

The poems of "Rock Bottom," especially those with titles, seem to stand more on their own, yet they also are part of a sequence mapping a period of personal change but continually shifting in terms of focalization, point of view, and pronominal indeterminacy. The writer appears more often as "I" here, addressing the lover as "you," but that "you" is open, sometimes clearly her, sometimes the generalized "one," and always capable of including us as we read. Sometimes from one line to the next, the "you" will shift to "her" as if unwilling to admit the intimacy "you" assumes. Some of the lyrics in this section have little obvious connection to the implied narrative of marital breakup and extramarital passion, yet they all fit into the whole. As perceived moments of change and process within the temporal boundaries of such a narrative, they render the "truth" that life does go on around the emotional upheavals such an affair causes.

The epigraph to part 1, by Robert Creeley, speaks to the sincerity of the declarative voice of love, which takes the foreground in the following lyrics. It is a voice confused, searching for some coherence in life and feeling but finding little, although what it does find, as the sequence goes on, is in relation to the new lover. Parataxis, sudden shifts of thought and perception, ambiguities of reference, and oddly aphoristic statements are the operative formal qualities of these poems. There are a few connective images, such as the moonlight invoked in the first line of the first poem (*SL,* 47), which surfaces at various times throughout and then attaches itself firmly to the lover in the final poem (*SL,* 82–83). But in some ways it is precisely the lack of connections that holds the narrative together, revealing the uncertainties inherent in the changes the protagonist has brought upon himself. The general lack of geographic markers emphasizes the novelistic rather than the autobiographical aspects of the sequence.

"Rock Bottom" begins as night thoughts, the jumble of desire and insight that comes to the person sleeplessly confronting the possibility that an affair elsewhere will go on and change his life. Desire is strong yet not clearly focused, as the typographical separation of "I want," ambiguously referring back to "what I know of passion" and forward to "the woman whose face / I could not believe in the moonlight" (*SL,* 47), indicates. But there was passion, "and both of us/ grim with situation" are caught up in its effects. The traditional appeal to art once again enters the realm of popular culture, the extremely short lines of the final stanza themselves implicating the lovers in the uncertainties they face, residing "near the delicate / heart / of Billie Holiday." The evocative power of this image, of finding a possible home near the core of a singer's vision of love and loss, hinges on the ambiguous relation of "delicate" to Billie Holiday's life and music.[11]

The poems move between addressing the lover and commenting on the ongoing life the writer leads. He fulfills the conventional role of a married lover well enough insofar as all the lyrics reflect his sense of his changed status. The writing, meanwhile, enacts the processes of desiring memory. A poem will slide easily from memory to action, as when his lover "said, this / doesn't happen so quick" (*SL,* 48), and he replies in the present tense, aware both then, when he was with her, and now, when he writes the scene, of "all the hunger / I didn't know I had." But the next lyric ironically places him in a summer domesticity of sorts, floating on an inner tube and seeing the world and "a blue heron . . . upside down" (*SL,* 49). This image of overturned perceptions leads to the more general question of which "of us is wrong // he / in his blue grey thud / thinking he knows / the blue way / out of here // or me," but the implied intertext with Ondaatje's own earlier poems on herons poignantly emphasizes the desperation he identifies with in seeking to find "the blue way / out of here" and out of the difficulties the affair has created.

The next few poems confront those difficulties, revealing a man feeling ever more trapped in his present situation. Formally, the choice of the man as a protagonist in this story of a disintegrating marriage is not new,[12] but Ondaatje's various methods of retaining distance from while invoking interest in his subject undermine the conventional figure somewhat. They include adapting the emotional understatement of hard-boiled writing to his purposes and extending certain syntactical tricks, such as dropping the subjects of verbs so as to create greater ambiguities of reference in what otherwise appear to be straightforward sentences. Similes and images that almost pass as "natural" statements also help to establish the emotional outlines of the poems: "The screen door in its suspicion / allows nothing in, as I allow nothing in" (*SL*, 50). That this insistence on refusing emotion is a carefully assumed mask emerges in the final image, where "the raspberries my son gave me," forgotten in his shirt pocket until late at night, become "the stain at my heart / caused by this gift" (*SL*, 50). This part of the book deals, precisely, with "the stain at my heart" caused by conflicting desires and loyalties.

Devastation materializes in the destruction "I" wreaks against himself and his home. Although his excesses seem too romantic (and even self-serving), his ironic statement that he is not exaggerating effects a slip away from pure lyric cry. As well, the simile "they were acts when words failed / the way surgeons / hammer hearts gone still" (*SL*, 55), maintains the central sense that his behavior is governed by his heart, while reminding us that in the act of writing words do not fail as they do within the written story. The glass sliver "on its voyage out / to the heart" will return (*SL*, 70); it, too, is a kind of inscription, in the body and the text.

Ironies play across many of these poems. His own behavior, as he continues to paint it, lacks a certain grace that romantic heroes are supposed to have. The periods after every word in the poem about Aeneas keeping "All. His. / Troubles. To. Himself" (*SL*, 58) score a series of pauses in the speech, while signaling a kind of psychological siege mentality. Each word is walled off from its neighbors. The poem is one of the few in which other voices get to speak for themselves, against the writer. He only gets to confess his own problems by letting two other voices speak of them in reference to the hero of an ancient masculine quest who betrayed his lover.

Throughout these poems the discourse seems "natural" and simple. The images and analogies appear to emerge from the ordinary activities of the writer, yet they are so varied and implicate such a wide range of knowledge that they have to be carefully constructed. What brings them all into the one inscribed space is the obsessive love that propels the poem, but their variety insists upon its written character. The argument he develops from "this small map / of stars" (*SL,* 59), for example, reverses the normal sense of distance in the sky and on earth, evokes the romantic worship of lovers, plays off the ancient connection between macrocosmic and microcosmic bodies to develop a delightful image of a bed in the sky (which becomes her bed "among" moonlight), and finally grounds the whole speculation in the language of astronautic technology. All this just to insist that they are separate and cannot touch each other. Or can they? The "('Envoi')" reiterates the night sky, "this tree of stars / map of the dreadful night" (*SL,* 60), as an image of hope and desire, for it stretches across the world to fall "over two children / and a woman driving." It seems they are driving in that faraway place, but there is some uncertainty as to where they may be going, which later sections will build on to suggest that they have begun a journey toward the writer. The final quatrain of part 1 leaves everything up in the air: "so this gratitude / friendship and / a little lust / for her left thigh via you." Since the lover is the third person here, the "you" might be the galaxy, but the title suggests it might be the poem itself, and if that is the case we readers may also be addressed in it.

The epigraph to part 2, "from *Cosmic Encounter, Rules to Expansion Set #5,*" refers to "this moon" and to "a player's past game performance or future game potential" (*SL,* 61). This neatly encapsulates the writer's predicament as he attempts to leave the old game and enter the new one the affair has made possible. Part 2 opens up both spatially and temporally, becoming more "social" as it moves to encounters with his lover, problems with his family, and what appear to be asides unconnected to the specific story although caught up in the themes its enactment explores. It begins with unanswerable or at least unanswered questions as the lovers drive through the Napa Valley. Places and lovers ambiguously share a state of being "stunned   lost" (*SL,* 63), but in their physical closeness the "blackness entering the car" has no power and under the light of "a star arch of dashboard" (an apt example of Ondaatje's ability to create new images of mythic dimensions out of the clutter of contemporary technology) he can celebrate her presence in a joyous affirmation: "I love this muscle / that tenses / and joins / the accelerator / to my cheek."

In the context of such affirmation, an interesting, and sometimes problematic, mixture of allusive and argumentative language occurs. In one fragment, he can say "there is nothing / I have taken from you / so I begin with memory / as old songs do," proceed to evoke the power of memory and song "to make ourselves whole," and then show them in action in the emblem of "your bright eyes / in a greek bar, the way / you wear your hat" (*SL,* 68). The light touch of the final allusion[13] gives the whole statement an aura of romantic comedy, but the next small attempt at explanation fails to maintain that light tone and, despite its playful acknowledgment of the lyric trope of love as an affliction, does not achieve a deeper romantic sincerity. Indeed, the playful allusions seem more sincere.

The pain of that sliver of glass provokes a troubling imperative—"let us go / under / loons going blind / going nowhere / murmuring heartbeat heartbeat" (*SL,* 70)—in which the confusing rush of thought and association intertwines intertextually with Buddy and Robin swimming "into the darkness into the complications" (*CTS,* 69). At this point in the story depressions still follow high moments. In the midst of emotional changes, the indecisive writer is "unable to make anything of this / who are these words for" (*SL,* 71), a confession that even the writing sometimes fails him. This moment of *mise-en-abyme,* in which the writing suggests it is occurring simultaneously with the action it records, leads to a discomforting final quatrain in which he admits whispering her name to the one member of the family who cannot betray his secret, the dog. This is one of the few moments where the text suddenly displays the negative moral effects of the affair upon the protagonist. It's not surprising, therefore, that he feels the need to defend both the writing and the loving in the next segment, where he declares that he does not own her, nor she him. By making this prosaic explanation in terms of writing, of "your fiction / or my story" (*SL,* 72), he simultaneously and paradoxically denies and affirms the autobiographical nature of the text. His assertion that "your entrance" scatters " 'poetic skill,' 'duty' " (*SL,* 73) similarly undermines and affirms the sense of invention in the poem. That invention is displayed in the way the epic simile of the snail's "journey over your shoulder" is transformed into a more complex one where "busy as snails / . . . / we enter each other's shells / the way humans at such times / wish to enter mouths of lovers" (*SL,* 74). The image of humans acting like snails in order to act like human lovers reveals the complexity of their relationship at a point "where the horizon [of her mouth]" (see *SL,* 47) is a sign of potential exploration of a still unknown future.

The contradictions of the title "(The Desire Under the Elms Motel)" comically undercut the potential tragedy of infidelity, which is, after all, what the affair is. The poem begins in a kind of comedy of eros, but as his attempt at seduction through playing a superior Canadian folk-rock group is displaced by her successful seduction simply through being herself, it reaches a kind of honest celebration of the power of love. Further allusions to romantic music of all kinds lead back to a dark awareness of the pain his actions are causing others. Speaking as a writer who has "lost the feather of poetry" (*SL*, 77), he nevertheless inscribes himself as a dramatic subject, telling his lover of his "wife's suffering / anger in every direction / and the children wise / as tough shrubs / but they are not tough." The final contradiction here suddenly undercuts the poet's attempt to salvage the situation in words; the words are inadequate to what he recognizes, and all he can say is that he is afraid, and does not know "how anything can grow from this." For the character in the story, awareness of others' pain is worthy; for the writer of the story in which he is a character, it is more complex and less noble. But he is inscribed as both character and writer, a figure in the ongoing novel that is *Secular Love*.

Because life goes on, because this is autobiography as well as fiction and therefore lacks the tidy resolutions of conventional romances, other parts of his life continue to impinge. In the midst of songs and memories, he creates a continuing present of sexual intimacy, "kissing your scarred / skin boat," in which he can acknowledge the "[h]istory . . . you've travelled on / and take with you" (*SL*, 81) without jealousy, asserting a new generosity in this new love. And finally, as he gathers her history, he celebrates the way "piece by piece / we put each other together" (*SL*, 82), although we only see his efforts. Her success in putting *him* together is seen in the poems that have accumulated to this point, for in being able to say this he has achieved it—in the text. Gathering some of the central images of earlier poems, especially the arrow and the moon, he asserts a ritualistic simplicity in their new love: "Ancient customs / that grow from dust / swirled out / from prairie into tropic" (*SL*, 83), following her trajectory to meeting him. "Rock Bottom" thus reaches an open conclusion that in their coming together "however briefly, bedraggled / history / focuses," but does not say on what. In fact, the focus of the following poems in "Skin Boat," itself titled after a description of her body (*SL*, 81), focus much more widely than those up to this point, as if to say that in the new life their love has brought them, he can cast his attention outward once again.

Another oddly appropriate epigraph, dealing with the unknown "intimate affairs of . . . diminutive mammals" (*SL*, 85), leads into a group of poems in which the lovers' communion allows glimpses of a larger communality, and the social becomes an extension of the intimate. Transferring "The Cinnamon Peeler," with its subtle comedy of marriage, and "Women like You," with its communal and ever-renewed romantic gestures, to *Secular Love* transforms them into part of the personal discourse of confession this book sometimes admits to being. But their presence as part of a "confessional" text equally deconstructs its personal aspects, making it part of an ongoing human and historical drama. Similarly, "The River Neighbour" and "Pacific Letter," which "are based on Rihaku–Tu Fu–Pound poems [, and] are not so much translations as re-locations into my landscape, the earlier poets making their appearance in these poems" (*SL*, [128]), tend to place this discourse as part of an ancient and ongoing poetic conversation crossing all boundaries but the largest one of art itself. They are poems of friendship, of the other connections everyone needs. In both the idiom is modern, the specific references contemporary and personal, yet the words and phrasings of poets centuries-old displace the autobiographical into what George Steiner once called "the gossip of eternity."[14] "The River Neighbour"[15] speaks of separation and addresses a "you" who could belong in either the original poem or the new one. Yet references to "the dust from my marriage" and to "you loung[ing] with my children" (*SL*, 93) in the writer's absence cement the poem to the present. The image of the dead bird and the "company of the leaf on the stairs" (*SL*, 93) belong to the ages while the "RCA Victor dog" is temporally local. The final quatrain, suggesting how these friends might get together, achieves an ahistorical voice that could belong to either Tu Fu or Ondaatje. "Pacific Letter,"[16] with its dedication to Stan Dragland, fellow riverman of "Walking to Bellrock" (*TK*, 81–83), fits into the slow accumulation of waterways that announces the general emotional health of the writer in this final part of the book. Playfully adapting Rihaku's ancient social mores to the lives of two contemporary English professors and their summer pleasures, alluding once more to traveling on the Mazinaw and walking Depot Creek, the poem speaks to the ways friendship continues against all the chance and change that work to destroy it. If "[a]ll this comes to an end," there is still "no conclusion in the heart" (*SL*, 102), as Rihaku also knew so many centuries ago.

"To a Sad Daughter" is one of the most direct addresses in the book. It is almost too pure an example of the plain style, an explanation and apology combined with advice the writer already knows she may reject. Its context therefore provides a lot of its emotional power, while its apparently casual use of her own image system of sports heroes, especially hockey goalies, holds its argument together. The poem works on the basis of speech: this is the confused and clumsy talk of a father to his daughter, somewhat estranged but still loved and cared for. It slides from gentle humor to awkward advice, to loving memories of watching her grow up, and back to that advice: "Want everything. If you break / break going out not in" (*SL*, 97). If the poem has problems, it is because its shifts from the personal plain talk of fatherly advice and love to the carefully patterned evocation of one girl's imaginative environment are themselves a bit too self-conscious; they do not successfully mask the writer behind the character in the poem.

After a couple of humorous poems that further demonstrate the writer's renewed engagement with the world at large, "7 or 8 Things I Know About Her / A Stolen Biography" explores "her" background in Topeka, Kansas. Refusing the political investigation implied in the title's allusion to Jean Luc Godard's *Two or Three Things I Know about Her,* it nevertheless plays off that film's insistence on placing its subject in a social context in seven laconically titled prose takes parodying sociological analysis. The eighth fragment gathers images from the previous seven to invent a "Reprise" into which the writer can insert himself as the fantasy lover she has always sought. Because it is comic, it works as a genuine valentine.

The next seven poems reach out again into the wider worlds of art, nature, and friendship. Just by being there, the two poems on great jazz singers argue a newfound return to outward vision as opposed to the intense self-scrutiny of the previous parts of the text. They are also brilliant evocations of their subjects, arguing the power of art to transcend temporal and social dislocation and reach any who will choose to pay attention. "The Concessions" is the first of two immigrant songs of belonging to a locality whose history is not yours but which you can join. A poem in four parts, it explores the way friends who work together can also join with one another and the people who have always lived there to make a place home. Beginning with a naming of towns that recalls Al Purdy's "The Country North of Belleville,"[17] it refuses the despair of that poem's representation of people leaving the land and revels in a "return" of folk who "are new and ancient here / talking through midnight's / tired arms, / letting go the newness" (*SL*, 110). Bringing "stories and a peace I want / to give," the writer receives the greater gift "of love / . . . I refuse to lose" in this "fragment of Ontario" (*SL*, 111). He situates himself among these people making their home, yet also addresses us—"Let me tell you, I love them more and more" (*SL*,

112)—and makes us part of the community he is conjuring in his writing. The poem, like the novel he is soon to write, articulates a postcolonial awareness new to Ondaatje's poetry: it insists on the local as ground, but also insists on enunciating that local as specifically Canadian. Yet it maintains the inherent undecidability of textuality, creating scenes of internal duplication that are richly indeterminate: "And so that yellow light / man or woman working inside / aware of the cricket night / *cricket cricket . . . cicada?* he writes, she says / to no one but the page" (*SL,* 113).

"Red Accordion—an immigrant song" picks up the threads of argument from "The Concessions" and revisits them in the context of a convivial drunken New Year's Eve party that stands in stark contrast to the desperate disconnection in "Claude Glass." Now the poet records a communal "us" sharing the pleasure of one another's company, "the 'gift' we can give each other" (*SL,* 116), and instead of drowning in a river flooding the house, he sees a different flow in which "[t]he years, the intricate / knowledge now of each other / makes love" (*SL,* 117). Against the darkness of that earlier vision he reveals "[a] full moon the / colour of night kitchen," in which the domestic is itself the charm. In the light of this moon, people dance to a music that is history, which is the "immigrant song": "a reel that carried itself generations ago / north of the border, through lost towns, / settled among the strange names, / and became eventually our own // all the way from Virginia" (*SL,* 118). This complex image brings the immigrant experience into the present, and in that "our" insists that it is always happening again, letting new people settle into and belong to the country.

The final poems return to the countryside, and especially to lakes and rivers, an "absolute landscape, / among names that fold in onto themselves" (*SL,* 124). Paddling into this other place, we discover once again that friendship is "an old song we break into / not needing all the words" and "[t]he reflections are never there / without us." The writing achieves a kind of clarity of speech that maintains the mystery against the propensity to interpret, and brings the trajectory of the book back to its beginning, as the writer, this time walking with his new love, becomes the riverman he desired (*SL,* 16). But Heraclitus was right, and you can't step into the same river twice: in "Escarpment," celebration and content oppose the disruption and estrangement of "Claude Glass," as the writer inscribes a waking dream of losing himself in river and woman and thus finding himself at home in the world. In a complex series of flashbacks from wakefulness to earlier dream to remembered walking in a stream, the prose poem moves from his lying awake holding his love's arm to the moment when he "slips under the fallen tree holding the cedar root the way he holds her forearm" (*SL,* 126). The tense here creates a small *mise-en-abyme,* by displacing the remembered act with the act of remembering, and leads into a greater one with its plunge into the further act of writing: "He holds it the same way and for the same reasons. Heart Creek? Arm River? he writes, he mutters to her in the darkness" (*SL,* 127). Yet the next sentence sets him back in the stream to follow this small tale to its conclusion here. The end of the poem returns to its beginning, but in reverse, as he "holds onto the cedar root the way he holds her forearm." World and woman have meshed to allow him to "hold on," and in that traditional image the gift of love is made palpably clear and the final chord of the narrative is sounded. But the penultimate sentence—"Turns upriver"—declares how open the ending is, leading him, and us, into whatever follows. As the ending has returned to the beginning, it has also become a new one, which we can imagine beyond the confines of the book, but which is beyond inscription, at least for now.

Chapter Eight
In the Skin of a Lion

In the Skin of a Lion's subtitle, "A Novel," calls attention to genre as none of Ondaatje's other books has done. Insofar as "the novel" itself is an almost infinitely malleable "mongrel" form (Bush, 94), all his longer works at least occasionally traverse its generic geography, but *In the Skin of a Lion* sets itself up as a novel in the larger sense of historical reclamation, multiple characters, interwoven narratives, and political reflection, the latter of which some critics find lacking in Ondaatje's earlier works. "One of the things a novel can do is represent the unofficial story, give a personal, complicated version of things, as opposed to competing with the newspapers and giving an alternate but still simplified opinion" (Bush, 96). This novel does not so much plot a single trajectory of narrative as offer moments of illumination and action in a number of lives, creating a larger, more complex collage than any of Ondaatje's previous books.

History, then, but the unacknowledged history left out of the official texts, is the matter of *In the Skin of a Lion*: " 'I can tell you exactly how many buckets of sand were used, because this is Toronto history, but the people who actually built the goddamn bridge were unspoken of. They're unhistorical!' " (Turner, 21). In seeking to redress the imbalance of official history, he joins a large group of contemporary postcolonial writers for whom "the novel is one way of denying the official, politicians' version of truth,"[1] and inscribing the "unhistorical" memories of immigrant populations.

Although Ondaatje began *In the Skin of a Lion* as "an investigation of the life of Ambrose Small, . . . a millionaire whose disappearance in 1919 occasioned the most vigorous man-hunt in Canadian history" (Turner, 21), he came to dislike Small and reduced his role in favor of more minor figures who "turned out to be immigrants who worked on things like bridges. The writing was a learning process, as the writing of books often is for me."[2] If "learning about things, discovering the work of Lillian Petroff, and so learning about where the Macedonians were living in Toronto and how they lived in this city" moved the writing "out from the self and into a wider sphere" (Hutcheon 1990, 199) than his previous works, it did not make his use of documentation any stricter than before. "This is a work of fiction and certain liberties have at times been taken with some dates and locales"[3] is this book's version of a by-now familiar warning, and it is worth noting that the liberties are sometimes immense.

In its multiplex presentation of various vital figures against a hitherto hidden but vibrantly exuberant ground, *In the Skin of a Lion* creates a mythical, magical realist portrait of the city popularized as "Toronto the Good and the Grey." Because even the facts seem so fantastic at times— Small's disappearance, the epic construction of the Bloor Street Viaduct and later the Victoria Park filtration complex, for example—it is all too easy to assume that Ondaatje has stuck to them, but in a novel where everything and everyone undergoes metamorphosis at some time or other,[4] we can expect that even the apparently fixed facts of geography and history will alter before our very eyes as the story progresses.

I have argued throughout this study that Ondaatje's texts are indeterminate, and that nothing, not even the documentation upon which they are based, escapes the rough if loving hands of change and chance. When everything is in flux and ambiguity rules over all, neither new writing nor the old upon which it is superimposed can be fixed. History as fiction and fiction as history keep writing over each other in the palimpsest of the novel. Ondaatje's cavalier distortion of his sources simply signals one more level of fictional invention working in the text. Nothing is certain, especially textuality. The concatenation of voices and narrative tropes throughout *In the Skin of a Lion* exemplifies Bahktin's concept of "carnivalization." Carnivalized writing "is heterogeneous and flagrantly 'indecorous,' interweaving disparate styles and registers. Where official genres are typically unitary, both generically and ontologically, projecting a single fictional world, carnivalized literature interrupts the text's ontological 'horizon' with a multiplicity of inserted genres—letters, essays, theatrical dialogues, novels-within-the-novel, and so on. Carnivalized literature, in other words, is characterized by stylistic heteroglossia and recursive structure" (McHale, 172).

Textual transformations begin with the epigraphs, where Ondaatje has just slightly "improved" the Sandars translation of *The Epic of Gilgamesh*.[5] Taken from a creation myth, the quotation concerns metamorphosis, the putting on of an other's skin, which is the imaginative act of both the novelist and his central character. The second epigraph warns us more particularly of the reading experience we are about to enter:

"Never again will a single story be told as if it were the only one." Although not fully credited, it comes from John Berger's historiographic metafiction, *G,* a book Ondaatje says "knocked me out."[6] It, too, is a complex historical invention, a carnivalesque fiction that seeks to give voice to those who have been silenced by official histories. The presence of more than one story makes metamorphosis not only possible but inescapable: in sliding from one story to another, characters necessarily change, especially as they move into the foreground of their own stories or retreat into the background of others'.

If so-called Great Men should appear in the text, its complex narrative weave reduces them to the same size as the ordinary laborers and others who inhabit these stories. In this, it assumes a postmodern stance, treading "a middle course on human ground and remain[ing] equally skeptical of heights and depths. . . . In place of Daedalus's labyrinthine artifice we find ordinary workers on straight bridges, in tunnels, or in tanning factories. Ondaatje deflates the hubris of modernism in his pastiche of labourer as young man, and artist as cityscape" (Greenstein, 117). This particular postmodern approach is partly determined by the postcolonial situation of the writer writing. As an immigrant, he sees the country from a new perspective and creates a protagonist who, despite belonging to the race and gender that control Canadian power, is alienated from them. A working-class country boy come to the city, he is as much an outsider as the immigrant workers he finds himself among and whose community he eventually joins.[7] Patrick is a person of continual change, in a text where change is the real sign of belonging, and stasis, like that of the hidden Ambrose Small, is a sign of decay and eventual death.

One of the most striking textual tropes of metamorphosis in the novel is its handling of time. Time is incredibly malleable in *In the Skin of a Lion*: figures remember within memories, and analepses contain Chinese boxes of further flashbacks and flash-forwards. Although generally the text moves forward in time from Patrick's childhood to his middle age, within each section there are anticipations and retrospections that interrupt any smooth progress and often remind us of the written and composed nature of the whole fiction. Formally, these shifts are marked by the typographical spacing of the text: three parts, each containing two or three chapters, each of which contains shorter sections divided by white space. An architectural rhythm emerges as we read.

A single short passage near the end of "Little Seeds" indicates the temporal complexity of the novel. Eleven-year-old Patrick sees what look like fireflies in the distance of a winter night: "Already he knew it could not be lightning bugs. The last of summer's fireflies had died somewhere in the folds of one of his handkerchiefs. (Years later, Clara making love to him in a car, catching his semen in a handkerchief and flinging it out onto bushes on the side of the road. *Hey, lightning bug!* he had said, laughing, offering no explanation.)" (*ISL,* 20). Although there will be many scenes of Patrick and Clara making love in "The Searcher," this is not one of them, yet its somewhat lighter view of his character during his obsessive relationship with her affects our reading of them all. A few paragraphs later, the young boy discovers that the lights are those of the alien workers skating at night, but he only finds out who they are in an even later section of the text, from Alice Gull's reminiscence of an earlier lover, Cato (*ISL,* 151). Thus, in less than a page, we have both a prolepsis and a scene integral to a later analepsis, and both occur within an analeptic passage following the narrative of his early life. Analysis of time anywhere in this novel would discover an equally complicated pattern of cross-references, yet the shifts are made so smoothly they pass almost unnoticed.

Before such temporal jumping about begins, however, there is an exergue somewhat like the first page of *Running in the Family,* that places the whole intertwined collection of narratives within an analeptic frame. This frame scene appears to situate the story as a series of anecdotes told by an unnamed *"man who is driving" "a young girl"* to Marmora. It specifically has to do with the telling of stories, and the images of that telling—*"a story a young girl gathers in a car"* and *"he picks up and brings together various corners of the story, attempting to carry it all in his arms"* (*ISL,* [1])—imply the multiplicity to follow. This frame is doubly outside the text in that within it something quite different happens. There, the young girl, now named as Hana, Patrick's adopted daughter, drives "adapting the rear-view mirror to her height" (*ISL,* 244) and thereby discovering the story behind her in her own way perhaps, while Patrick talks the gears to her. This small alteration breaks the frame just enough to destablize any notion of conventional narration: the text we have been reading is multiple and its narrators many. The telling shifts from one narrative level to another just as the time shifts back and forth across the whole period the novel covers. Flux and metamorphosis are the governing tropes at every turn.

The three books of the novel cover a period from about 1913 to 1940, the years in which Toronto, and Canada, came of age. Each book covers approximately a decade, and figures emerge, fade, and emerge again.

Because he will encounter them all, if only through others' stories and various forms of documentation, the text presents Patrick first, giving him the only childhood background of all the characters. Though born in this country, he comes from beyond its known boundaries, a native outsider. From his "abashed" (*ISL,* 15) father he learns to stand apart, to find a job that allows him to remain separate, to deny community. Isolated in a home bereft of women, he desires to know more, perhaps to identify with the alien loggers who work there in the winter months. But even during the strange moment of illumination when he discovers them skating with their cattail torches, savors the romance of their disruption of the boundaries of day and night, and knows that "nothing would be the same" for him again, he does "not trust either himself or these strangers of another language enough to be able to step forward and join them" (*ISL,* 22). This refusal to "step forward and join" others marks much of Patrick's behavior throughout the novel. Although his difficult struggle to find a community makes up one of the central narrative lines of the novel, he is often absent from the stories it presents. Despite the way this overview of his young life appears to be setting up a life-story, that is precisely what it is not doing, and the personal epic of a heroic life is exactly what this novel refuses to become.

One of the major reasons for the book's popularity is the sense of "realistic" representation of history and people in history it offers,[8] yet "Little Seeds" gives us a fragmented and opaque view of character, imaged moments rather than psychological explanations. These moments are so artfully arranged we might also believe they reveal the inner man, but the theory of character the text offers is almost wholly one of surfaces: "It was strange for Patrick to realize later that he had learned important things, the way children learn from watching how adults angle a hat or approach a strange dog" (*ISL,* 19). Once again, gesture lies at the heart of the writing and represents all we can really know of another.

In "The Bridge," the novel begins its turn away from private lives toward the public history in which they occur. The shift is a large one, as Patrick disappears from the text for the entire section. Most of the gestures here are public, although the central ones concerning Nicholas Temelcoff inextricably conflate the private with the public, revealing the personal contexts official history tends to ignore. Essentially Temelcoff's story, it also introduces various other figures who will return in later sections. "The Bridge," in fact, is almost a textbook example of "the discontinuous drama" of postmodernist fiction, which is mimetic,

"but. . . . at the level of form. . . . what postmodernist fiction imi-
tates, the object of its mimesis, is the pluralistic and anarchistic ontological landscape of advanced industrial cultures . . . [in which
characters move from] fictional worlds to the paramount reality of
everyday life, or from paramount reality to fiction" (McHale, 38). This is
a passage Temelcoff crosses many times during his story.

If the first section entered a world outside of history's inscription, not
yet mapped although inhabited, "The Bridge," as its title announces,
enters a world all too fully documented. The narrative voice here moves
confidently from the documentation and photographs of city archives
and multicultural histories to an invented action that conjures the sense
of process in the constructions of an industrial culture. The first descriptions move from photographic absorption in the machines of construction to the perceptions of the workers, made and kept anonymous by the
method and attitude of documentation. If "[t]he bridge goes up in a
dream" (ISL, 26), it is because their knowledge and feelings have never
been acknowledged. In a cinematic rush of scenes, the text leaps forward
to the bridge's completion, its naming, and to the cyclist who *escaped*
police to cycle anonymously across the bridge before the dignitaries did
so for their place in posterity's archive. "In the photographs he is a blur
of intent," but even he is not the first, for the "previous midnight the
workers had arrived and brushed away officials who guarded the bridge
in preparation for the ceremonies the next day, moved with their own
flickering lights—their candles for the bridge dead—like a wave of
civilization, a net of summer insects over the valley" (ISL, 27). This is
how the analogic layering of the text works: the image of the moving
lights and the metaphor of summer insects remind us of the men skating,
and in that way claiming their place of work for themselves, in "Little
Seeds." But the metaphor also argues both their real presence in the work
and their evanescence as workers in any one place, which is how they are
seen by the powerful, named men who use them to complete their
projects.

The text now jumps back to the actual building of the bridge,
enunciating the physical, human labor of the effort in a series of images
that evoke the sensual engagement of these men with their work. It
briefly mentions Caravaggio, telling us he will quit but not what he will
do (we'll find that out 54 pages later, and finally get his story in the
section of book 3 named after him), and then introduces the figure of the
major boss, "Rowland Harris, Commissioner of Public Works" (ISL,
29).[9] The first paragraph on Harris places him in the ongoing civil dream

of which the bridge is a first part, and its historical information is accurate even as it helps to create an image of a visionary public builder. Having generalized Harris's passionate involvement with his bridge across the whole period of its construction, the scene stops at a particular moment, "[a]n April night in 1917" (*ISL,* 30) when five nuns suddenly walk onto the unfinished bridge. The wind suddenly throws one off the bridge: "She disappeared into the night by the third abutment, into the long depth of air which held nothing, only sometimes a rivet or a dropped hammer during the day" (*ISL,* 31). The careful use of terms from construction, and the dying fall of the final phrase with its specific objects of the trade, provide the necessary verisimilitude to the description. The scene ends with Harris at one end of his bridge, staring "along the mad pathway. This was his first child and it had already become a murderer" (*ISL,* 31).

But closure for Harris is an opening of the field for both the nun and Nicholas Temelcoff (who, although far less documented, is a historical figure like Harris and Small). In one of many moments of "ontological flicker"[10] in this text, the wind tosses the nun off the bridge from one story into a different, hidden fiction. "The man in mid-air," not yet named, grabs a pipe with one hand and the falling nun with the other, hauling her into his story. A statement of outrageous logic confirms the shift into a new world of events within the text: "The new weight ripped the arm that held the pipe out of its socket and he screamed, *so* whoever might have heard him up there would have thought the scream was from the falling figure" (emphasis added). The second half of the sentence displaces the event even further into a conditional state. The description of their slow climb back to land, her silence, his directing her down Parliament Street to the Macedonian district on Eastern Avenue, mixes puns, technical terminology, oblique narrative, complex imagery, and quick shifts of perspective to achieve a sense of verisimilitude, yet it is all based on a magical moment beyond the scope of history and documentation. Although most of the passage is focalized through Temelcoff, it shifts to her—anonymous and without any context—near the end, as she perceives his "abrupt requests" (*ISL,* 33), the restaurant, and its owner, then, in the final paragraph, it returns to his perception: "She still hadn't said a word. He remembered she had not even screamed when she fell. That had been him" (*ISL,* 34). The almost analytic tone of the final sentence distances the event, and points the narrative back to what he "had been." The rest of "The Bridge" deals with Temelcoff, who "is famous on the bridge, a daredevil" and whose "work is so exceptional and

time-saving he earns one dollar an hour while the other bridge workers
receive forty cents" (ISL, 35),[11] shifting between his past and the present
encounter in the Ohrida Lake Restaurant.

Although Temelcoff has been named, he has not been seen: "Even in
archive photographs it is difficult to find him. . . . He floats at the
three hinges of the crescent-shaped steel arches. These knit the bridge
together. The moment of cubism" (ISL, 34). Mise-en-abyme takes over
here as we are implicated in the search for his presence; but he is present,
as a figure in and of the text, described in terms that allude to earlier
Ondaatje poems of the artist yet present this artist as part of a human
project, happily engaged in making his own life out of the work, rather
than vice versa. The final sentence fragment alludes to another intertext,
John Berger's famous essay, and thereby reflexively calls attention to the
complex representation the text seeks to enact.[12] Back in the restaurant,
another anachronistic radio program, a parrot named Alicia, drink, and
her silence surround him. The focus slides from him to her, his concern
for and desire to know her conflicting with her concern for him and desire
to elude anyone's knowing. The narration seems to work at a strictly
realistic level, yet somewhere among the allusions, the metaphoric
destabilization, and the floating referentiality of some phrases, it slips
slightly off balance, toward an indeterminacy that renders all historical
records at least partially suspect. This story may supplement the official
version, but in doing so it holds all writing up to skepticism. Nothing is
what it seems, change is the only constant—the bar whose outside is
Toronto and whose inside is the Balkans, a language learned from songs
on a radio program that does not yet exist, a nun thrown out of her world
into something new and strange.

Another fragment renders Nicholas's usual days at work, in "the fairy
tale" (ISL, 39) of construction, including his fairy-tale escape from death
when a traveller collapses. The narrative shifts back to the nun's transformation, stepping out into the new day, but in the midst of that story
it informs us of Temelcoff's past and future as a baker; then it returns to
his work in the world of Commissioner Harris, and his isolation from the
other workers, who watch and listen to him although he "never realizes"
it (ISL, 42). In another of the short circuits by which the novel is
constructed, the narrator passes from Nicholas's love of his new language
to a future of immigration that Nicholas has anticipated in his own life.
Although the talking picture "will light the way for immigration in
North America" (ISL, 43; emphasis added), it was a different "spell of
language that brought Nicholas here," a "fairy tale of Upper America"

(*ISL*, 44) told by "those first travellers who were the judas goats to the west." Daniel Stroyanoff's tale of losing an arm and gaining the money to return to Macedonia is only an extreme version of the lives of many Macedonian migrants in Canada.[13] The story of Nicholas's own trip to the new country reads as if it belonged to a conventional historical novel, but it takes off into the comically absurd in the fantasia of immigrants learning English "through mimicking actors on stage . . . at the Fox or Parrot Theatres" (*ISL*, 47). After this comic displacement, the text returns to the image of Nicholas speaking and singing in his privacy, then leaps back to the morning of the fall, as he wakes to find the nun gone but his memories of their intimacy leading him (or is it only the narrator and us?) into a notion of a "long silent courtship, her absence making him look everywhere" (*ISL*, 49). In context, it is difficult to know if he is courting the nun or only the world she has brought into being with her sudden fall into his life. That is the ambivalence he lives when he "releases the catch on the pulley and slides free of the bridge," which is the last glimpse the text offers of him in this section.

"The Searcher" entwines a different set of fictional and documentary lives, beginning a process that will bring all the figures from these different ontological levels in the text into relation with one another. Becoming "an immigrant to the city" (*ISL*, 53), Patrick joins the other immigrants from other countries "in the belly of a whale" (*ISL*, 54). Locking away the sensual memories of his past, he becomes "new even to himself," in an act reminiscent of Buddy Bolden's "landscape suicide." Yet, while sharing some structural traits with earlier Ondaatje protagonists (including, most obviously perhaps, intimate relationships with two women), he differs from both Billy and Buddy in not being a tortured artist, nor a man doomed to isolated death.

A literary jump cut takes us into a strange world of police documentation concerning the disappearance of millionaire Ambrose Small in 1919. Ondaatje mixes fact and fiction seamlessly in the section on Small's "deliberate" disappearance, inventing at least as much "documentary evidence" as he finds.[14] For example, there is no mention anywhere "that the police had his Bertillon record" (*ISL*, 55), but the Bertillon method of measurement worked more or less as Ondaatje describes it.[15] And he has altered the quotations from newspapers in his usual manner. Although the tone of the documentation brooks no questioning, the key shift of Small's lover's name from Clara Smith to Clara Dickens allusively indicates the transition from documented reality to fictional invention. When Patrick becomes a searcher, he does so in the fictional world of the novel (there is no mention of the searchers in any of the commentaries on the Small case). Yet the letters that interest him and by which he is led to Clara are part of the documented story.

Once again, in a historical lacuna, a man is "dazzled by" a woman, stunned into obsessive love "as if she without turning had fired a gun over her shoulder and mortally wounded him. The 'rare lover,' the 'perfect woman' " (*ISL*, 61). In this book, however, neither the woman nor the romantic obsession will prove quite as dangerous to the lover as their earlier counterparts. Patrick gives himself up to Clara, yes, but their affair has as many moments of light comedy as it does of dark dejection, and although devastated by his eventual loss of her, he will recover. Moreover, her sexuality is alluring but not frightening; delight rather than suffering is the ruling passion in their affair.

When Patrick meets Clara, the text shifts gears, becoming much more obviously cinematic: a series of carefully observed scenes follow, full of shifting focalization, cryptic verbal exchanges, quick emotional transitions, and complex images of feeling and sensation. As figures on a stage of passion, Patrick and Clara achieve an opaqueness that simultaneously humanizes and textualizes them. But then, she is an actress and he is in her play. The text suggests his encounter with her marks a small beginning in his movement out of the self and into fuller engagement with the world; thus, he feels "happier and more at ease than he had ever been" in the jealous contemplation of her past lovers, partly because he recognizes that he is caught up in both "the spell of her body [and] the complex architecture of her past" (*ISL*, 66).

As we read through the text, the various narratives simultaneously uncover and hide certain kinds of knowledge. One pleasure of any text is unraveling what the plot has hidden, but Ondaatje has shaped a narrative in which plot disperses into plots, and stories intertwine across various levels of textual reality. On first reading we will not necessarily realize until much later how the text has woven various strands of narrative together within this section, connecting Patrick through Clara and her friend Alice Gull to the level of documentary reality where the world of Ambrose Small suddenly connects with that of Harris and Temelcoff (much later, Patrick will piece together the evidence and realize that Alice Gull is the anonymous nun, who took her name from the parrot Alicia when she entered the world as a new person). Within the story of "The Searcher," the three fictional figures assume different degrees of character depth: Clara's delight in recounting her past provides her with a history; Patrick's tendency to withhold his is alleviated by our textual knowledge of "Little Seeds"; but Alice Gull appears to have no past at all. Patrick delights in "the eroticism of [Clara's] history," and for him, her earlier discovery that "[s]eduction was the natural progression of curiosity" translates into his deepening interest "only in her" (*ISL*, 69). But everything he learns suggests the breadth of her previous experience and the impossibility of containing and holding her. Even after she has told him all about her relations with Small, he realizes only that her character is complex and that "he still didn't know who she was" (*ISL*, 72). As a reader representing us, Patrick has run into the wall for which psychology only pretends to provide a door.

Clara sees more deeply into him, recognizing the "wall in him that no one reached . . . though she assumed it had deformed him" (*ISL*, 71); given its presence, she understands his isolation from other people—as he admits, he has no other friends than her. Perhaps it is this recognition that prompts her to tell him he has no remorse, in a passage more deliberately "literary" than their other conversations. His response anticipates the change that will lead him to act in the section of that title: "A strange word. It suggests a turning around on yourself" (*ISL*, 67). The many such bridges among the text's various parts defeat the conventional assumptions of time built into traditional plotting, but are often invisible at their beginnings. Alice Gull, Clara's actress friend, is one such bridge, but for most of this section she is simply a near tabula rasa upon which both Clara and Patrick write their own fleeting interpretations of themselves and each other: an audience for their little drama, albeit a somewhat interactive one. The narration continually shifts focus from Patrick to the women and back again: they perform for him, then talk to each other, then do a spirit painting of him, and then he wakes to leave the cottage and sees Alice for herself alone, even if only because Clara touched her. The alternating points of view ensure that we remain as puzzled by these characters as they are.

Despite their comic tone, Patrick's reflections on the women reveal the dark undercurrents of his isolated life even as they also anticipate a time when he will join in the ceremony of fellowship: "He feels more community remembering this than anything in his life. Patrick and the two women. A study for the New World. Judith and Holofernes. St. Jerome and the Lion. Patrick and the Two Women. He loves the tableau, even though being asleep he had not witnessed the ceremony" (*ISL*, 79). Standing in for us, Patrick reads community into the tableau he did not witness. But the two intertexts, themselves a conflation of writing and painting, contradict each other—Judith's cutting off Holofernes's head is an emblem of violent revolt; St. Jerome's removing the thorn from the lion's paw, one of profound compassion. This juxtaposition of opposing stances anticipates Patrick's encounter with both in his deepening involvement with the two women. "A study for the New World" cannot escape the inheritances from the old. The intertexts insist this is a fiction, and that all its figures are themselves continually textualized, part of a writing that at this point is going on.

The violence of love makes itself felt first in the scene of Patrick's blind dance for Clara. The writing catches his desperation and his exhilaration, her delight in his act and her refusal of the binding implied in it. When she leaves him, he retreats from the world entirely, obsessively cleaning his room and reading "novels and their clear stories. Authors accompanying their heroes clarified motives. World events raised characters from destitution. The books would conclude with all wills rectified and all romances solvent. Even the spurned lover accepted the fact that the conflict had ended" (*ISL,* 82). The irony is clear: this text offers none of these consolations, and although "Patrick believed in archaic words like *befall* and *doomed*" (*ISL,* 83), the conditional mood of his desire to be a hero and "come down on Small like an arrow" signals his continuing failure to do so. Instead, he writes imaginary letters, another genre woven into the novel; and other stories, like that of Caravaggio the thief, slip into his, only to retreat until the text can fit them in.

In another sudden time jump, the text creates a confusing ambiguous reference: "He opened the door to her and stepped back quickly, appalled. He had not expected her" (*ISL,* 86). The visitor is Alice, not Clara, and two years have passed. While she appears older and more confident, "[h]e felt dangerous" (*ISL,* 87), the odd choice of adjective suggesting anger rather than fear. Yet the scene reveals that she has the power to change him, not the other way around. Shifts of focus and ambiguous pronoun references make the two women one in his mind. But if his perception is eclipsed by romantic dreams, her behavior differentiates her from Clara, especially when she tells him—after they have been to bed together—"You must remove her shadow from you" (*ISL,* 89). Her final remark, "Then when we meet again we can talk . . . we can say hello," might have been written for one of her performances at the Parrot Theatre. "She said that so strangely he would later recall it differently— clothed in sarcasm or tentative love or sadness." His confusion about her behavior and motives matches ours at this point.

Every move forward in the plot of any of the stories in *In the Skin of a Lion* complicates the text: while the necessary explanations bring Patrick closer to Clara, the erotic imagery of "the faint impression of her backbone on the white paint" (*ISL,* 92) of a hotel wall implies that her textual presence and absence are identical. Images press home the nonrepresentational aspects of the writing even as the narrative pretends to realism. The Ambrose Small Patrick finds has escaped documentation; but he is not a character even in the sense that Patrick, Clara, and Alice are, for the text suggests no inner life for him at all. Indeed, Patrick denies him the chance to create a history for himself, denies him any depth whatever. He exists only to push Patrick's story a bit further on, by attempting to burn him to death in an attack where sensual imagery and suspense narration mix. Patrick's last scene with Clara returns to the dramatic/cinematic mode of the earlier ones. She comes to him to help, and tells him not to lose his sense of being "on the verge" (*ISL,* 97), but although her perception of him is compassionate, she will not stay with him. The final pages of "The Searcher" focus through her, as they make love and she leaves quietly in the middle of the night. The final sentence drifts above them all, focusing on the triangle from a great height, and leaves them all "between the two points of this journey": "The dressings hung off him like a limp white rib while Ambrose came down from the house and saw her there thinking, looking at Patrick's river" (*ISL,* 100).

"Palace of Purification,"[16] leaps ahead in time to 1930 and outward in focus to a more particularly political vision. Like "The Bridge," it begins by arguing with the photographic documentation of the titular structure's construction, revealing the public lies of the official city photographs. The picture is still, but the work is a long and continuing effort, and Patrick is a part of it, working in the tunnel being built under Lake Ontario. The text itself digs beyond the archives' numbers and facts to put a human face upon the backbreaking work that brought the tunnel into being. Although Patrick is the focus of a perceptual description in which all the senses are implicated, unlike the conventional realist novel, this text offers no reason for his presence in the tunnel. Because the actual story of what went on there is a historical lacuna, the text can slip him into that empty space where images of the muck, the explosions, the mules and pit-horses, combine to fill in the spaces left empty by official photographs and publicity.

Something of the official view appears in the following fragment, representing Harris's dream of the plant. Ironically, while no names of the workers survive (the only name the text can offer is Patrick's, and he is entirely an invention), the names of the various companies and towns that contributed to the construction are all available. The irony is political, yet Harris emerges as something more than a mere capitalist boss. The material poetry of his dream, in which the sumptuous and elaborately expensive building "would be an image of the ideal city," the statement that he "could *smell* the place before it was there, knew every image of it as well as his arms" (*ISL*, 109), as well as his quotation from Baudelaire, invoke him as a visionary force able to turn dream into reality. By itself, the passage might idolize Harris, but after the *Inferno*-like vision of workers toiling in the tunnel, it creates a tension that complicates the arguments and actions of the rest of the novel.

Even as the text represents Harris as the master builder providing jobs and keeping the wheels of industry turning, it shines a light upon the lives of those lost in "labour and darkness" in the "unfinished world" of the tunnels. The narrative foregrounds him just long enough to register his dream in all its megalomania, simultaneously exploitative and truly visionary: "Such a strange dream for him. The silence of men coming out of a hole each within an envelope of steam. Horses under Lake Ontario. Swallowing the water one-and-a-quarter miles away, bringing it back into his body, and spitting it out clean" (*ISL*, 111). Even as he identifies his body with that of the city, the text insists on acknowledging the unknown, unnamed men who make his dream possible; focusing through Patrick, it turns back to them, away from Harris. Nevertheless, the glory of Harris's dream remains as palpable as the suffering its realization creates.

Having "reduced himself almost to nothing" (*ISL*, 113), Patrick experiences a delirious anonymity. But a compassionately comic passage whose tenses render temporal causality insecure translates him into the Macedonian community. Kosta, the owner of the Ohrida Lake Restaurant, who reappears to negotiate Patrick's acceptance into his new group, is a sign of connections in the text, but they are connections that tend to ignore realistic plotting. As he drifts away from Patrick after inviting him to the waterworks on Sunday night, he drifts out of the story once again. A psychopomp who initiates Patrick into the communal dream life of his people, he does not participate in Patrick's story once he has brought him into the public world again.

In a phantasmagoric scene in the half-built waterworks, Patrick watches an allegorical puppet play enacting the fears and sufferings of the immigrants in the movements of a single "male" hero who confronts the power, laws, and authority of the rich. As he perceives that story, it pulls him into its orbit, and he rushes to the stage to prevent the young hero from hurting himself; there he discovers the man is a woman, but she slips away into the darkness backstage. He follows her and finds the puppets, now an image of "a king's court, silent—a custom of the east" (*ISL*, 120), but the story that image conjures is not so much his as a higher-level narrator's. It ironically recalls Harris's power over the workers' bodies even as it demonstrates his lack of control over their imaginations. Focalization shifts back to Patrick, "locked within metamorphosis" like the puppets, but unlike them able to recognize how puppetlike he is and so prepare himself for the changes that will follow his finally meeting Alice Gull again. The scene concludes with him washing her makeup off, "cloth over one finger for precision, the blue left iris wavering at the closeness . . . so that it was not Alice Gull but something more intimate—an eye muscle having to trust a fingertip to remove that quarter inch of bright yellow around her sight" (*ISL*, 121), another act of metamorphosis, and one that underlines the uncertainty of all naming and self-representation in this novel.

As rich in drama as this scene is, it is also an extraordinary collage of images allusively connected to Patrick's past and future. Targets, dark spaces, flashlit bodies, even the water Alice is washing in: all have their analogues elsewhere in the text. The serial movement of imagery parallels the narrative movement of character and event here. Ondaatje has threaded a series of intertwining image systems throughout the work, all of which emphasize the nonrepresentational aspects of this "mongrel" text. For example, Patrick is associated with water from the very beginning, hauling the cow out of the river, watching the men skate, working the rivers with his father. He throws himself into Depot Creek to escape Small's fiery assault; later he works in the tunnel beneath the lake; later still, he travels the Muskoka Lakes to set his own fire; and finally, he returns to the tunnel from the lake in order to sabotage the water filtration plant. In the middle of the story, he tells Alice he has "a passive sense of justice" (*ISL*, 122). Agreeing, she worries that, "Like water, you can be easily harnessed, Patrick. That's dangerous." But he tells her, "I don't believe the language of politics, but I'll protect the friends I have. It's all I can handle." This conflict, which exists even in the midst of their love, connects the imagery to the narrative, for her insight suggests why he does become a revolutionary of sorts after her death.

This discussion follows directly upon his finding her at the waterworks. Although she can speak for a particular politically revolutionary point of view, the dialogue prevents the text from becoming a tract, as does the description of the other workers and their families. Alice says you must "name the enemy and destroy their power" (*ISL*, 124), and tells him to begin "with their luxuries—their select clubs, their summer mansions" (*ISL,* 125), which is what he will do when she is killed. But in the light of this conversation, will his act be political or romantic? It is by not resolving such questions that this novel achieves its most complex effects. Although Patrick responds to Alice's comments, the scene is mainly hers, and she proves incapable of holding to a single perspective. Though she wants to involve him in her political agenda, she also admits that she's not "big enough to put someone in a position where they have to hurt another;" and in her final comment that she feels her daughter Hana is only "loaned to [her]. We're veiled in flesh. That's all," she reveals (to us, though not to Patrick) that the nun still inhabits the revolutionary.

Patrick's memory of Clara telling him about Alice, Cato, and Hana demonstrates the way this text constantly returns on itself, as it enters their earlier talk, comes back to Patrick breakfasting at the Thompson Grill, then returns to the conversation with Clara, and finally to his memory of his first love, which elicits this meditation: "He saw something there he would never fully reach—the way Clara dissolved and suddenly disappeared from him, or the way Alice came to him it seemed in a series of masks or painted faces, both of these women like the sea through a foreground of men" (*ISL,* 128).[17] But romantic imaginings quickly give way to the life of the present. Slowly growing into his relationship with both Alice and her daughter, Patrick also enters more fully and consciously into the life of the working class. Moving to a tannery, he experiences the truth of Alice's comments on the suffering of the men who work there. Once again, the writing captures the physical experience of the place through a series of images utilizing all five senses. When Patrick thinks of painting his fellow workers, the text overturns the traditional cliché by presenting through a thousand words an analytic interrogation of the visual surfaces the picture would create. As it expands to analyze the dyers' early deaths due to the dye invading their bodies, the writing enters into the processes of historical time in a way no painting could. Although the focalization is through Patrick, the questions seem to come from a narrative level that includes his thinking as well as what he is thinking about. The dramatic images underwrite a political vision of compassion and empathy, like Alice's.

Alice's gift of Conrad's words creates another intertext in the novel, invoking the central immigrant writer of early modernism to support her arguments about the power the rich WASPs hold over the immigrant population in Canada (*ISL,* 134).[18] But from Conrad's political insights she immediately turns to her "favourite lines," which simultaneously assert her mysticism and her sense of the contingency of all things: "I have taught you that the sky in all its zones is mortal. . . . Let me now re-emphasize the extreme looseness of the structure of all objects" (*ISL*, 135).[19] The quotation also points self-reflexively at the structure of the text we are reading. Between Alice's words and his work, Patrick discovers a place for his life in Alice's and Hana's, expanding his sense of self to include a community within his personal horizon. All this happens within the metaphoric "Palace of Purification" that is the text itself, and the purification is what washes away Patrick's self-absorption and frees him to research Alice's past.

In a processual *mise-en-abyme*, Patrick performs the authorial research authenticating the story of "The Bridge" we have already read, except that the photograph and letters of Cato, Hana's father, are inventions within the text placed at the same level of ontological reality as the photographs and newspaper stories on the building of the Bloor Street Viaduct. The juxtaposition of "real" and invented documents creates another instance of "ontological flicker" (McHale, 90) in the text, implying the instability of all writing. Suggesting how new generations embed themselves ever deeper in their country, Hana ties the disparate strands of the narrative together for him, first by introducing him to Nicholas Temelcoff at her "favourite place of spells . . . the Geranium Bakery" (*ISL*, 138), then by giving him the objects of Alice's past, "[t]hree other photographs: a group of men working on the Bloor Street Viaduct, a photograph of Alice in a play at the Finnish Labour Temple, three men standing in snow in a lumber camp. A sumac bracelet. A rosary" (*ISL*, 139). Patrick's subsequent research, paralleling that which made the writing of the book possible, leads to a moment of illumination that nestles his story into a junction of multiple fictional and real narratives as he suddenly realizes that "[h]is own life was no longer a single story but part of a mural, which was a falling together of accomplices. Patrick saw a wondrous night web—all of these fragments of a human order, something ungoverned by the family he was born into or the headlines of the day. A nun on a bridge, a daredevil who was unable to sleep without drink, a boy watching a fire from his bed at night, an actress who ran away with a millionaire—the detritus and chaos of the age was realigned" (*ISL*, 145). This moment of apparent psychological naturalism also insists that the realignment Patrick perceives is the novel of which he is a part: the various levels of ontological reality collapse into the single "night web" of textuality, and the implied author steps forth to remind us that however much Patrick knows, we know more (and even what he can learn from the juxtaposition of "real" and invented news about the nun and the daredevil could not possibly include Temelcoff's time with her at the Ohrida Lake Restaurant). He tells us how the official photographers of Toronto lacked anyone like Lewis Hine, whose work Patrick "would never see" even though the author describes some examples in precise and empathetic detail. As he mixes quotations[20] and historical meditation to speak directly to us of the nature of this text of realignment, he argues the power of art despite its slowness, compared to the speed with which "[o]fficial histories [and] news stories" manage to simplify *"the chaotic tumble of events"* (*ISL,* 146). And he proposes a different way, exemplified by the text we are reading: "The chaos and tumble of events. The first sentence of every novel should be: 'Trust me, this will take time but there is order here, very faint, very human.' Meander if you want to get to town."

The disturbance of ontological levels in the novel continues as the text shows Patrick in the midst of suppositions—"If Alice Gull had been a nun?"—only to suddenly slide from third-person to first-person pronoun in a bleaker supposition of death—"She could move like . . . she could sing as low as . . . Why is it that I am now trying to uncover every facet of Alice's nature for myself?" (*ISL,* 147)—which merges Patrick with the author in a moment of literary desire. Pronominal slippage throughout the rest of this fragment links character, writer, and reader in literature's desire to overcome death. Now the supposition is desperate: "As if he can be given that gift, to relive those days when Alice was with him and Hana, which in literature is the real gift. He turns the page backwards. Once more there is the image . . . All these fragments of memory . . . so we can retreat from the grand story and stumble accidentally upon a luxury, one of those underground pools where we can sit still. Those moments, those few pages in a book we go back and forth over" (*ISL,* 148). Even as it announces the *mise-en-abyme,* this passage paradoxically generates a sense of Patrick's genuine pain—a slightly different testament to the power of art within the text.

An analeptic jump cut to Nicholas's response to Patrick's discoveries subtly suggests that Patrick's gift of his past to Nicholas is identical with literature's real gift: it "shows him the wealth in himself, how he has been sewn into history. *Now he will begin to tell stories"* (*ISL,* 149; emphasis added). A further analepsis—itself indicative of both Patrick's and the author's desire to defer confronting Alice's death—presents stories of Cato, once Alice's lover and, inescapably in a writing trying to put off death, now dead. But Cato's actions when alive were for Alice, still alive in the memory of her telling of them. Through her, he provides an answer to a riddle Patrick had never thought to ask, that the skaters of his childhood were Finns. But however much he learns of her, he cannot learn who she is. Instead, she delivers him to himself as "the sum of all he had been in his life" (*ISL,* 152) even as she lives a life of transformation, metamorphosis, a refusal to be summed up by anything. Yet memory or fiction cannot prevent the death from slipping in, if only as an image of a her as "a fabulous heron in flight . . . fallen dead at his feet," an image full of resonance for readers of Ondaatje's poetry.

In a complex passage that argues the power of reading as an imaginative act (and therefore invites our complicity in such reading), Patrick reads Cato's letters to Alice, imagining what they represent—the further story of what happened to Cato after he sent them and escaped the work camp (itself an almost Conradian adventure of pursuit and courage)—as well as Alice's response to them.

In his remembered life with Alice and Hana, Patrick wants to formalize the relationship, to become a father to Hana, but Alice resists the legality as she has resisted all laws since she escaped the law of gravity in her fall from the bridge. Then the text returns to the present, in which "he aches for her smallness, her intricacy" (*ISL,* 159), invoked in self-reflexive terms of art and science: an artist drawing and a lunar eclipse. The narrative slips into Patrick's voice as he recalls the tenderness that made him trust her, then back into the third person for one last image of their happiness together. The section ends with a final merging of author and character in a conditional desire that once more defers the actual moment of her death (a full description of which won't appear in the text until five pages from the end): "He has come across a love story. This is only a love story. He does not wish for plot and all its consequences. Let me stay in this field with Alice Gull. . . ." (*ISL,* 160). The sentence-to-sentence translation from character to author and back again induces a literary vertigo.

At the beginning of the section entitled "Remorse," Patrick does turn around on himself, returning in his pain to a solitary figure of romantic angst. Despite earlier expressions of fatherly love for Hana, he mourns alone in a highly romantic language of castles and moats, a conditional revolutionary: "As if, having travelled all that distance to enter the castle in order to learn its wisdom for the grand cause, he now turns and walks away" (*ISL,* 164). But he walks away only far enough to bomb the Muskoka Hotel—an essentially romantic, sentimental gesture to Alice more than an act of faith in her politics. Ondaatje demonstrates his mastery of different modes and tones in this Conradian adventure. The jumps forward and backward in time provide a psychological verisimilitude to a narrative whose playful juggling with geography and documented fact emphasizes how much more fictional than historical the story has become.[21] While exploding a fictional bomb in a fictional hotel takes up a small part of Patrick's adventure, his almost magical encounter in "the Garden of the Blind" (ISL, 168) with a blind woman who *shows* him how to read it through other senses than sight, and so helps him take a first tentative step outside his narcissistic self-pity, is far more important to his ongoing story. She is an oracle of sorts, and Patrick will spend the rest of the novel puzzling out her central message—"Don't resent your life" (ISL, 170). Here as elsewhere, the sentences articulate the subtlest shifts of feeling, yet refuse to expose personality or psychology.

Part 3 both widens and narrows the general focus of the narrative, first seeming to unravel into a separate story, and then bringing that story to bear on the larger mural Patrick's figure crisscrosses. "Caravaggio" is a complex Chinese box of analepses within a narrative of escape. It begins with another apparently natural moment of magical realism, as Patrick and another prisoner at the Kingston Penitentiary paint the painter Caravaggio (who, aside from his name, seems to have nothing in common with his seventeenth-century namesake) into the sky and out of sight. Painting a roof blue becomes an exercise in trompe l'oeil, as the text conveys a magical sense of perceptual loss in a prose of journalistic flatness. First seen as a worker on the viaduct, then as a thief, Caravaggio now becomes the spokesman for a marginalized awareness of the various and subtle demarcations in society. The offhand tone describing their painting him blue so that the guards could not see him against the sky renders the scene as something akin to silent comedy, a metaphysical slapstick out of Charlie Chaplin that places the whole chapter, even its worst violence, under the aegis of comedy.

Ironic internal references—such as "the stiffness [of the paint] which encased him" (ISL, 180), with its echo of the tunnel mud in Patrick's clothes (ISL, 108), the one a sign of freedom, the other a sign of economic entrapment—tie this story to the larger social one. Caravaggio's escape depends upon his charm and the craft he has learned as a thief, which allows the narrative to turn further and further back into his past. His meeting with the young boy Al (Purdy: a major Canadian poet) has the same, slightly comic, resonance as Clara's walk home past the farm where young (Canadian philosopher) George Grant is bringing in the cows

(*ISL,* 100). Whereas the major figures from history in the text are figures of power, these two, just mentioned in passing, are part of the Canadian literary heritage, and exemplify the best aspects of settler colony culture,[22] especially Al, who is happy to help a member of a cultural minority.

As a painter, Caravaggio is as much a part of "the moment of cubism" as Temelcoff earlier was. Moving through a landscape marked by industrialization, he catches the intersections of the natural and the manufactured world: "When he ran he saw it all. The eye splintering into fifteen sentries, watching every approach" (*ISL,* 183). And when he finds a refuge, it is in the culturally spruced-up "nature" of a summer cottage. Throughout this passage, the narration focuses through Caravaggio, but at the end, before the first major analepsis, it pulls back from his specific knowledge to a more general awareness couched in a self-reflexive simile that can only be the author's: "He would sleep as insecurely as a thief does, which is why they are always tired" (*ISL,* 184).

Emerging from a dream that could as well occur in the cottage, the first flashback presents the viewpoints of Caravaggio and Patrick as the thief is savagely attacked by "[t]hree men who have evolved smug and without race" (*ISL,* 185). The text formally renders the violence through surreal imagery and sudden shifts of perspective. Temporally, this is the second time Caravaggio has noticed Patrick, while textually it is the third time their names have been connected. Such textual inversions continually remind us of the nonrepresentational patterning upon which this novel is built. Caravaggio falls into his bed in the cell, and awakes the next morning in cottage country. Finally the text returns to the first time Caravaggio notices Patrick, a scene in which Patrick mentions his earlier awareness of the thief and his red dog. Mention of the dog creates an analepsis within the analepsis, back to Caravaggio's training as a thief. A series of temporal shifts delineates a comedy of apprenticeship and love, as the young thief learns his craft, gets hurt on his first solo job, hides in a mushroom factory, and in a delightful erotic farce meets Giannetta, his wife. The sequential ordering of even this small part of the "Caravaggio" section suggests the complexity of *In the Skin of a Lion* as a whole, yet Ondaatje's prose carries us across its many lacunae with casual grace.

Watching a woman write and remembering hiding among books, Caravaggio recognizes that "there was such intimacy in what he was seeing that not even a husband could get closer than him, a thief who saw this rich woman trying to discover what she was or what she was capable of making" (ISL, 198). That this woman is the poet Anne Wilkinson is only barely intimated by her introducing herself as "Anne" (ISL, 187), and by a cryptic reference among the acknowledgments. Erasing class lines, this paradigmatic moment of empathy ignores Caravaggio's own insistence on demarcation, somewhat confusing the issue. The liberal sympathies of the text often clash with its leftist political agenda: here it takes Patrick's individualistic point of view rather than Alice's communal one. Cut off from the signs of power attached to her class, the woman can define herself as artist, while Caravaggio becomes "anonymous, with never a stillness in his life like this woman's. . . . an outline of a bear in her subconscious" (ISL, 199). And the text self-reflexively allows him to deny that he will ever sign himself into art, even as it does so for him.

After the narrative turns back to Caravaggio's early career as a thief, a further comedy of failure until he steals the dog, and then a comedy of manners between him and the dog, it returns to the scene of his coming home, and to the rich sensuality of his making love to his wife. The narration here affects a completely different tone from the rest of the chapter (except, perhaps, the scene of his beating), fragmenting perception and event to create a metonymy of process that evokes the erotic through allusive and elusive imagery. Like the thief it's named after, "Caravaggio" seems to steal away from the rest of the novel, yet it also moves Patrick's story, only alluded to in passing, forward in time, shows him emerging from the self-pitying narcissism under which he made his "criminal" or "revolutionary" gesture of bombing the Muskoka Hotel, and sets up his collaboration with the thief in the final section of the book.

"Maritime Theatre" begins with a list of occurrences, ostensibly set in the year 1938, when Patrick is released from prison. With its carefully ironic juxtapositions of high and popular culture, working-class life and antirevolutionary activity, the opening passage reminds some readers of Doctorow's Ragtime (see Hutcheon 1988b, 101–2), but Ondaatje's temporal displacement of "facts" (the film of Tolstoy's Anna Karenina, T. S. Eliot's Murder in the Cathedral, and the assassination of Huey Long all occured in 1935) creates an uncertainty effect missing from the earlier novel. "Patrick suddenly had no idea what year it was" (ISL, 210); nor do we, if we have paid any attention to the dating of the information provided. Indecisively balanced between his past and his future, Patrick recalls Clara's face but is unable to evoke Alice's, partly because Clara's seems fixed while Alice's was a site of continual transformation. On the streets, he feels invisible, but his invisibility is different from Caravaggio's, for the thief chose his while Patrick hasn't. Slowly making his way back into the eastern part of the city, he enters the Geranium Bakery, where Temelcoff hugs him, "[a] bear's grip. The grip of the world" (*ISL*, 210). Only now do we learn that Patrick had taken care for Hana, placing her with Temelcoff before he went to Muskoka. A comment that he has been away for five years helps to explain the temporal uncertainty here: when he met Hana in 1930, she was nine years old, but now, five years after he lost her mother and went to prison, she is supposed to be sixteen, and it is supposed to be 1938. These discrepancies undermine the general air of representation all the factual data appear to support.

Herself a young woman, "[s]he watched him, understanding what kind of love was behind his stare" (*ISL*, 211). With this sentence, she enters the realm of mystery in which all of Patrick's women live, and by not naming the kind of love she understands, she renders his emotional life equally mysterious. As he sits with her, "gathering her perspective" (*ISL*, 212), he recalls how the racist attack on Caravaggio had led him back from solitary confinement in his own pain to community.

If Patrick can return to the world from the bottom of the social ladder, Ambrose Small can only retreat further and further into the isolation of megalomania. The scene of his dying accentuates the years of separation from the world Clara has endured for his sake. Her shock, now, "attacked by all the discontinuous moments of his past" (*ISL*, 214), parallels Patrick's earlier shock at her true confessions of Small's treatment of her before he disappeared. Two images, one central to the novel, one to Ondaatje's whole oeuvre, fix Small in his final relation to the other figures in the text. As he spews his past into the air, Clara realizes that "there was no horizon" (*ISL*, 215) to it, a remark that connects to all the other allusions to horizons and, in the image of her speeding over the scenes he discloses, to "the moment of cubism" alluded to at various points.[23] The image of Small as a heron, especially the final apotheosis in which "the mouth of the heron touched the blue wood floor and his head submerged under the water and pivoted and saw in the fading human light a lamp that was the moon" (*ISL*, 215), is especially problematic. Within the novel, it recalls Patrick's earlier vision of Alice as "a fabulous heron in flight" (*ISL*, 152), an image of death that connects her to all the heron heroes of Ondaatje's poetry, but does it therefore imply Small's heroism as well? Everything she performs, as well as every textual comment on her, insists upon her heroic resistance to all that Small represents. If this later metaphor aligns him with the "[m]ad kings" and "their heritage of suicides" (*TK*, 55) in "Heron Rex," does it not lower their symbolic worth? A gorgeously surreal image, this final sentence seems to contradict the diminution of Small that the rest of the section has accomplished. On the other hand, Clara's loyalty to Small, given her place in the story as an object of desire for Patrick—clearly a figure we are meant to identify with, at least partially—has always given him an aura of nobility nothing else in his story supports. Our difficulty in placing him in the implied hierarchy of characterization in the text may reflect no more than the difficulties the popular media have in doing the same thing with so many of the rich and famous.

The next section, following immediately upon Small's death but switching to Patrick's point of view, initiates the finale hinted at in the beginning of the book. A casual reference to Patrick's broken arm also reveals that the narration has leaped ahead in time and will have to backtrack to fill in what turns out to be Patrick's final attempt to make a statement on behalf of the social underdogs he has adopted as his community. Clara is asking for Patrick's help, and as their deliberately witty dialogue proceeds, he makes his largest gesture of affiliation by telling her that he is Hana's father.

Instead of the drive, however, the text jumps back six months to present a picture of social unrest by juxtaposing the Spanish Civil War (1936–39), union dissidence, and the police crackdown initiated by Toronto's "rich and powerful" (*ISL,* 220). Sliding easily once again from facts to invention, it returns its focus to Commissioner Harris, determined to protect his dreams—especially the water filtration plant—from any attack. Harris's earlier unconscious dream of the plant as his body has now become a conscious vision of it as a body vulnerable to crippling. In this version of history, he spends his nights there, meditating upon the materialization of his civic desires. Moving from the brightness of the plant at night to an overview of the summer costume ball at the Toronto Island Yacht Club, and ironically emulating the descriptions of such events that appear in the social columns, the narrative slips into the tone of a comedy/thriller, focusing on the "image of Caravaggio among the rich which Patrick will always remember: meticulous, rude, and confident" (*ISL,* 222). In another of the story's transformations, Patrick, Caravaggio, and Giannetta enter this world uninvited in order to steal a yacht. The writing slides easily from one focal character to another, evoking a complex range of perceptions as it dramatizes their "sting." While some sentences seem straight out of a light thriller, the perceptual intensity of others interferes with any straight generic reading.

In the passages of preparation for and entry into the intake tunnel, a similar sensuous intensity simultaneously reinforces and interrupts the buildup of dramatic tension. Still, the description of Patrick's swim and of the small detonation he uses to break through the final metal screen is powerfully physical. As guardian of the place, Harris notices everything, but he cannot imagine an attack via the underwater tunnel. When Patrick confronts him, the epic nature of his approach may be what Harris appreciates most. Patrick's unconscious parroting of the popular songs of his day, even as he sets the charges, demonstrates his ability to separate himself from the larger culture they represent. It is another manifestation of the political ambivalence that drives this narrative, as is, perhaps, the surreally comical image of "the blasting-box carried like a chicken under his right arm" (*ISL*, 234).

The confrontation between Patrick and Harris replays but does not resolve the opposing political visions the novel has articulated. Theirs is a dialogue serving a dialogic text, as two voices, two different stories, vie for supremacy. Harris sweeps Patrick's generalizations aside with his assertion of the aesthetics of pure construction, and then he accuses Patrick of failing to understand or respect power. He refuses the easy assignment of a villain, implying that there is no such thing. His are the arguments of the powerful, and they have a logic of power that the general populace—including most of us—has been taught throughout our lives. Ondaatje captures the tone and rationalizations of such arguments with parodic clarity, but as Harris expands his rhetoric to include his dream, the parody falls away, and it's hard not to think that the rhetoric has won the author's assent. Certainly there is no touch of irony to Harris's speech at this point (*ISL*, 237). As he turns the argument back against Patrick in "a *mise en abyme* of this entire novel's mixing of history and fiction and its focus on class politics" (Hutcheon 1988b, 103), he uses one of Ondaatje's key positive metaphors to denigrate Patrick's refusal to engage power: "But you're among the dwarfs of enterprise who never get accepted or acknowledged. *Mongrel* company. You're a lost heir" (*ISL*, 238; emphasis added). That "mongrel" is derogatory in Harris's speech only adds to the ambivalence of the whole scene.

At this point, Patrick's only rejoinder is another story, the analeptic explanation, finally, of how Alice died through a gruesome mistake. Harris's shocked response to the information that meetings had been held in his palace provides a dark satiric edge to the conversation. As a sigh of his lack of empathy, it undercuts his position somewhat. Yet, he does show sympathy, and his knowledge of Alice's sources, like Diogenes, suggest that in some ways he is closer to her than Patrick is. The emotional drama of the scene is carried through its multiple shifts of focus. Patrick's first-person narrative of searching for Alice collapses immediately after the explosion kills her to a third-person description of his behavior. As Temelcoff lets him go and walks "over to the body of Alice" (*ISL,* 241), the sound of his name announces a return to Harris's office, where he has fallen asleep, still not having set off his dynamite. In this anticlimactic moment, it is Harris's thoughts the text offers us, and he is a man of wider political awareness than we might have expected: "Earlier Harris had understood why the man had chosen him, knew he was one of the few in power who had something tangible around him. But those with real power had nothing to show for themselves. They had paper" (*ISL,* 241–42). That this description also excludes Small means that this text can only define such power by its absence. Perhaps because writers also have paper, like "those with real power," they are able "to change how we read history and fiction, the change how we draw the lines we like to draw between the real and imaginary. The ex-centric, those on the margins of history—be they women, workers, immigrants (or writers?)—have the power to change the perspective of all the centre, and that power is given voice in *In the Skin of a Lion*" (Hutcheon 1988b, 103). All of which may be true, but this power of naming is not the same as the power of owning to which Harris's thinking alerts us, even as his use of another quotation from *The Epic of Gilgamesh* aligns his vision with that of the author in a strange loop of reference. In terms of both action and argument, this segment of the text remains unresolved; an earlier anarchist revolutionary act went terribly wrong, while this one fails. Nothing has changed in the novel's world, as nothing happened in the historical one. Ambiguity prevails.

The calling of his name that Patrick did not hear in Harris's office does wake him up in his and Hana's apartment. It is just before dawn, a dawn carefully rendered nonsymbolic at the end of a novel that might all too easily be read as allegory. Instead, Patrick and Hana get into the car, in a manner contradicting while recalling the beginning of the novel. Patrick's first order to Hana as she gets ready to drive also invokes the image of a movie director getting ready to shoot; the final words of the novel thus return us to its beginning, or perhaps just to beginnings: "Lights, he said" (*ISL,* 244).

The very title of the final section, "Maritime Theatre," intimates the ambiguous politics of the whole novel. The text has been a series of performances whose fluidity and transformations resist the stasis of authority that builds monuments to men like Harris. The stories are there, the ordinary people whose effort has built the country have been named, but the text refuses to pretend that this naming can replace the official histories; at best it can supplement them and demonstrate the contingency of their truths. Although *In the Skin of a Lion* sometimes betrays a confused ideology, its power lies in its ability to express the variety of stances to be found in any society, not as arguments but as visceral gestures, to make us see the lives of all these figures most feelingly.

Afterword

The English Patient

As this book was going to press, it had been five years since the publication of Michael Ondaatje's last novel, *In the Skin of a Lion* (in terms of new work, *The Cinnamon Peeler: Selected Poems* does not count). If that seems a long time readers need only remember the care he takes with each of his books. Although *The English Patient* may be Michael Ondaatje's blandest title yet, he once again provides the real thing in a novel whose sensuous prose and poetic perceptions are exquisitely seductive and provocative.

Despite its "local" and defiantly Canadian concerns, *In the Skin of a Lion* gained for Ondaatje perhaps the widest international audience of his career. A big novel, it helped him build upon the reputation he had gained as one of Canada's most exciting poets and innovators, especially for his longer works, but it still did not quite gain him the kind of reputation that breaks beyond the boundaries of the so-called "literary world" (the reputation, it could be argued, that Australian Peter Carey and New Zealander Keri Hulme did not gain until their Booker Prize winning *Oscar and Lucinda* and *The Bone People*). *In the Skin of a Lion* won or was listed for a number of major literary awards, and garnered rave reviews in England and the United States as well as in Canada; it made Ondaatje a much more recognizable name but not quite a heralded one. Now *The English Patient* has become the first Canadian book to win Britain's prestigious Booker Prize, and Ondaatje's first bona fide bestseller; and it will likely make him as well known as Carey, Hulme, or Rushdie. The good thing about it, as about those writers' winning novels, is that it manages to be ideally "international" in scope without in any way betraying his artistic principles. A richly and intricately woven tapestry of fragmented tales, it offers readers the solace of representation but refuses to deny the power of artifice; the authority to make such a complicated bargain with his readers stick has always been one of Ondaatje's most precious gifts as a writer.

As this study has shown, Ondaatje has always been fascinated by history—seen as a series of arcane stories about the past. And ever since his second book, *the man with seven toes*, that phantasmagoric and fragmented narrative poem set in Australia during the early days of settlement, he has cobbled together history's idiosyncrasies into luminous and complex *bricolages*. Because history itself can be defined as a kind of invention, Ondaatje has taken great pleasure in reinventing various episodes that have caught his fancy. In his hands, even the documents of history slide away from factual representation toward a haunting apprehension of indeterminacy. Perhaps his almost infinite curiosity concerning the tidbits of marginal information that can surround various subjects has led him more and more toward the novel, because the novel provides larger spaces in which to disperse the disparate nuggets of knowledge that provide such strange pleasure. In his last novel, he reinvented, and made wonderfully strange and exotic, the building of early twentieth-century Toronto, and the people involved in that grand modern project. In *The English Patient*, he returns to a major turning point in our near past, the end of World War II, and explores its impact on the lives of four people.

In a deserted Italian villa, once an army hospital, a young nurse continues to give aid to her final patient, a pilot whose plane had crashed in the Libyan desert, "someone who looked like a burned animal, taut and dark."[1] To the villa come a thief from Toronto and a young Sikh soldier in the British Army, a sapper whose business it is to defuse bombs. As the complexly ordered fragments of the novel accumulate, their pasts, their present, and their possible futures intertwine in an intricate collage that can best be described as labyrinthine. One of the most interesting aspects of this novel, especially given Ondaatje's declared aim to begin writing anew with each book, is that for the first time he has brought characters forward from his last novel into this one: Hana, the nurse, is the adopted daughter of Patrick, a major viewpoint figure in *In the Skin of a Lion*, while Caravaggio, the thief who has been turned into a spy by the war, was one of Patrick's and Hana's friends, and the eponymous subject of a major section of that book. It is oddly delightful to meet them again, and both their presence in a new text and our pleasure at reading them five years later (in both writer's and characters' time) raise intriguing questions about the novelty of the novel and its characterizations. Robert Kroetsch, one of Ondaatje's fellow Canadian novelists, who has also published a new book this year featuring characters from his last novel, puts an argument I suspect Ondaatje would generally agree with: "How I see it now is this: I would like, every decade or so, to drop in on these characters and see what's happening in their lives. So I'm in no sense writing a sequel. I'm really returning to these characters, because I think it's a shame to leave characters and never see them again."[2] Certainly, both Hana and Caravaggio have changed during, or more to the point, have been changed by, the war. And the two new characters with whom their lives intertwine provide further changes, beyond measurement but not beyond figuration.

Despite the complexity of its time scheme, and the range of its historical and geographical references—from India to Arabia to England to Italy to Canada; from desert exploration in the thirties to bomb disposal in Britain during the war to spying everywhere—*The English Patient* is possibly Ondaatje's most accessible fiction. Yet it rejects nothing of the style and intensity of vision that mark his earlier works. As I have tried to demonstrate in this study, Ondaatje's language has a hallucinatory intensity of focus, a passionate perception at work in images that seem absolutely right once you have read them. He is interested in mood and feeling, and in how they can suddenly transform people and lives. He creates characters who behave with such velocity of feeling they seem transparently familiar, yet in fact remain opaque to any rational understanding: as such they are the figures of a wild romanticism, a desire to sink into the sea of feeling in which we all swim, and sometimes drown. These characters hold on to their secrets even as they demonstrate the depths of feeling to which such secrets lead.

A by now familiar trope in Ondaatje's writing, the passionate, duplicitous, and destructive adulterous affair is the center of the maze the English patient creates as he tells the story of his life as a desert geographer in the 1930s. His story, with its fascinating vision of the singular, obsessed men who spent years returning to the desert, "[l]ooking for the lost army of Cambyses. Looking for Zerzura" (*TEP,* 138), a long-lost oasis known as "[t]he City of Acacias" (*TEP,* 135), slowly shapes its various fragments into a narrative of another, even more dangerous obsession, his love affair with the wife of a young pilot, whose single-engined craft ferries them back and forth from Cairo to the desert. As he tells his story, sometimes to Hana, more often to Caravaggio, whose own obsession at this time is with discovering who "the English patient" really is, Hana and the young Sikh, Kirpal Singh, enter a love affair as doomed as his, if for entirely different reasons. In another series of analepses, Singh's other and ethnically complex "affair" with the best of English character in the persons of his mentor in bomb defusing, the nonconformist Lord Suffolk and his secretary Miss Morden, has its shades of blindness and duplicity too. As a spy, Caravaggio, who eventually sacrificed his thief's hands to his mission, knows only too well how much of human behavior is based on illusion and lies, perhaps especially the lies we don't even know we are telling by our conduct. Ondaatje reveals all this while maintaining his and our liking for all his characters: they are, after all, only human.

Ondaatje's always powerful narrative images—girl with piano and rifle-toting soldiers, boy in ditch with bomb, burned pilot with bedouins and shaman-healer, spy sneaking naked into a room containing woman and commandant-lover—affect a perverse permanence in the minds of characters and readers both. But the sense of permanence is illusory, of course, as these scenes deliquesce, waver into insubstantiality, hover at the edge of memory: "When we meet those we fall in love with, there is an aspect of our spirit that is historian, a bit of a pedant, who imagines or remembers a meeting when the other has passed by innocently. . . . " (*TEP*, 259). It is that "imagines" that puts all memory in the novel in question, not to mention all historical documentation. Nothing— especially not the heart's desired ends—lasts in this shimmering and seemingly infinite branching of stories, except in memory, the one place they might be expected to rest, and even there they fragment, lose their sharp edges, become part of an indeterminate flow of events. Ondaatje's carefully casual *bricolage* of disassociated moments, the accumulation of narrative fragments, never quite solidifies into a plot, never quite denies us the traditional pleasures of narrative movement.

Yet, there is a sweeping subtlety to the way these image fragments manage to incorporate so much diachronal implication. Hana is playing the piano that may or may not be mined, when "two men slipped through the French doors and placed their guns on the end of the piano and stood in front of her. The noise of chords still in the air of the changed room" (*TEP*, 63). The scene, as it develops through remembrance and perception, perfectly demonstrates Ondaatje's particular poetic power:

A lightning flash across the valley, the storm had been coming all night, and she saw one of the men was a Sikh. Now she paused and smiled, somewhat amazed, relieved anyway, the cyclorama of light behind them so brief that it was just a quick glimpse of his turban and the bright wet guns. The high flap of the piano had been removed and used as a hospital table several months earlier, so their guns lay on the far side of the ditch of keys. The English patient could have identified the weapons. Hell. She was surrounded by foreign men. Not one pure Italian. A villa romance. What would Poliziano have thought of this 1945 tableau, two men and a woman across a piano and the war almost over and the

guns in their wet brightness whenever the lightning slipped itself into the room
filling everything with colour and shadow as it was doing now every half-minute
thunder crackling all over the valley and the music antiphonal, the press of
chords, *When I take my sugar to tea* . . .
Do you know the words?
There was no movement from them. She broke free of the chords and released
her fingers into intricacy, tumbling into what she had held back, the jazz detail
that split open notes and angles from the chestnut of melody.

> *When I take my sugar to tea*
> *All the boys are jealous of me,*
> *So I never take her where the gang goes*
> *When I take my sugar to tea.*

Their clothes wet while they watched her whenever the lightning was in the
room among them, her hands playing now against and within the lightning and
thunder, counter to it, filling up the darkness between light. Her face so
concentrated they knew they were invisible to her, to her brain struggling to
remember her mother's hand ripping newspaper and wetting it under a kitchen
tap and using it to wipe the table free of the shaded notes, the hopscotch of keys.
After which she went for her weekly lesson at the community hall, where she
would play, her feet still unable to reach the pedals if she sat, so she preferred to
stand, her summer sandal on the left pedal and the metronome ticking.
She did not want to end this. To give up these words from an old song. She
saw the places they went, where the gang never went, crowded with aspidistra.
She looked up and nodded towards them, an acknowledgement that she would
stop now.

(*TEP*, 63–65)

Such references to jazz, recalling *Coming Through Slaughter* and its self-
referential evocation of the interaction of passion and art, occur throughout *The English Patient*; and in this scene, the writing, in all its
improvisational complication, its rendering of language down to its
most sensitive alertness, seems to explain its own power in the description of another act of art.

Perhaps then, although there is a kind of spy story hidden in the
labyrinth of *The English Patient*, it is nearer the mark to say that the spy
story is the labyrinth, its various by-ways the darkly radiant narratives
that intertwine and interfere with one another until we forget we might
have been looking for a center, or a way out. Ondaatje's great generosity
as a writer here, to his characters, and to us, is his willingness to let them
go in the end, to allow them their human silences. They leave the story as

solid and impenetrable as when they entered it, yet they leave us enriched by our involvement in their narratives. *The English Patient* is as much about the power of written narratives as it is about the power of passion. Early on, the text calls attention to the obsessive strength books can exert: "This was the time of her life that she fell upon books as the only door out of her cell. They became her world. She sat at the night table, hunched over, reading of the young boy in India who learned to memorize diverse jewels and objects on a tray, tossed from teacher to teacher—those who taught him dialect those who taught him memory those who taught him to escape the hypnotic" (*TEP,* 7). Of course, her reading of *Kim* (carefully left unnamed here), or later of *The Last of the Mohicans,* cannot be, textually, innocent: soon enough Kirpal Singh will arrive and she will become his lover; too soon he will find it necessary to leave Europe and all it stands for, and therefore also leave her. By then, their own stories, as well as those of Caravaggio and "the English patient" himself, will have become labyrinths they escape into and cannot escape. But see how the text also describes its own workings, as in the description of Hana's reading to her patient: "books for the Englishman, as he listened intently or not, had gaps of plot like sections of a road washed out by storms, missing incidents as if locusts had consumed a section of tapestry, as if plaster loosened by the bombing had fallen away from a mural at night" (*TEP,* 7).

Ondaatje has tended to resist overt politicalization of his texts, and his texts have tended to resist the usual forms of political exploration. Yet, because of his choice of subjects, they also refuse to become truly apolitical. A Ceylonese-born Canadian, he is necessarily in one way or another a postcolonial writer, and seemingly off-hand allusions, like the one to perhaps the most famous novel in praise of colonization, or the various references in the chapter on Kip's training in Britain when he falls under the spell of an eccentric paragon of the best British values, create a climate in which the sudden and final break Kip makes with his three chosen comrades seems sadly inevitable, and for precisely the political reasons the novel seems to ignore. I believe Ondaatje is determined not to write from a program, and this is why he seeks to begin each new project anew, as if learning how to write again for the first time. Nevertheless, he does not ignore the political in his work; rather he seeks to place it in a human, fallible context, complicated by the force of powerful and contradictory emotions, and "the emotions are not skilled workers."[3]

A novel of international scope, set at a time of terrible and triumphant change in the world, *The English Patient* focuses primarily on the way-ward ways of the human heart among a small number of people inden-tifiably ordinary. Even its ending, which invokes one of our time's most terrifying images of slaughter of the innocents to break its tentative community apart, manages to avoid melodrama. The eponymous char-acter at one point tells Caravaggio about words: "They have a power" (*TEP*, 234), he says. As I have tried to show in this study, when wielded by an artist with the grace and force of Michael Ondaatje, they have the power to move.

Notes and References

Chapter One

1. Margaret Atwood, ed., *The New Oxford Book of Canadian Verse in English* (Toronto: Oxford University Press, 1982), xxxvi; hereafter cited in text.

2. Interview with Michael Ondaatje, *Manna* 1 (March 1972): 19; hereafter cited in text.

3. Coach House Press was one of many small presses that began life in the 1960s in Canada; from the beginning it attracted innovative Canadian writers, as well as some important U.S. ones. Ondaatje joined Coach House's editorial board in the 1970s and has seen a number of important books through the press. House of Anansi Press also began life in the late 1960s, and has managed to maintain a small list of books regularly taught in Canadian literature courses; two of its best-sellers are *The Collected Works of Billy the Kid* and *Coming Through Slaughter*. McClelland and Stewart published Ondaatje's selected poems in 1979 as well as *Running in the Family* and *In the Skin of a Lion* (like *Coming Through Slaughter*, these were also published in New York and London). His individual books of poetry have continued to appear from Coach House Press.

4. Ann Mandel, "Michael Ondaatje," *Canadian Writers since 1960: Second Series*, ed. W. H. New (Detroit: Gale Research Company, 1987), 274; hereafter cited in text. Mandel provides the most complete outline of Ondaatje's life, and it is her account I follow.

5. Mark Witten, "Billy, Buddy, and Michael," *Books in Canada* 6, no. 6 (June–July 1977): 9; hereafter cited in text.

6. *Running in the Family* (Toronto: McClelland and Stewart, 1982), 206; hereafter cited in text as *RF*.

7. Barbara Turner, "In the Skin of Michael Ondaatje: Giving Voice to a Social Conscience," *Quill & Quire* 53, no. 5 (May 1987): 21; hereafter cited in text. Ondaatje has since revised this claim; see chapter 8.

8. *The Collected Works of Billy the Kid* was designed and printed at Coach House: *Coming Through Slaughter* was designed there; *In the Skin of a Lion* was designed and typeset there.

9. Marjorie Perloff, *The Poetics of Indeterminacy: Rimbaud to Cage* (Princeton: Princeton University Press, 1981), 4; hereafter cited in text. The whole of Perloff's first chapter provides a comprehensive comparison of the two traditions, that of high modernist symbolism and that of "undecidability" or "indeterminacy" (see 3–44). I think it important to note, in the context of Ondaatje's later long works, which either mix poetry and prose or are wholly prose, Perloff's comment that, in her argument, "'poetry' is construed not as

'verse' (which is not, in fact, the dominant medium of the poets concerned) but as *language art* or 'word-system'" (43).

10. See Marjorie Perloff, "Pound/Stevens: Whose Era?" in her *The Dance of the Intellect: Studies in the Poetry of the Pound Tradition* (New York: Cambridge University Press, 1985), 1–32; hereafter cited in text.

11. George Bowering puts it this way: "The development of Ondaatje's poetry, from his early years in this country to the present, resembles the development of the main currents of Canadian verse over a period perhaps twice as long. Unlike the Vancouver poets with their advocacy of open-ended, process form, Ondaatje emerged from the school that believes the poem to be an artifact, something well-made and thus rescued from the chaos of contemporary world and mind. If the Vancouver poets might be loosely said to descend from Duncan, and Victor Coleman from Zukofsky, Ondaatje might be said to descend from Yeats and Stevens" ("Ondaatje Learning to Do," in *Imaginary Hand: Essays by George Bowering* [Edmonton: NeWest Press, 1988], 163); hereafter cited in text.

12. On the general problems with the terms, and their many interpretations, see, among others, the entry in Chris Baldick, *The Concise Oxford Dictionary of Literary Terms* (New York: Oxford University Press, 1990), 174–75; Linda Hutcheon's three volumes on the topic, *A Poetics of Postmodernism: History, Theory, Fiction* (London: Routledge, 1988a), *The Canadian Postmodern: A Study of Contemporary English-Canadian Fiction* (Toronto: Oxford University Press, 1988b), and *The Politics of Postmodernism* (London: Routledge, 1989); Brian McHale's lucid exploration of the problem in the opening chapter of *Postmodernist Fiction* (New York and London: Methuen, 1987), 3–25; and Robert Rawdon Wilson's remarks on the "two distinct archives, two sets of relevant primary and secondary texts, behind the usage of 'postmodern'" in "SLIP PAGE: Angela Carter, In / Out / In the Postmodern Nexus," *Ariel* 20, no. 2 (October 1989): 99 (his whole argument covers 96–104); hereafter cited in text. These writers all point to a vast number of other studies, every one of which would add to both one's understanding and one's confusion, but this seems to be the basic situation of postmodernism, as such.

13. McHale's larger, and more complex, argument is that the difference between modernism and postmodernism can best be seen in terms of "Jacobson's concept of the dominant" (6). He argues that "the dominant of modernist fiction is *epistemological*" (9) while "the dominant of postmodernist fiction is *ontological*" (10). Modernist fiction asks questions about knowledge and interpretation; postmodern fiction asks questions about being and acting. Of course, as McHale readily acknowledges, writers continually pass from one mode to another, as do various of their works; these are not inviolable categories. Perloff does not make this argument, exactly, yet one of the clear differences she sees between Stevens and Pound is that the poems of the former lead to "this formulation from Harold Bloom": they are "'more advanced as *interpretation* than our criticism as yet has gotten to be," yet no one claims Pound "is great because his work constitutes an advanced form of 'interpretation'" (1985, 3),

which is to say, Pound's is not an epistemological poetics, but more an ontological one, a question not of why but of how (and see McHale's lists of typical questions for each dominant [9–10]).

14. See Robert Kroetsch, "For Play and Entrance: The Contemporary Canadian Long Poem," in *The Lovely Treachery of Words* (Toronto: Oxford University Press, 1989), 119 (originally published in 1981), and Frank Davey, "The Language of the Contemporary Canadian Long Poem," in *Surviving the Paraphrase* (Winnipeg: Turnstone Press, 1983), 186, 192; hereafter cited in text.

15. The two most important essays on the documentary poem are Dorothy Livesay's original essay coining the term, "The Documentary Poem: A Canadian Genre?" in *Contexts of Canadian Criticism*, ed. Eli Mandel (Toronto: University of Toronto Press, 1971), 267–81, and Stephen Scobie, "Amelia or: Who Do You Think You Are? Documentary and Identity in Canadian Literature," *Canadian Literature* 100 (Spring 1984): 264–85, the most important parts of which were reprinted in Stephen Scobie, "Documentary : the Forged Signature," in *Signature Event Cantext* (Edmonton: NeWest Press, 1989), 119–27; hereafter cited in text. That by 1979, when he edited an anthology of Canadian long poems, Ondaatje was fully aware of the documentary tradition is attested to by his introduction, where he refers to Livesay's essay and then suggests that "What is needed now is perhaps a new look at the documentary poem in Canada—how it has changed in intent, how it has become (in Susan Sontag's term) 'infradidactic.' For in spite of the poems being *long,* there is little evidence of a didactic formal voice" (Introduction to *The Long Poem Anthology* [Toronto: Coach House Press, 1979], 15; hereafter cited in text as *LPA*.

16. See M. M. Bakhtin, "Discourse in the Novel," in *The Dialogic Imagination,* ed. Michael Holquist, trans. Caryl Emerson and Michael Holquist (Austin: University of Texas Press, 1981), 259–422; hereafter cited in text. One major point in this essay is that while the traditional language of poetry is "monologic" rather than "dialogic" ("The language in a poetic work realizes itself as something about which there can be no doubt, something that cannot be disputed, something all-encompassing" [286]), the language(s) of that transgeneric genre, the novel, is "dialogic," a "double-voiced discourse" (324) that "can never be exhausted thematically" (326). See also the "Glossary," especially its definitions of "dialogism" (426) and "heteroglossia" (428).

17. In my "Transformations of (the Language of) the Ordinary: Innovation in Recent Canadian Poetry" (*Essays on Canadian Writing* 37 [Spring 1989]: 30–64), I argue that the innovative poetry of our century "is 'novelized,' in Bakhtin's sense of the term: it is a poetry of voices in concert and argument, not a singular voice speaking a centripetal 'unitary language,'" and I suggest that heteroglossia "emerges most strongly in the long poem" (31). But my other major point is that poetry also insists on being read as poetry, not as novel, and it does so by taking heteroglossic, dialogic "speech, with its reflection of the social languages around us, and render[ing] it mysterious, delivering the word

as simple signifier back to its numinous position as object. The poetry of innovation does so most often by engaging the signifier as an open space of possibility beneath which the potential signifieds slide but never come to rest: the poetic word as heteroglossic speech rather than polysemic trope" (32). As I will argue in later chapters, Ondaatje's longer works are "open" in precisely this manner.

18. In the introduction to his most recent interview, Catherine Bush says of Ondaatje's four larger works: "Each work summons up a whole world, combining varied voices, encompassing real and imagined history, collapsing time within the clear, refracting lens of Ondaatje's original vision. Genre boundaries blur. Often simultaneously, Ondaatje manages to be both lyrical and outrageous. His language, honed to a precise clarity, is deeply sensual" ("Michael Ondaatje: An Interview," *Conjunctions* 15 [1990]: 87; hereafter cited in text). Fully attentive to generic slippage, Bush also recognizes how much of Ondaatje's appeal lies in his evocative language.

19. On the concept of "carnivalization" and how it applies to literary texts, see Mikhail Bakhtin, introduction to *Rabelais and His World,* trans. Hélène Iswolsky (Cambridge, Mass.: MIT Press, 1968), 1–58; Tzvetan Todorov, *Mikhail Bakhtin: The Dialogic Principle,* trans. Wlad Godzich (Minneapolis: University of Minnesota Press, 1984), 78–80; and, perhaps most pertinent to Ondaatje's work, Robert Kroetsch, "Carnival and Violence: A Meditation" (Kroetsch, 95–107).

20. While both McHale (4–5) and Hutcheon (1989, 11 ff.) allow for the possibility of various "constructions of postmodernism" (McHale, 4), they do not make the same allowance for modernism, at least not explicitly. But it seems clear by now that there were, even just in the realm of English poetics, at least two modernist traditions, as Perloff so cogently argues in both texts referred to above. That, in fact, a number of modernisms interacted with and countered one another seems clear: it also seems likely that most later writers were influenced by contradictory impulses from the various modernisms and postmodernisms. This is, in fact, McHale's point when he argues that the same writer can shift dominants from one book to another or even within a single text (McHale, 9–11, 12–25).

21. A good introduction to the concept as it affects literary studies is Bill Ashcroft, Gareth Griffiths, and Helen Tiffin, *The Empire Writes Back: Theory and Practice in Post-colonial Literatures* (London: Routledge, 1989); hereafter cited in text. On the complex relationship between postmodernism and postcolonialism, see Stephen Slemon, "Modernism's Last Post" and Linda Hutcheon, "'Circling the Downspout of Empire': Post-Colonialism and Postmodernism," in the special issue of *Ariel* on "Post-Colonialism and Post-Modernism," *Ariel* 20, no. 4 (October 1989): 1–17, 149–75; hereafter cited in text.

22. Sam Solecki, "An Interview with Michael Ondaatje (1975)," in *Spider*

Blues: Essays on Michael Ondaatje, ed. Sam Solecki (Montreal: Véhicule Press, 1985), 24–25; hereafter cited in text as Solecki 1975.

23. Because "[c]onsciously or unconsciously we burn the previous devices which have got us here but which now are only rhetoric" (Sam Solecki, "An Interview with Michael Ondaatje (1984)," in *Spider Blues,* 325; hereafter cited in text as Solecki 1984).

Chapter Two

1. *The Collected Poetry of W. H. Auden* (New York: Random House, 1945), 185–88; hereafter cited in text. The earliest version of the poem, including the stanza Ondaatje quotes, appeared in the *Listener,* 12 July 1933, and was written between September 1932 and January 1933 (see *The English Auden: Poems, Essays, and Dramatic Writings,* ed. Edward Mendelson [London: Faber and Faber, 1977], 130, 422–23).

2. J. E. Chamberlin, "Let There Be Commerce between Us: The Poetry of Michael Ondaatje," in Solecki, ed., *Spider Blues,* 31; hereafter cited in text.

3. Stephen Scobie, "His Legend a Jungle Sleep: Michael Ondaatje and Henri Rousseau," in Solecki, ed., *Spider Blues,* 51; hereafter cited in text as Scobie 1985a.

4. Susan Glickman, "From 'Philoctetes on the Island' to 'Tin Roof': the Emerging Myth of Michael Ondaatje," in Solecki, ed., *Spider Blues,* 80; hereafter cited in text.

5. Tom Marshall, "Layering: The Shorter Poems of Michael Ondaatje," in Solecki, ed., *Spider Blues,* 84–85; hereafter cited in text.

6. Lynette Hunter, "Form and Energy in the Poetry of Michael Ondaatje," *Journal of Canadian Poetry* 1, no. 1 (Winter 1978): 50; hereafter cited in text.

7. Sam Solecki, "Nets and Chaos: The Poetry of Michael Ondaatje," in Solecki, ed., *Spider Blues,* 93; hereafter cited in text as Solecki 1985a.

8. See *The Collected Poems of Wallace Stevens* (New York: Alfred A. Knopf, 1967), 526. This is the title of the second section of "The Rock."

9. Michael Ondaatje, *The Dainty Monsters* (Toronto: Coach House Press, 1967), 11; hereafter cited in text as *DM.* Where the poems are reprinted in Michael Ondaatje, *There's a Trick with a Knife I'm Learning to Do* (Toronto: McClelland & Stewart, 1979; New York: W. W. Norton & Co., 1979), I will also give the page number of that volume, hereafter cited in text as *TK.*

10. Perhaps. It is "because the term 'surrealism' is used so freely now, having passed into common currency rather as 'romantic' did " (Dawn Ades, "Dada and Surrealism," in *Concepts of Modern Art,* ed. Tony Richardson and Nikos Stangos [Harmondsworth: Penguin Books, 1974], 133), that one refers to it as a generalized 'influence' on young writers. The following statement on metaphor is most relevant to my purpose here: "The surrealist image is born by the chance juxtaposition of two different realities, and it is on the spark struck by

their meeting that the beauty of the image depends, the more different the two terms of the image are, the brighter the spark will be" (125).

11. *The Compact Edition of the Oxford English Dictionary* (New York: Oxford University Press, 1971), 1303; hereafter cited in text as *OED*. It is an early sign of Ondaatje's ability to play the language for effect, that he creates his neologism out of the half of the compound that has no separate existence.

12. See: J. E. Cirlot, *A Dictionary of Symbols,* trans. Jack Sage (1971; reprint, London: Routledge & Kegan Paul, 1983, 28; hereafter cited in text.

13. On the "perfectly coherent symbolic structure" (13) of poems in the symbolic tradition, see Perloff 1981, 11–18.

14. See Ezra Pound, "A Retrospect," in *Literary Essays of Ezra Pound,* ed. T. S. Eliot (London: Faber and Faber, 1960), 5. This essay, along with Pound's poetry, remains one of the central teachings of modernist poetry.

15. In *TK,* this final couplet is removed. This does not essentially affect my argument.

16. Stephen Scobie has written a whole essay on this affinity, in which he argues that both depict "the coexistence, amounting to interpenetration, of a domestic scene and a jungle." But he argues that although "Ondaatje's poetry reaches towards the kind of balance found in the visual composition of *The Dream,* . . . for him it is more difficult to attain. Rousseau's jungle is more exotic than violent; but for Ondaatje, violence is the essence of the jungle, and time after time it breaks through his poems with disturbing effect" (Scobie 1985a, 47–48).

17. Symbolically, the dragon is "an amalgam of elements taken from various animals that are particularly aggressive and dangerous" (Cirlot, 85), and as a symbol of the instincts it is also perceived as "adversary" or "primordial enemy" (Cirlot, 86), in its relation to "the concept of chaos . . . and of dissolution" (Cirlot, 88). It is, then, a highly symbolic figure.

18. On this, see Sharon Cameron, *Lyric Time: Dickinson and the Limits of Genre* (Baltimore and London: Johns Hopkins University Press, 1979), 23, where she argues that "the lyric voice is solitary and generally speaks out of a single moment in time." See also Bakhtin's comments on the unified, singular, and bounded language of poetry (Bakhtin, 284–87).

19. On the nature of writing as supplement, see Jacques Derrida, *Of Grammatology,* trans. Gayatri Chakravorty Spivak (Baltimore and London: Johns Hopkins University Press, 1976), especially, "That Dangerous Supplement," 141–64; hereafter cited in text. See also Stephen Scobie, "Amorce: Always Already," *Signature Event Cantext* (1989), 1–8.

20. See Guy Davenport, "The Symbol of the Archaic," in *The Geography of the Imagination* (San Francisco: North Point Press, 1981), 27; hereafter cited in text.

21. T. S. Eliot, "Ulysses, Order, and Myth," in *Selected Prose of T. S. Eliot,*

ed. Frank Kermode (London: Faber and Faber, 1975), 177. The article originally appeared in the *Dial* 75, no. 5 (November 1923): 480–83.

22. Ondaatje's epigraph refers only to the character, not even to the novel. One critic suggests that the epigraph "invites us to search for Ondaatje in the guilty Paris, for his wife Kim in Helen, the stolen bride. Here, the poet appropriates exotic *characters*, rather than magical beasts, to be the carriers of personal symbols" (Glickman, 72). I would be very careful in making such biographical analogies.

23. In Canada, bpNichol's *The Martyrology* is the most sustained systematic example of a continuing poem that contains stories but is, instead, in Robert Kroetsch's terms, a "method, then, and then, and then, of composition; against the 'and then' of story" (Kroetsch, 120). I use Shlomith Rimmon-Kenan's version of the terms, *story, text,* and *narration* here, although she applies them only to a narrow definition of "narrative fiction [that] gives rise to a classification of its basic aspects: the events, their verbal representation, and the act of telling or writing. In the spirit of Genette's distinction between '*histoire*', '*récit*' and '*narration*' . . . , I shall label these aspects 'story', 'text' and 'narration' respectively" (Shlomith Rimmon-Kenan, *Narrative Fiction: Contemporary Poetics* [London: Methuen & Co., 1983], 3; hereafter cited in text).

24. For the whole Wayland Smith tale, see Brian Branston, *The Lost Gods of England* (London: Thames and Hudson, 1957), 6–9. Ondaatje has told me in conversation that he did not have the story of Wayland Smith consciously in mind when he wrote "Peter," but he did recall having come across the legend in an English class once.

25. Gillian Harding-Russell, "A Note on Ondaatje's 'Peter': a Creative Myth," *Canadian Literature* 112 (Spring 1987): 205; hereafter cited in text.

26. They are not usually linked together: Jason belongs to Greek mythology as the leader of the Argonauts and the lover of Medea (Hamilton, 118–30); Tara "at once recalls the Irish home of kings and a Buddhist deity who provides essential life energy to *everyman*" (Harding-Russell, 207).

27. Harding-Russell argues that although "Peter has caused the girl all this suffering, his guilt and sorrow identify him with his victim, even as the artist is identified with the subject matter of his art" (Harding-Russell, 209), and then adds that "Here is an almost ritual view of mourning in which the artist's 'face' or identity is 'glued' to the girl's neck through his tears of remorse. A certain redemption attends the artistic process even if it is not strictly therapeutic" (Harding-Russell, 209–10). Aside from my disagreement with her personalist view of the artist's identification with his subject matter (although it is the romantic view of extremist art this poem interrogates), I also feel her misreading of "his tears of remorse" when the text mentions only *her* tears, has led her astray at this point.

28. Sam Solecki, "Making and Destroying: *Coming Through Slaughter* and

Extremist Art," in Solecki, ed., *Spider Blues,* 247; hereafter cited in text as Solecki 1985c.

29. Leslie Mundwiler argues that it is a complete failure, "the 'myth' of the artist . . . undercut completely by the abstraction from time and place and by the improbability of Peter's development." Clearly, he does not respond to the tone of folktale that I suggest hovers over the whole sequence. See Leslie Mundwiler, *Michael Ondaatje: Word, Image, Imagination* (Vancouver: Talonbooks, 1984), 33; hereafter cited in text.

30. Michael Ondaatje, *the man with seven toes* (Toronto: Coach House Press, 1969).

31. Kenneth Clark, Colin MacInnes, and Bryan Robertson, *Sidney Nolan* (London: Thames and Hudson, 1961); hereafter cited in text. The first major book on Nolan, it remains one of the best basic studies of his work. The "version of the story" is MacInnes's, which Ondaatje creatively quotes at the end of his book.

32. Michael Ondaatje, "O'Hagan's Rough-Edged Chronicle," *Canadian Literature* 61 (Summer 1974): 24, 25; hereafter cited in text as ORC.

33. See Michael Alexander, *Mrs. Fraser on the Fatal Shore* (New York: Simon and Schuster, 1971); Stephen Tatum, *Inventing Billy the Kid: Visions of the Outlaw in America, 1881–1981* (Albuquerque: University of New Mexico Press, 1982); and Donald M. Marquis, *In Search of Buddy Bolden, First Man of Jazz* (Baton Rouge and London: Louisiana State University Press, 1978); hereafter cited in text.

34. "There's a series of paintings by Sidney Nolan on this story and I was previously interested in Nolan's Ned Kelly series. I got fascinated by the story of which I only knew *the account in the paintings* and the quote from Colin MacInnes. That's how it grew. It had to be brief and imagistic because the formal alternative was to write a long graphic introduction explaining the situation, setting, characters, and so on. All the geographical references in the book are probably wrong and I'm sure all Australians think that the book is geographically ridiculous, just as the people of the south-west might think *Billy the Kid* is" (Solecki 1975, 20; emphasis added).

35. See Marshall McLuhan and Wilfred Watson, *From Cliché to Archetype* (New York: Viking Press, 1970), 48–51, 117–30, 158–66, 168–70.

Chapter Three

1. Annie Dillard, *Living by Fiction* (New York: Harper & Row, 1982), 21–22.

2. See Frank Davey, "Surviving the Paraphrase," in *Surviving the Paraphrase* (Winnipeg: Turnstone Press, 1983), 1–12; and his later reconsideration of that essay and the problems it addressed in "Reading Canadian Reading," in *Reading Canadian Reading* (Winnipeg: Turnstone Press, 1988), 1–18.

3. Stephen Scobie, "Two Authors in Search of a Character: bp Nichol and

Michael Ondaatje," in Solecki, ed., *Spider Blues,* 188; hereafter cited in text as Scobie 1985c.

4. Judith Owens, "'I Send You a Picture': Ondaatje's Portrait of Billy the Kid," *Studies in Canadian Literature* 8, no. 1 (1983): 117; hereafter cited in text. Other essays with a similar view of Billy include: Dennis Lee, "Savage Fields: *The Collected Works of Billy the Kid,*" in Solecki, ed., *Spider Blues,* 166–84; Percy M. Nodelman, "The Collected Photographs of Billy the Kid," *Canadian Literature* 87 (Winter 1980): 68–79; and Dennis Cooley, "'I Am Here on the Edge': Modern Hero / Postmodern Poetics in *The Collected Works of Billy the Kid,*" in Solecki, ed., *Spider Blues,* 211–39. See also T. D. MacLulich, "Ondaatje's Mechanical Boy: Portrait of the Artist as Photographer," *Mosaic* 14, no. 2 (Spring 1981): 110 (Garrett "possesses the perfectly controlled personality that Billy wishes for"); hereafter cited in text.

5. Kent Ladd Steckmesser, in *Western Outlaws: The "Good Badman" in Fact, Film, and Folklore* (Claremont, Calif.: Regina Books, 1983), takes an introductory chapter to establish the paradigms of "The Robin Hood Legend," before showing how certain legendary figures of the Old West took on the coloring of Robin Hood in their own tales. As he points out, "[t]o some people, Billy the Kid is the perfect folk hero" (79), and, whether he merits it or not, "'the mantle of Robin Hood has descended on his narrow, bottle shoulders'" (79).

6. Walter Noble Burns, *The Saga of Billy the Kid* (New York: Doubleday, Page & Co., 1926); hereafter cited in text.

7. Michael Ondaatje, *The Collected Works of Billy the Kid* (Toronto: House of Anansi Press, 1970), 110; hereafter cited in text as *CWBK.*

8. See Jack David, "Michael Ondaatje's *The Collected Works of Billy the Kid,*" *Canadian Notes & Queries* 13 (June 1974): 11–12. David suggests Ondaatje's book was influenced by the Spicer book, which Ondaatje had reviewed favorably in *Quarry.*

9. Using the term *fabula* where I use *story,* Barbara Godard makes this point, too: "the fabula is always already there, a legendary fabula accessible to the reader in the cultural intertext" (Barbara Godard, "Stretching the Story: the Canadian Story Cycle," *Open Letter* 7, no. 6 [Fall 1989]: 42; hereafter cited in text).

10. Manina Jones, "*The Collected Works of Billy the Kid*: Scripting the Docudrama," *Canadian Literature* 122–23 (Autumn–Winter 1989): 29; hereafter cited in text.

11. Smaro Kamboureli, *On the Edge of Genre: The Contemporary Canadian Long Poem* (Toronto: University of Toronto Press, 1991), 192; hereafter cited in text as Kamboureli 1991. As will become clear, I am more indebted to the two recent readings of *The Collected Works of Billy the Kid* by Manina Jones and Smaro Kamboureli than to any of the others; I recommend both to anyone interested in the complexities of this text.

12. As Jones points out, the term *pronominal* is Benveniste's (Jones, 29). According to Benveniste, "these 'pronominal forms' do not refer to 'reality' or to 'objective' positions in space or time but rather to the utterance, unique each time, that contains them" (Emile Benveniste, "The Nature of Pronouns," in *Problems in General Linguistics,* trans. Mary Elizabeth Meek [Coral Gables: University of Miami Press, 1971], 219).

13. "*Exergue* derives from the Greek *ex-ergon,* literally 'outside the work.' . . . it also has the sense of an epigraph, of something 'outside the work'" (Jacques Derrida, "White Mythology: Metaphor in the Text of Philosophy," in *Margins of Philosophy,* trans. Alan Bass [Chicago: University of Chicago Press, 1982], 209).

14. Sheila Watson, "Michael Ondaatje: the Mechanization of Death," in Solecki, ed., *Spider Blues,* 157; hereafter cited in text. See Kamboureli 1991, 189.

15. I am using these terms as Rimmon-Kenan does: " 'Story' designates the narrated events, abstracted from their disposition in the text [or the intertext] and reconstructed in their chronological order, together with the participants in these events. . . . 'text' is a spoken or written discourse which undertakes their telling . . . [it] is what we read. . . . The act or process of production is . . . 'narration.' . . . [S]tory and narration may be seen as two metonymies of the text, the first evoking it through its narrative content, the second through its production" (Rimmon-Kenan, 3–4).

16. From the book *Huffman, Frontier Photographer,* according to Ondaatje's end note (*CWBK,* 110). It is really a carefully edited pastiche of two separate letters from Huffman to Perrin Cuppy Huffman, 18 January 1885 and 7 June 1885; the *name* of the person photographed is *Bessie,* Huffman's daughter, and the letters are found in the *chapter* titled "L. A. Huffman, Frontier Photographer," in Mark H. Brown and W. R. Felton, *The Frontier Years: L. A. Huffman, Photographer of the Plains* (New York: Henry Holt and Company, 1955), 43.

17. J. M. Kertzer, "On Death and Dying: *The Collected Works of Billy the Kid,*" *English Studies in Canada* 1, no. 1 (Spring 1975): 92, 93; hereafter cited in text.

18. Cooley argues that while the text of *The Collected Works* presents such a world, the character of Billy the Kid tries to freeze it in a still-camera shot, and fails to do so over and over again (224, 228). For him, Billy is a "[w]ould-be modernist" caught in the flux of an "essentially postmodern" world (232). With its narrow definition of modernism, this analysis also reads Billy as a singular character.

19. Robert Kroetsch in conversation, Edmonton, 13 October 1985: his point was that the notion of the Freudian fixed self that ruled over much modern poetics (and, I would argue, the criticism that emerges from them) is obsolete. He suggested that what we find in a long poem like *The Collected Works* is an *emptying* of the traditional monologic self, so that inconsistencies are allowed their full place.

20. "Ondaatje's favourite films [include] the Italian Westerns of Sergio Leone, [and] John Boorman's *Point Blank.* . . . *Point Blank*'s female lead is Angie Dickinson" (Scobie 1985c, 192). The comment "it is difficult to find books in which the original myth is given to us point blank," appears in Ondaatje's essay on *Tay John* ("ORC," 24).

21. For a useful overview of reader-response criticism, see Elizabeth Freund, *The Return of the Reader* (London: Methuen & Co., 1987), especially her conclusion, which argues in a manner that seems to parallel my own feelings about Ondaatje's writing that "[i]ndeterminacy invites a resistance to closure and an insistence on greater reflection and self-reflection," and that "[d]ialogue [is] a trope for reading that stands in opposition to the authority of monological discourse, whether the text's or the reader's. . . . [Therefore] reading continues, ever more closely and patiently, because, as de Man puts it . . . , the 'dialogue between work and interpreter is endless'" (156).

22. Anne Blott, "'Stories to Finish': *The Collected Works of Billy the Kid,*" in *Minus Canadian: Penultimate Essays on Literature,* ed. Barry Cameron and Michael Dixon (*Studies in Canadian Literature* 2, no. 2 [Summer 1977]), 190, 191; hereafter cited in text.

23. How a reader's bias can lead to misreading emerges in Nodelman's insistence that "when she actually captures him, he is 'blurred in the dark' himself [the line refers to her (*CWBK,* 64)], having totally lost his clarity and shouting 'stop'" (72). But Billy only shouts "stop" to one woman, and that is Sallie as she approaches to rub his burned legs (*CWBK,* 34).

24. We would, for example, read "[t]he smell of her sex strong now daubing my chest and shirt where she rubs it" as a sign of Billy's arousal rather than his "disgust" at Angela's "offensive odours" (Nodelman, 74).

25. According to Ondaatje, "[t]he last piece of dialogue between Garrett and Poe is taken from an account written by Deputy John W. Poe in 1919" (*CWBK,* 110), but in Poe, the dialogue appears thus:

"That was the Kid that came in there onto me, and I think I have got him." I said, "Pat, the Kid would not come to this place; you have shot the wrong man."

Upon my saying this, Garrett seemed to be in doubt himself as to whom he had shot, but quickly spoke up and said, "I am sure that was him, for I know his voice too well to be mistaken." (John W. Poe, *The Death of Billy the Kid* [Boston & New York: Houghton Mifflin Co., 1933], 37–38)

Ondaatje's comment appears to be another of the many little games he plays with documentation in this book. He actually quotes, with slight emendations, Burns's *Saga,* 284.

Chapter Four

1. Michael Ondaatje, *Rat Jelly* (Toronto: Coach House Press, 1973), hereafter cited in text as *RJ*. Where the poems appear in *Trick with a Knife,* I will cite *TK* as well.

2. Ondaatje let Stephen Scobie and me have the poem to publish in *White Pelican* 1, no. 2 (Spring 1971) when we interviewed him on 3 March 1971; so it was written at the very latest in February 1971. I suspect it had been written earlier, as he usually waits a while before publicly reading or publishing his work. He began serious work on *Running in the Family* when he traveled to Sri Lanka in the spring of 1978.

3. Roger Shattuck, *The Banquet Years: The Origins of the Avant Garde in France 1885 to World War I,* rev. ed. (New York: Vintage Books, 1968), 221; hereafter cited in text.

4. Susan Glickman argues that his father "is evoked continually in Ondaatje's work" (78), and that, like Bolden, he "becomes one of those 'people who disappear'" (79), commemorated in "White Dwarfs."

5. From Howard O'Hagan, *Tay John* (New York: Clarkson N. Potter, 1960), 28, which Ondaatje would have been reading when he wrote many of these poems, as the publication of his article on the novel in the summer of 1974 indicates.

6. See *RJ,* 49; Herman Melville, *The Confidence Man: His Masquerade,* ed. Hershel Parker (New York: W. W. Norton & Co., 1971), 57–58. The ambiguous relation between "confidence" and "truth" in Melville's fiction plays across all the poems in "White Dwarfs."

7. T. S. Eliot, "Sweeney Agonistes," in *Collected Poems 1909–1962* (London: Faber and Faber, 1963), 131.

8. I could also describe this passage as "magical realist," in that there was such a fishbowl full of book in the editorial office of Coach House Press, which was founded by Stan Bevington. The effect in the poem is definitely one of defamiliarization.

9. Solecki makes some similar points in his reading of the poem, insisting that it represents "an ideal which [Ondaatje] feels he has not yet achieved. I would suggest that it is a mark of Ondaatje's integrity as a poet that his most successful poems raise this kind of question" (Solecki 1985a, 105). Solecki's reading of the whole poem can be found on pp. 104–6.

10. "The white dwarfs comprise a group of stars . . . [that] are of interest for several reasons, not the least of which is that they represent the last stage of stellar evolution, the last feeble glow of a dying star" (L. W. Aller, "Star," *Encyclopædia Britannica* [Chicago: Encyclopædia Britannica, 1970], 21:131).

11. See the Bible, Matt. 19:24; Mark 10:25; and Luke 18:25.

12. "The human function, which *is* here the artistic function, is as always

to give form, to exercise control, to maintain equilibrium, to 'shape / and lock the transient'" (Scobie 1985a, 59–60).

13. In January 1978, Ondaatje took a sabbatical leave to travel across the Indian subcontinent to Sri Lanka, where he spent five months with his sister and other relatives. It was the first time he had returned to his birthplace, and while there he began keeping a journal, recording family stories and responding anew to the exotic qualities of what was to him an essentially new place. Many of the prose and verse entries found their way into a special issue of the *Capilano Review* 16/17 (1979): 5–43, the selection clearly intimating that a larger work was under way. He returned in 1980 to do further research on his own and his family's past in order to complete *Running in the Family*, but from this first trip he produced a number of travel poems that found their way into *Trick with a Knife* (see Mandel, 279).

14. But see Chamberlin for a different argument aligning Ondaatje with "other contemporary poets writing out of situations that define essentially colonial predicaments, where language or audience or the identity or role of the poet are indeterminate. . . . Canada offers Ondaatje a geography, but no inheritance; Sri Lanka offers him a family history, but no tradition, no way of passing things on; the English language offers him both an inheritance and a history, but no time and place" (Chamberlin, 41).

15. Italo Calvino, *Invisible Cities,* trans. William Weaver (London: Pan Books, 1979), 20; hereafter cited in text.

16. "Indeed, in all of these poems we get the sort of arrangement of objects indicated in the epigraph from Calvino" (Marshall, 88).

17. Readers who know Dewdney's writing and his interest in geology might decide that "pure memory" can only be found in rock or "a piece of wood 120 million years old from the tar sands" (*TK,* 101). Written, therefore fictionalized, memory is never pure.

Chapter Five

1. Smaro Kamboureli, "The Poetics of Geography in Michael Ondaatje's *Coming Through Slaughter,*" *Descant* 14, no. 4 (Fall 1983): 117; hereafter cited in text. Kamboureli adds, "Be it a long poem or a poetic novel, *Coming Through Slaughter* as a text reflects the poetics of geography" (117), a point I will return to later in this chapter.

2. Susan MacFarlane, "Picking Up the Pieces: *Coming Through Slaughter* as Paragram," *Open Letter,* 7th ser., no. 6 (Fall 1989): 73; hereafter cited in text.

3. Michael Ondaatje, *Coming Through Slaughter* (Toronto: House of Anansi Press, 1976), 134; hereafter cited in text as *CTS.*

4. Scobie in conversation with the author, 19 October 1990.

5. The stories, and in the latter case the photograph, can be found in the two sources Ondaatje acknowledges: William Russell and Stephen W. Smith, "New Orleans Music," in *Jazzmen,* ed. Frederic Ramsey, Jr., and Charles Edward

Smith (1939; New York: Harcourt Brace Jovanovich, 1967, 10–18); and Martin Williams, *Jazz Masters of New Orleans* (New York: Macmillan, 1967), esp. 10–19; hereafter cited in text.

6. John Szarkowski, ed., E. J. Bellocq: *Storyville Portraits* (New York: Museum of Modern Art, 1970), 6; hereafter cited in text.

7. See Al Rose, *Storyville, New Orleans: Being an Authentic, Illustrated Account of the Notorious Red-Light District* (University: University of Alabama Press, 1974), 59–60; hereafter cited in text.

8. Marquis says that Bolden "may have played a few jobs for whites" and that some whites came "to Lincoln Park to hear him play" but seems to feel that he had little if any contact with white society, including white musicians (Marquis, 73).

9. Sam Solecki, "Making and Destroying: *Coming Through Slaughter* and Extremist Art," in *Spider Blues*, 247–48; hereafter cited in text as Solecki 1985c.

10. See also Arun Mukherjee, "The Poetry of Michael Ondaatje and Cyril Dabydeen: Two Responses to Otherness," in *Towards an Aesthetics of Opposition: Essays on Literature, Criticism, & Cultural Imperialism* (Toronto: Williams-Wallace Publishers, 1988), 32–40; hereafter cited in text. Discussing his poems and *Running in the Family,* she argues that "Ondaatje, coming from a Third World country with a colonial past, does not write about his otherness" (33) and "that Ondaatje's masters in the art of poetry have led him away from an exploration of his own realities. The Romanticist line of poetry is essentially ahistorical as it sings only of the intensities of the present" (37). Although this is a not inaccurate description of Ondaatje's poetic, Mukherjee finds no value whatever in it. In this she stands apart from most of Ondaatje's readers.

11. My colleague Stephen Slemon developed many of the points in this paragraph in a conversation with me, 10 April 1991.

12. Solecki 1985c, 248–49 and Scobie 1978, 6 both discuss these themes.

13. "Endings constitute a special case of self-erasing sequences, since they occupy one of the most salient positions in any text's structure." Typically postmodern texts have endings "that seem both open and closed, somehow poised between the two, because they are either *multiple* or *circular*" (McHale, 109).

14. "In addition to . . . strategies for soliciting the reader's involvement in 'unreal' hypodiegetic worlds, there are other devices designed to encourage him or her to mistake nested representations for 'realities.' Among the simplest is the device of the missing end-frame: dropping down to an embedded narrative level without returning to the primary diegesis at the end" (McHale, 117). The final image of *Coming Through Slaughter* may or may not be an example of this, but its diegetic indeterminacy marks it as postmodern, as does the slippage between "nested" representations."

15. He later elaborates: "George Bowering was talking about the derivation of the word 'order' as coming from 'to begin.' I don't know if that's true or

not but it's interesting that in writing *Running* and *Slaughter* the two pieces I wrote to *order* the book were written last—but went in at the beginning. I'm always preoccupied over what should be left in and what should be left out. I love restructuring things" (Solecki "1984", 327).

16. A. D. Coleman, *Light Readings: A Photography Critic's Writings, 1968–1978* (New York: Oxford University Press, 1979), 61–62, as quoted in Lorraine M. York, *"The Other Side of Dailiness": Photography in the Works of Alice Munro, Timothy Findley, Michael Ondaatje, and Margaret Laurence* (Toronto: ECW Press, 1988), 110; hereafter cited in text. York adds that "Bellocq, like Buddy, finds it difficult to give this 'intuition, spontaneity, and improvisation' a form."

17. Moreover, "the metafictional gesture for sacrificing an illusory reality to a higher, 'realer' reality, that of the author, sets a precedent: why should this gesture not be *repeatable*? What prevents the author's reality from being treated in its turn as an illusion to be shattered? Nothing whatsoever, and so the supposedly absolute reality of the author becomes just another level of fiction, and the *real* world retreats to a further remove" (McHale, 197).

18. From this point on, rather than refer to "Ondaatje" or even "the author," I will follow Rimmon-Kenan in focusing on the narrator and the narratee while generally ignoring the implied author and the implied reader in the text (see Rimmon-Kenan, 86–89). This approach maintains "the author" as part of the fiction, if at the highest diegetic level. The fact that "[n]arration is always at a higher narrative level than the story it narrates" (Rimmon-Kenan, 92) suggests how complex the relations among embedded stories is in *CTS*. Even "the narrator" is ambivalent; for there are more than one, not counting Bolden-as-narrator, but I think I can differentiate between the one who acts as "the author" or "Ondaatje" and the invisible commentator who simply delivers information.

19. Ray Wilton, *Order as Process: Narrative Structure in the works of Michael Ondaatje* (M. A. thesis, University of Manitoba, 1986), 76; hereafter cited in text.

20. Scobie suggests Webb's usefulness as a narrative device but argues at length his "thematic as well as structural significance" (1978, 9) by showing how the "complex of images around Webb defines one of Bolden's options" (1978, 11), which is to give in to or else override, as Robichaux does, the power of his audience and its demands that he repeat himself.

21. Linda Hutcheon argues that parody is a significant marker of postmodern writing. See *A Theory of Parody: The Teachings of Twentieth-Century Art Forms* (New York and London: Methuen, 1985) and *A Poetics of Postmodernism: History, Theory, Fiction* (New York and London: Routledge, 1988), 22–36, 124–40.

22. The actual name is "Wolfe-Rayat Stars," and "[a] large fraction of the known Wolfe-Rayat stars are close binaries" in which one member of the binary could be *a white dwarf*. See O. Struve and P. C. Keenan, "Spectroscopy,

Astronomical," *Encyclopaedia Britannica,* 20: 1181, and L. H. Aller, 137. Ondaatje has altered astronomical facts as he has altered historical ones in order to provide metaphoric substance for his inventions.

23. York observes that "many readers probably read the testimonies by the band members in the book, flip to the photograph key, and then to the photograph itself, to see the image behind the word—a fluid reading style which forms a perfect testimony to the complex interrelationships between the image and the word which Ondaatje has created in *Coming Through Slaughter"* (York, 115).

24. See Constance Rooke, "Dog in a Grey Room: The Happy Ending of *Coming Through Slaughter,"* Solecki, ed., *Spider Blues,* 268–92; hereafter cited in text.

25. See Kamboureli's argument that "[b]y means of elimination, Ondaatje deconstructs the original landscape that the poetic image evokes, while at the same time he foregrounds language by creating its own terrain" (Kamboureli 1983, 119), and her explication of some of the ambiguities in the *"Train Song."* See also MacFarlane, 75–76.

26. "As Bolden returns to Storyville his contact with the story increases, the story becomes increasingly emphasized in discourse: in his walks to Nora's house, with the kids, while looking for Pickett, along the waterfront. There is . . . a sense of convergence between story and discourse that culminates in the parade" (Wilton, 93).

27. Given the situation he finds himself in (and the story Ondaatje found), for "Bolden the only escape from becoming a convention himself . . . is destroying the conventions upon which sanity and order depend. As he moves into silence he takes with him the 'mood of sound.' Bolden's story never concludes, never achieves the order that would capture and kill his music" (Wilton, 93). Perhaps that escape from story is "[w]hat [Bolden] wanted."

28. Most critics speak of "Ondaatje's" presence in the text at this point, but given McHale's comments on the further fictionality of authorial intervention in a text (McHale, 197), I will continue to refer to the author-narrator as a fictional/textual construct.

29. Scobie explores the problems of identification and concludes that "Ondaatje's most successful identification in the book is not with Bolden but with Webb. If he is drawn toward Bolden, it is because he too is 'Attracted to opposites' (p. 96). The kind of artist that Ondaatje describes Bolden as being could not have created the structure that is *Coming Through Slaughter"* (Scobie 1978, 20). See also Solecki 1985c, 264–65.

30. The slippage from "art" to "artist" in Rooke's sentence suggests the deeply personal nature of her reading, which takes Bolden as a "realistic" presence, a historical figure, rather than the figure of this particular text.

Chapter Six

1. Smaro Kamboureli, "The Alphabet of the Self: Generic and Other Slippages in Michael Ondaatje's *Running in the Family,"* in *Reflections: Autobiog-*

raphy and Canadian Literature, ed. K. P. Stich (Ottawa: University of Ottawa Press, 1988), 80; hereafter cited in text.

2. See Hutcheon 1988, 83–85, on the ways the readers are implicated in the performance of the text, sharing with the writer a sense of breaking down boundaries between genres and even between art and life.

3. An ambiguous comment: does it imply that imagination precedes conception or that conception cannot come to fruition without imagination? Even the acknowledgments defer meaning and undermine conventional thinking about the imaginative process in writing.

4. On this group, see Ernest MacIntyre, "Outside of Time: *Running in the Family,*" in Solecki, ed., *Spider Blues,* 315–16; hereafter cited in text.

5. Although *Running in the Family* is essentially a text of private familial mythology, it does take account, if only by implication, of the political realities of a colonial country. Against the absolute dismissal of "Ondaatje's unwillingness or inability to place his family in a network of social relationships" and his "sentimental tone and lack of perspective" (Mukherjee, 40), I would place the native awareness of Ernest MacIntyre, already referred to, and suggest that Ondaatje's duplicitous language is not only not sentimental but self-reflexively cognizant of the political implications of his peoples' apolitical behavior. It simultaneously asks us to enjoy and criticize it.

6. The title and the "false maps" allude to a central imperial intertext, Conrad's *Heart of Darkness,* in which Marlow talks of his boyhood passion for maps with "many blank spaces on the earth" before entering one of them via a river of narrative. See Joseph Conrad, *Heart of Darkness,* ed. Leonard F. Dean (Englewood Cliffs, N.J.: Prentice-Hall, 1960), 5.

7. As usual, Ondaatje has "adapted" Knox, quoting, but not quite accurately. See Robert Knox *"An Historical Relation of Ceylon,"* introduction by S. D. Saparamadu, reprinted in *Ceylonese Historical Journal* 6, nos. 1–4 (July 1956–April 1957): 49–50; hereafter cited in text.

8. Ondaatje quotes the last two of four stanzas. See Lakdasa Wikkramasinghe, "Don't Talk to Me about Matisse," in *An Anthology of Modern Writing from Sri Lanka,* ed. Ranjini Obeyesekere and Chitra Fernando (Tucson: University of Arizona Press, 1981), 113.

9. It is a creative translation, altering the original and adding to it. See "The Sigiri Graffiti," trans. S. Paranavitana and W. G. Archer, in *An Anthology of Sinhalese Literature up to 1815,* ed. C. H. B. Reynolds (London: Allen & Unwin, 1970), 27–31.

10. Even later, as he excavates the sites of their incompatibility, he will insist that "[m]y mother loved, *always* loved, even in her last years long after their divorce, his secretive and slightly crooked humour. It bound them together more than anything. They were in a world to themselves, genial with everyone but sharing a code of humour" (*RF,* 170).

11. The phrases come from *King Lear,* 4. 6, where Edgar leads Gloucester

to the imaginary cliff, and afterward they meet the mad King Lear. See William Shakespeare, *King Lear,* ed. Kenneth Muir (London: Methuen, 1982), 160–64.

12. The ambiguous use of *their* as referring to both the stories and the people they are about is deliberate.

Chapter Seven

1. *Secular Love* (Toronto: Coach House Press, 1984), 128; hereafter cited in text as *SL*. Ondaatje himself says, "you know, *Tin Roof* was being written during the same time I was working on *Running* so I remember the two works as being together" (Solecki 1984, 332).

2. Patricia J. Eberle, review of *Secular Love, Journal of Canadian Poetry* 1 (1986): 74; hereafter cited in text.

3. Those names that do appear in either the poems or the occasional dedications are of famous figures in art or entertainment or of writing friends; while the latter names definitely imply that the "I" of their poems is the named author of the book, even that "I" is always already an other.

4. It might recall J. D. Salinger's famous Glass family, to which Ondaatje actually refers in a discussion of novelistic form and *Secular Love* (Solecki 1984, 325).

5. Eberle suggests an allusion to Yeats's "The Second Coming" in this line, and adds, "the center, like his anchor to the past in the images of his family, cannot hold; and the 'rough beast' heralded in Yeats's poem, in Ondaatje's poem looks unnervingly like the poet himself" (Eberle, 77). As the poem mentions "fucking Yeats" a few lines further on, I can admit the allusion, but refuse to go quite as far as Eberle in wholly identifying the "he" of the poem with "the poet himself." Which may only demonstrate how much each reader creates the poem he or she reads.

6. Ondaatje dedicates the following poem, "Tin Roof," to Webb, and has indicated the importance of "Naked Poems" to all later long poems (*LPA,* 12); as well, "Naked Poems" uses "plum" as an image of sensual delight and speaks of the writerly desire to speak reality in terms similar to "but the mouth / wants plum" (*SL,* 15). See Phyllis Webb, *The Vision Tree: Selected Poems,* ed. Sharon Thesen (Vancouver: Talonbooks, 1982), 74, 75, 104; hereafter cited in text.

7. The poem flows like a river (Depot Creek) even as it moves awkwardly and noisily to accumulate and accommodate reiteration. The repetition of the phrase emphasizes what it does.

8. On the definition of the serial poem, see Robin Blaser, "The Fire," in *The Poetics of the New American Poetry,* ed. Donald Allen and Warren Tallman (New York: Grove Press, 1973), 235–46; and his "Statement" in *The Long Poem Anthology,* especially the comments that "[s]uch poems deconstruct meanings and compose a wildness of meaning in which the I of the poet is not the centre but a returning and disappearing note" and that "[t]he serial poem . . . gives

a special meaning to time—poem following poem in sequence of writing" (*LPA,* 323).

9. Most readers will first hear "heart like a wheel," the well-known song by Anna McGarrigle, which appeared on *Kate and Anna McGarrigle* in 1975, and on Linda Ronstadt's *Heart Like a Wheel* in 1974. But there is also the possible allusion to "the sleeve of the pillowing arm" in "*The Diary of Izumi Shikibu*" in *Japanese Poetic Diaries,* ed. and trans. Earl Miner (Berkeley: University of California Press, 1969), 125–31.

10. See "Poetics against the Angel of Death" with its final line, "long lines, clean and syllabic as knotted bamboo. Yes!" (Webb, 60). Webb also addresses Rilke in her poem of that title (Webb, 120).

11. Interestingly, such an allusion clearly implies both age (the actors are at least in their late thirties) and a certain kind of cultural knowledge (they [and we] have some knowledge of jazz and of Holiday's music specifically).

12. "Confessional poetry" as such is full of such first-person protagonists. Robert Lowell's work is exemplary in this regard.

13. The final allusion to George and Ira Gershwin's "They Can't Take That Away from Me" evokes a whole arsenal of romantic belief, associated with the sadness of torch songs and the freedom of jazz.

14. George Steiner, "Dante Now: The Gossip of Eternity," in *On Difficulty and Other Essays* (New York: Oxford University Press, 1978); see esp. 176–77.

15. See Tu Fu, "To My Younger Brother," in *Poems of the Late T'ang,* trans. A. C. Graham (1965; Harmondsworth: Penguin Books, 1977), 47. It is a short poem, from which Ondaatje has borrowed phrases and imagery for the beginning and end of his poem. Tu Fu addressed his poem to his brother, while Ondaatje appears to be addressing a friend.

16. The specific intertext here is Ezra Pound's rendering of Rihaku's "Exiles Letter," in *Personae: The Shorter Poems,* rev. ed., ed. Lea Baechler and A. Walton Litz, (New York: New Directions, 1990), 137–39. Of the 73 lines of Ondaatje's poem, 16 are direct quotes and another 4 are close approximations of Pound's.

17. Al Purdy, *The Collected Poems of Al Purdy* (Toronto: McClelland & Stewart, 1986), 61–62.

Chapter Eight

1. Salman Rushdie, "Imaginary Homelands," *London Review of Books* 7, no. 20 (October 1982): 18.

2. Linda Hutcheon, "Interview: Michael Ondaatje," in *Other Solitudes: Canadian Multicultural Fictions,* ed. Linda Hutcheon and Marion Richmond (Toronto: Oxford University Press, 1990), 199; hereafter cited in text.

3. *In the Skin of a Lion* (Toronto: McClelland and Stewart, 1987), vii; hereafter cited in text as *ISL*.

4. On this, see Michael Greenstein, "Ondaatje's Metamorphoses: *In the*

Skin of a Lion," Canadian Literature 126 (Autumn 1990): 116–30; hereafter cited in text.

5. See *The Epic of Gilgamesh,* ed. and trans. N. K. Sandars, (Harmondsworth: Penguin Books, 1960), 96. There is a further unacknowledged, slightly altered transcription from Sandars, 97, near the end of the novel (*ISL,* 242).

6. Cary Fagan, "Where the Personal and the Historical Meet: An Interview with Michael Ondaatje," *Paragraph* 12, no. 2 (1990): 5; hereafter cited in text. See John Berger, *G* (Harmondsworth: Penguin Books, 1973), 149.

7. See Hutcheon, 1988b, 94, on Patrick's social alienation. She adds that "the novel is the tale of his re-insertion into community and connection," but it is much more than just one tale; that is its point.

8. "*In the Skin of a Lion* is one of the few works of fiction that makes Toronto something more than itself, a city of story and image. I am amazed how many people I know have read it. And *loved* it" (Fagan, 4).

9. Roland C. Harris was appointed commissioner of public works in 1912 and served in that position until his death in 1945 ("Veteran Head of Civic Works Once Office Boy," *Toronto Globe and Mail,* 3 September 1945). Although a very powerful figure in civil administration, he stayed out of the public eye, was seldom referred to in the press, and never mentioned in books on Toronto history. (As Ondaatje points out, when he "started to find out about him . . . none of the books mentions this guy" [Fagan, 5].) In the few photographs extant, he appears to be a "[s]tout, smiling, engaging . . . man on whom the duties of his office weigh but lightly" (*Globe,* 1 May 1913), which makes all the more interesting Ondaatje's refusal to describe him physically at any point in the novel. Ondaatje is interested in him as a voice expressing certain perceptions and beliefs, not as a rounded character per se.

10. When postmodernist fiction deals with history, it violates "the constraints on 'classic' historical fiction: by visibly contradicting the public record of 'official' history; by flaunting anachronisms; and by integrating history and the fantastic. Apocryphal history . . . revises the *content* of the historical record, reinterpreting the historical record, often demystifying or debunking the orthodox version of the past. . . . [it] operates in the 'dark areas' of history, apparently in conformity to the norms of 'classic' historical fiction but in fact *parodying* them. . . . the effect is to juxtapose the officially-accepted version of what happened and the way things were, with another, often radically dissimilar version of the world. The tension between these two versions induces a form of ontological flicker between the two worlds: one moment, the official version seems to be eclipsed by the apocryphal version; the next moment, it is the apocryphal version that seems mirage-like, the official version appearing solid, irrefutable" (McHale, 90). The relevance of these remarks to *In the Skin of a Lion* seems obvious.

11. This is fact: Temelcoff is specifically mentioned as earning this kind of money in Lillian Petroff, "Macedonians in Toronto: Industry and Enterprise,

1903–40," *Polyphony: The Bulletin of the Multicultural History Society of Ontario / Toronto's People*, 6, no. 1 (Summer 1984): 39. Ondaatje told me that he once met Temelcoff, who said in response to a question about his work on the bridge only that it was "difficult" (in conversation, 10 June 1991).

12. Discussing this intertextual allusion to "The Moment of Cubism," Greenstein concludes that "Ondaatje displaces an interlocking system with his cinematic intertext replete with poststructural possibilities coursing through metallic surfaces. Cubists may have imagined the world transformed, but Canada's post-cubist imagines the very process of transformation" (Greenstein, 122).

13. See Harry Vjekoslav Herman, *Men in White Aprons: A Study of Ethnicity and Occupation* (Toronto: Peter Martin Associates, 1978), 17–25, on the early migration of workers to Canada, most of whom planned to return to Macedonia.

14. Much has been written on the Small case, the most complete reportage being found in Fred McClement, *The Strange Case of Ambrose Small* (Toronto: McClelland and Stewart, 1974). McClement paints a very different picture of Small's wife than does Ondaatje, mentions a girlfriend named Clara Smith, but no Clara Dickens, says nothing about a Bertillon record for Small, yet does present evidence of Small's sexual peccadilloes, including a hidden office in his theater, which Ondaatje ignores. Ondaatje probably lost interest in Small's story because of its inescapably crude pulp-fiction aspects.

15. See Alphonse Bertillon, *Signaletic Instructions, Including the Theory and Practice of Anthropometrical Indentification* (no translators names given), edited under the supervision of Major R. W. McClaughry, late general superintendent of police of Chicago (New York, London, Chicago: Werner Co., 1896), 5.

16. "The R.C. Harris Filtration Plant sits majestically in extensive landscaping addressing both Queen Street and Lake Ontario. The sumptuous interiors with finished detailing of brass and marble were considered excessive when completed. They remain unparalleled in Toronto architecture and even today the filtration plant is referred to as a 'Palace of Purification'" (*The Architecture of Public Works: R. C. Harris Commisioner 1912–1945* [Toronto: The Market Gallery of the City of Toronto Archives, 1982], 22).

17. His thinking at the end of this short analepsis also reveals his (and perhaps the text's) cultural entrapment in a form of "gynesis." See Alice A. Jardine, *Gynesis: Configurations of Woman and Modernity* (Ithaca and London: Cornell University, 1985). Very simply, "gynesis" is the effect of male projection in the representation of women in texts, where "man" still functions as a seeker, but "woman" is no longer fixed as the object of the search. Some readers might feel that Patrick is awfully lucky in having one woman replace the other so simply in this otherwise extremely complex narrative. On the other hand, Alice's story, at least, has a degree of self-sufficiency. To apply gynesis in an analysis of all of Ondaatje's representative woman figures would require a book-length study of its own.

18. Several editions of Conrad's letters had been published by 1930. The first quotation on p. 134, however, is taken from "The Informer," in Joseph Conrad, *A Set of Six* (New York: Doubleday, Page & Co., 1924), 78. I have not been able to discover the source of the second quotation.

19. These two sentences are taken from Lucretius, *The Nature of the Universe,* trans. R. E. Latham (Harmondsworth: Penguin Books, 1951), 218, 245, with no acknowledgment, and the usual sly editing.

20. The two quotations in italics concerning Hines's work are taken from Judith Mara Gutman, *Lewis W. Hine and the American Social Conscience* (New York: Walker and Co., 1967), 22, 33.

21. Ondaatje has created a fictional crazy quilt of document and invention in his Muskoka: there was no passage for steamers across North Portage; although the *Algonquin* and the *Iriquois* were real steamers, they sailed in separate lakes and never met; Bigwin Island was on Lake-of-Bays, but the *Royal Muskoka Hotel* (there was no Muskoka Hotel) was on Lake Rosseau, which could not be reached from Lake-of-Bays; there is no Page Island (its name an obvious hint at the fictionality of the whole scene) on the topographical maps of the region. See, e.g., Barbaranne Boyer, *Muskoka's Grand Hotels,* ed. Richard Talley (Erin, Ont.: Boston Mills Press, 1987); Geraldine Coomb, *Muskoka Past and Present* (Toronto: McGraw-Hill Ryerson, 1976); and Richard Talley, *The Steamboat Era in the Muskokas, Vol. II: The Golden Years to the Present* (Erin, Ont.: Boston Mills Press, 1984).

22. On "settler colonies," see Ashcroft, et.al., 25, 133–45.

23. On Ondaatje's playing "with notions of horizon in his cinematic levelling and dissolving" and his opening "horizons to admit history and politics from a newer perspective that endlessly questions," see Greenstein, 119.

Afterword

1. Michael Ondaatje, *The English Patient* (Toronto: McClelland & Stewart, 1992), 41; hereafter cited in text as *TEP*.

2. Interview, Edmonton, 2 October 1992.

3. Chris Wallace-Crabbe uses the phrase, borrowed from a poem by "Ern Malley," as a title of his book, *The Emotions Are Not Skilled Workers* (London & Sydney: Angus & Robertson Publishers, 1980).

Selected Bibliography

PRIMARY SOURCES

1. Longer Works

The Collected Works of Billy the Kid: Left Handed Poems. New York: Norton; Toronto: House of Anansi, 1970.

Coming Through Slaughter. New York: Norton; Toronto: House of Anansi, 1976. London: Marion Boyars, 1979.

Running in the Family. New York: Norton; Toronto: McClelland and Stewart, 1982.

In the Skin of a Lion. New York: Alfred A. Knopf; Toronto: McClelland and Stewart, 1987.

The English Patient. New York: Alfred A. Knopf; Toronto: McClelland and Stewart; London: Bloomsbury, 1992.

2. Poetry

The Dainty Monsters. Toronto: Coach House Press, 1967.

the man with seven toes. Toronto: Coach House Press, 1969.

Rat Jelly. Toronto: Coach House Press, 1973.

Elimination Dance. Ilderton, Ont.: Nairn, 1978.

There's a Trick with a Knife I'm Learning to Do: Poems 1963–1978. New York: Norton; Toronto: McClelland and Stewart, 1979.

Rat Jelly and Other Poems: 1963–78. London: Marion Boyars, 1980.

Tin Roof. Lantzville, B.C.: Island, 1982.

Secular Love. Toronto: Coach House Press, 1984.

The Cinnamon Peeler: Selected Poems. London: Pan Books, 1989. New York: Alfred A. Knopf, 1991; Toronto: McClelland and Stewart, 1992.

Elimination Dance/La Danse éliminatoire. Translated by Lola Lemire Tostevin. London, Ont.: Brick Books, 1991.

3. Books Edited

The Broken Arc: A Book of Beasts. Illustrated by Tony Urquhart. Ottawa: Oberon Press, 1971.

Personal Fictions: Stories by Munro, Wiebe, Thomas, & Blaise. Toronto: Oxford University Press, 1977.

The Long Poem Anthology. Toronto: Coach House Press, 1979.
From Ink Lake: Canadian Stories Selected by Michael Ondaatje. New York: Viking Penguin; Toronto: Lester & Orpen Dennys; London: Faber & Faber, 1990.

4. Criticism

Leonard Cohen. Toronto: McClelland and Stewart, 1970.
"O'Hagan's Rough-Edged Chronicle." *Canadian Literature,* no. 61 (Summer 1974): 24–31.
"García Márquez and the Bus to Aracataca." In *Figures in a Ground: Canadian Essays on Modern Literature Collected in Honor of Sheila Watson,* edited by Diane Bessai and David Jackel, 19–31. Saskatoon, Sask.: Western Producer Prairie Books, 1978.

5. Dramatic Works

the man with seven toes. First produced at the Vancouver Festival, Vancouver B.C., 1968.
The Collected Works of Billy the Kid. First produced at St. Lawrence Centre, Toronto, 23 April 1971.
Coming Through Slaughter. First produced at Theatre Passe Muraille, Toronto, 5–27 January 1980.

6. Films and Screenplays

Sons of Captain Poetry. Mongrel Films/Canadian Film-Makers Distribution Centre, 1970 (director).
Carry On Crime and Punishment. Mongrel Films, 1972 (director).
The Clinton Special. Mongrel Films/Canadian Film-Makers Distribution Centre, 1972 (producer and director).
"The William Dawe Badlands Expedition 1916." *Descant* 14, no. 4 (Fall 1983): 51–73.
Love Clinic. Canadian Centre for Advanced Film Studies, 1990 (writer). *Border Crossings* 9, no. 4 (October 1990): 14–19.

7. Interviews

Barbour, Douglas, and Stephen Scobie. "A Conversation with Michael Ondaatje." *White Pelican 1,* no. 2 (Spring 1971): 6–15.
Interview (by mail) with Michael Ondaatje. *Manna,* no. 1 (March 1972): 19–22.
Bush, Catherine. "Michael Ondaatje: An Interview." *Conjunctions,* no. 15 (1990): 87–98.
Fagan, Cary. "Where the Personal and the Historical Meet: An Interview with Michael Ondaatje." *Paragraph* 12, no. 2 (1990): 3–5.
Hutcheon, Linda. "Interview." In *Other Solitudes: Canadian Multicultural Fic-*

tions, edited by Linda Hutcheon and Marion Richmond, 196–202. Toronto: Oxford University Press, 1990.

Pearce, Jon. "Moving to the Clear: Michael Ondaatje." In *Twelve Voices: Interviews with Canadian Poets,* edited by Jon Pearce, 131–43. Ottawa: Borealis Press, 1980.

Solecki, Sam. "An Interview with Michael Ondaatje." *rune,* no. 2 (Spring 1975): 39–54. Reprinted as "An Interview with Michael Ondaatje (1975)" in *Spider Blues: Essays on Michael Ondaatje,* edited by Sam Solecki, 13–27. Montreal: Véhicule Press, 1985.

———. "An Interview with Michael Ondaatje (1984)." In Solecki, ed., *Spider Blues,* 321–32.

[Whiten, Clifton.] "PCR Interview with Michael Ondaatje." *Poetry Canada Review* 2, no. 2 (Winter 1980–81): 6.

SECONDARY SOURCES

Bibliography

Brady, Judith. "Michael Ondaatje: An Annotated Bibliography." In *The Annotated Bibliography of Canada's Major Authors,* edited by Robert Lecker and Jack David, 6: 129–205. Toronto: ECW Press, 1985. Lists Ondaatje's books, broadsides, films, dramatic productions, editorial work, manuscripts, and contributions to periodicals and books. Secondary materials are provided with lengthy commentary.

Books and Articles

Bjerring, Nancy E. "Deconstructing the 'Desert of Facts': Detection and Antidetection in *Coming Through Slaughter.*" *English Studies in Canada* 16, no. 3 (September 1990): 325–38. Argues that the tension between the detective in the story and the antidetective narrating it reveals its postmodern subversion of epistemological realism.

Blott, Ann. "Stories to Finish: *The Collected Works of Billy the Kid.*" *Studies in Canadian Literature,* no. 2 (Summer 1977): 188–202. Refers to photography and cinema in a discussion of the book's attempt to collect a picture of Billy.

Bowering, George. "Ondaatje Learning to Do." In Solecki, ed., *Spider Blues,* 61–69. Reprinted in *Imaginary Hand,* 163–70. Edmonton: NeWest Press, 1988. Discusses Ondaatje's development from a poet of artifact to one of open form and process.

Chamberlin, J. E. "Let There Be Commerce between Us: The Poetry of Michael Ondaatje." *Descant* 14, no. 4 (Fall 1983): 89–98. Reprinted in Solecki, ed., *Spider Blues,* 31–41. Posits Ondaatje's position as a contemporary postcolonial poet in terms of the way his poetry deals with its inheritances.

Clarke, George Elliott. "Michael Ondaatje and the Production of Myth." *Studies in Canadian Literature* 16, no. 1 (1991): 1–21. Develops an interpretation of "myth" that applies to all of Ondaatje's works from *The Dainty Monsters* to *Secular Love.*

Cooley, Dennis. "'I Am Here on the Edge': Modern Hero/Postmodern Poetics in *The Collected Works of Billy the Kid.*" In Solecki, ed., *Spider Blues,* 211–39. Reprinted in *The Vernacular Muse: The Eye and Ear in Contemporary Literature,* 277–311. Winnipeg: Turnstone Press, 1987. Argues that Billy exists in postmodern flux, but he seeks to be as oblivious to pain and suffering as his antagonist, Pat Garrett.

Glickman, Susan. "From 'Philoctetes on the Island' to 'Tin Roof': the Emerging Myth of Michael Ondaatje." In Solecki, ed., *Spider Blues,* 70–81. Argues that Ondaatje's organization of his first volume of selected poems reveals his changing evaluation of the romantic code by which his early artist figures live.

Godard, Barbara. "Stretching the Story: The Canadian Story Cycle." *Open Letter* 7th ser., no. 6 (Fall 1989): 27–71. Includes a narratological reading of *Billy the Kid* in terms of "a poetics of the fragment."

Harding-Russell, Gillian. "A Note on Ondaatje's 'Peter': A Creative Myth." *Canadian Literature,* no. 112 (Spring 1987): 205–11. On how Ondaatje presents the artist as victim and victimizer through an allusive mixing of mythologies.

Heighton, Stephen. "Approaching 'That Perfect Edge': Kinetic Techniques in the Poetry and Fiction of Michael Ondaatje." *Studies in Canadian Literature* 13, no. 2 (1988): 223–43. Studies Ondaatje's growing use of cinematic and other techniques for invoking physical movement in his writing.

Hunter, Lynette. "Form and Energy in the Poetry of Michael Ondaatje." *Journal of Canadian Poetry* 1, no. 1 (Winter 1978): 49–70. An overview of Ondaatje's poetry up to *Rat Jelly* in terms of its use of metaphor to achieve imaginative equilibrium.

Hutcheon, Linda. "*Running in the Family*: The Postmodernist Challenge." In Solecki, ed., *Spider Blues,* 301–14. Reprinted (edited with additional material on *In the Skin of a Lion*) in *The Canadian Postmodern: A Study of Contemporary English-Canadian Fiction,* 81–106. Toronto: Oxford University Press, 1988. Discusses the ways in which Ondaatje's longer works operate as historiographic metafictions.

Jones, Manina. "*The Collected Works of Billy the Kid*: Scripting the Docudrama." *Canadian Literature,* nos. 122–23 (Autumn–Winter 1989): 26–38. Discusses the long poem as "documentary-collage," and Billy as a body of texts resistant to interpretation as a character.

Kamboureli, Smaro. "The Poetics of Geography in Michael Ondaatje's *Coming*

Through Slaughter. " *Descant* 14, no. 4 (Fall 1983): 112–26. Discusses Bolden as the subject of geography in its largest sense of social and cultural, as well as physical, environment.

————. "The Alphabet of the Self: Generic and Other Slippages in Michael Ondaatje's *Running in the Family.*" In *Reflections: Autobiography and Canadian Literature,* edited by K. P. Stich, 79–91. Ottawa: University of Ottawa Press, 1988. Demonstrates how this "autobiographical" work resists being read as autobiography or as any other single-genre text, and therefore how its narrator also evades every attempt at categorization.

————. "Outlawed Narrative: Michael Ondaatje's *The Collected Works of Billy the Kid.*" *Sagetrieb,* no. 1 (Spring 1988): 115–29. Reprinted (as "Outlawed Narrative") in *On the Edge of Genre: The Contemporary Canadian Long Poem.* Toronto: University of Toronto Press, 1991. Complex discussion of both Billy and his death as "exergues," lying outside the story yet influencing its discontinuous narrative.

Kertzer, J. M. "On Death and Dying: *The Collected Works of Billy the Kid.* " *English Studies in Canada,* no. 1 (Spring 1975): 86–96. Analyzes how the poetry presents "a violent world in which life is suffused with death."

Lane, M. Travis. "Dream as History: *the man with seven toes.*" *Fiddlehead,* no. 86 (August-September-October 1970): 158–62. Reprinted (as "Dream as History: A Review of *the man with seven toes*") in Solecki, ed., *Spider Blues,* 150–55. Psychoanalytic reading of the poem.

Lee, Dennis. *Savage Fields: An Essay in Literature and Cosmology.* Toronto: House of Anansi, 1977. Excerpts reprinted (as "Savage Fields: *The Collected Works of Billy the Kid*") in Solecki, ed., *Spider Blues,* 166–84. Explores Ondaatje's book as an example of the dualistic cosmology Lee is attempting to construct.

MacFarlane, Susan. "Picking Up the Pieces: *Coming Through Slaughter* as Paragram." *Open Letter* 7th ser., no. 6 (Fall 1989): 72–83. Discusses how this fragmentary text undermines conventional reading habits through inexact repetition, self-directed textual violence, mirroring, and discontinuity.

MacLulich, T. D. "Ondaatje's Mechanical Boy: Portrait of the Artist as Photographer." *Mosaic* 14, no. 2 (Spring 1981): 107–19. Argues that, although there can be no single interpretation of Billy's story, he is a mechanized killer in retreat from his own humanity.

Marshall, Tom. "Layering: The Shorter Poems of Michael Ondaatje." In Solecki, ed., *Spider Blues,* 82–92. Argues that the layering of contradictory states or images over one another is the central metaphoric gesture of the poetry.

Maxwell, Barry. "Surrealistic Aspects of Michael Ondaatje's *Coming Through Slaughter.*" *Mosaic* 18, no. 3 (Summer 1985): 101–14. Compares the novel to various works of the surrealists.

Mukherjee, Arun. "The Poetry of Michael Ondaatje and Cyril Dabydeen: Two Responses to Otherness." In *Towards an Aesthetic of Opposition: Essays on Literature, Criticism, & Cultural Criticism*, 32–51. Toronto: Williams-Wallace Publishers, 1988. Argues that "a universalist poetic" leads Ondaatje to ignore the political realities of his own situation as a postcolonial writer.

Mundwiler, Leslie. *Michael Ondaatje: Word, Image, Imagination*. Vancouver: Talonbooks, 1984. A study, mixing phenomenological and political analyses, of all of Ondaatje's works up to *Running in the Family*.

Nodelman, Perry M. "The Collected Photographs of Billy the Kid." *Canadian Literature*, no. 87 (Winter 1980): 68–79. Sees Billy as a photographer attempting to maintain emotional distance from the events he describes and seeking an insane control over mutability.

Owens, Judith. "'I Send You a Picture': Ondaatje's Portrait of Billy the Kid." *Studies in Canadian Literature* 8, no. 1 (1983): 117–39. A reading, through the metaphor of photography, of Billy's problems as narrator in controlling and "fixing" the world of his life and death.

Rooke, Constance. "Dog in a Grey Room: The Happy Ending of *Coming Through Slaughter*." In Solecki, ed., *Spider Blues*, 268–92. Reprinted in *Fear of the Open Heart: Essays on Contemporary Canadian Writing*, 93–112. Toronto: Coach House Press, 1989. Takes Bolden to be a hero who knows the extremist artist's necessity to break through boundaries and move beyond our understanding.

Scobie, Stephen. "Two Authors in Search of a Character." *Canadian Literature*, no. 54 (Autumn 1972): 37–55. Reprinted (as "Two Characters in Search of an Author: bpNichol and Michael Ondaatje") in *Poets and Critics: Selections from "Canadian Literature" 1966–1974*, edited by George Woodcock, 225–46. Toronto: Oxford University Press, 1974. (Reprinted with additions (as "Two Authors in Search of a Character: bpNichol and Michael Ondaatje") in Solecki, ed., *Spider Blues*, 185–210. Comparing the two poets' treatment of the legend, Scobie argues that Ondaatje's text is a form of mythmaking in the Romantic tradition of the outlaw as outsider.

———. "His Legend a Jungle Sleep: Michael Ondaatje and Henri Rousseau." *Canadian Literature*, no 76 (Spring 1978): 6–21. Reprinted in Solecki, ed., *Spider Blues*, 42–60. Explores areas of affinity between Rousseau and the writer, especially their shared vision of the artistic function as giving form, exercising control, and maintaining equilibrium between jungle violence and domestic peace.

———. "*Coming Through Slaughter*: Fictional Magnets and Spider's Webbs." *Essays on Canadian Writing*, no. 12 (Fall 1978): 5–23. Complex exploration of the relationships of Webb, Bellocq, Nora, and Robin to Buddy Bolden, especially in terms of Ondaatje's own relation to the protagonist of his book.

Solecki, Sam. "Nets and Chaos: The Poetry of Michael Ondaatje." *Studies in Canadian Literature,* no. 2 (Winter 1977): 36–48. Reprinted in *Brave New Wave,* edited by Jack David, 24–50. Windsor, Ont.: Black Moss Press, 1978. Reprinted in Solecki, ed., *Spider Blues,* 93–110. Argues that Ondaatje's poetry attempts to compel the reader to reperceive reality; its language and metaphors attest to the paradoxical dualities of chaos and nets in our experience.

————. "Making and Destroying: Michael Ondaatje's *Coming Through Slaughter* and Extremist Art." *Essays on Canadian Writing,* no. 12 (Fall 1978): 24–47. Reprinted in Solecki, ed., *Spider Blues,* 246–67. Compares Bolden to other suicidal twentieth-century artists and argues that there is a radical difference between him and his creator, Ondaatje.

————. "Point Blank: Narrative in Michael Ondaatje's *the man with seven toes.*" *Canadian Poetry: Studies, Documents, Reviews,* no. 6 (Spring–Summer 1980): 14–24. Reprinted in Solecki, ed., *Spider Blues,* 135–49. Argues that *the man with seven toes* is pivotal in Ondaatje's development toward longer and more experimental forms.

————. "Michael Ondaatje." *Descant* 14, no. 4 (Fall 1983): 77–88. Reprinted (as "Michael Ondaatje: A Paper Promiscuous and Out of Forme with Several Inlargements and Untutored Narrative") in Solecki, ed., *Spider Blues,* 333–43. Argues that the "I" is a third-person pronoun in Ondaatje's work, which is full of rhetorical reluctance to give anything away.

Van Wart, Alice. "The Evolution of Form in Michael Ondaatje's *The Collected Works of Billy the Kid* and *Coming Through Slaughter.*" *Canadian Poetry: Studies, Documents, Reviews,* no. 17 (Fall–Winter 1985): 1–28. Argues that Ondaatje develops the formal methods of the long poem in the later novel, creating a hybrid that blurs the distinctions between poetry and prose.

Watson, Sheila. "Michael Ondaatje: The Mechanization of Death." *White Pelican* 2, no. 4 (Fall 1972): 56–64. Reprinted in *Sheila Watson: A Collection, Open Letter* 3d ser., no. 1 (Winter 1974–75): 158–66. Reprinted in Solecki, ed., *Spider Blues,* 156–65. Places Ondaatje's use of mechanical violence in the context of modernist art and thought.

Wilson, Ann. "*Coming Through Slaughter:* Storyville Twice Told." *Descant* 14, no. 4 (Fall 1983): 99–111. Compares the novel and the play as explorations of identity.

York, Lorraine M. "'The Making and Destroying': The Photographic Image in Michael Ondaatje's Works." In *"The Other Side of Dailiness": Photography in the Works of Alice Muro, Timothy Findley, Michael Ondaatje, and Margaret Laurence;* 93–120. Toronto: ECW Press, 1988. Analyzes Ondaatje's use of photographs and photographic and cinematic metaphors.

Index

The Author

Douglas Barbour is a poet and professor of English at the University of Alberta. He is the author or editor of over a dozen books and monographs, including *Worlds Out of Words: The SF Novels of Samuel R. Delany, Daphne Marlatt and Her Works, John Newlove and His Works,* and *bpNichol and His Works.* He most recently edited *Beyond Tish: New Writing Interviews Critical Essays. Visible Visions,* a volume of his selected poems, won the 1984 Stephan Stephansson Award for Poetry. *Story for a Saskatchewan Night* was published in 1990. He has read and performed his poetry, and lectured on Canadian literature, in Canada, the United States, Europe, Australia, and New Zealand.

DATE DUE

GAYLORD			PRINTED IN U.S.A.